What the Tortoise Taught Us

What the Tortoise Taught Us

The Story of Philosophy

Burton F. Porter

ROWMAN & LITTLEFIELD PUBLISHERS, INC.
Lanham • Boulder • New York • Toronto • Plymouth, UK

Published by Rowman & Littlefield Publishers, Inc.
A wholly owned subsidiary of The Rowman & Littlefield Publishing Group, Inc.
4501 Forbes Boulevard, Suite 200, Lanham, Maryland 20706
http://www.rowmanlittlefield.com

Estover Road, Plymouth PL6 7PY, United Kingdom

Copyright © 2011 by Burton F. Porter

All rights reserved. No part of this book may be reproduced in any form or by any electronic or mechanical means, including information storage and retrieval systems, without written permission from the publisher, except by a reviewer who may quote passages in a review.

British Library Cataloguing in Publication Information Available

Library of Congress Cataloging-in-Publication Data

Porter, Burton Frederick.
  What the tortoise taught us : the story of philosophy / Burton Porter.
    p. cm.
  Includes bibliographical references and index.
  ISBN 978-1-4422-0551-2 (cloth : alk. paper) — ISBN 978-1-4422-0553-6 (electronic)
  1. Philosophy—History. I. Title.
  B74.P67 2011
  190—dc22
                                                                        2010019909

∞™ The paper used in this publication meets the minimum requirements of American National Standard for Information Sciences—Permanence of Paper for Printed Library Materials, ANSI/NISO Z39.48-1992.

Printed in the United States of America

For Barbara, Mark, Sarah, and Ana,
who are most precious to me, and to all who
relish the teachings of the tortoise

Contents

	List of Illustrations	ix
Chapter 1	The Beginning of Reflection	1
	Glimpses of Light: Ancient Philosophy	1
	The Unexamined Life Is Not Worth Living: Socrates	13
Chapter 2	Being Governed by the Mind: Rational Thought	25
	Learning Is Recollection: Plato	25
	The Path of Moderation: Aristotle	37
	Accept What You Cannot Change: The Stoics	45
Chapter 3	Religious Faith: The Philosophy of Religion	57
	The Glorification of God: St. Thomas Aquinas	58
	Love One Another: Christian Agape	69
Chapter 4	Personal Identity and Human Nature: Metaphysics	81
	I Think, Therefore I Am: René Descartes	81
	Beasts, Angels, and Machines: Hobbes and Rousseau	95

Chapter 5	How Things Seem and What They Are: Epistemology	109
	Thinking Makes It So: Bishop Berkeley	113
	Seeing Is Believing: David Hume	120
Chapter 6	The Purpose of Living: Ethics	131
	Doing the Right Thing: Immanuel Kant	131
	The Greatest Happiness Principle: John Stuart Mill	142
	Investing Life with Meaning: Jean-Paul Sartre	152
Chapter 7	Contemporary Trends	161
	Fiddling with Words While the World Burns: Linguistic Philosophy	162
	The Voices of Women: Feminist Perspectives	168
	Current Moral Issues: Abortion and Racism	177
	Notes	191
	Selected Bibliography	195
	Index	201
	About the Author	205

List of Illustrations

Figure 1.1.	Bust of Socrates (National Archaeological Museum in Athens).	2
Figure 2.1.	*School of Athens*, by Raphael, 1509 (Vatican).	26
Figure 3.1.	The so-called Flammarion woodcut, an anonymous wood engraving of the heavens that first appeared in the work of French astronomer Camille Flammarion, 1888.	57
Figure 3.2.	*Saint Thomas Aquinas*, by Carlo Crivelli, 1476 (National Gallery, London).	59
Figure 4.1.	René Descartes, 1596-1650. Engraving by W. Holl after painting by Franz Hals. (Courtesy of the Library of Congress)	82
Figure 5.1.	*Portrait of David Hume*, by Allan Ramsay, 1766 (Scottish National Portrait Gallery, Edinburgh).	110
Figure 6.1.	Immanuel Kant, black-and-white reproduction of eighteenth-century portrait.	132
Figure 7.1.	Mary Wollstonecraft, photograph of a stipple engraving by James Heath, ca. 1797, after a painting by John Opie. (Courtesy of the Library of Congress)	161

"Why did you call him Tortoise, if he wasn't one?" Alice asked.
"We called him Tortoise because he taught us."

—Lewis Carroll, *Alice in Wonderland*

Note to the Reader:
The phrase "What the Tortoise Taught Us" first appeared as the title of an article by D. G. Brown in *Mind*, 1954 LXIII (250), 170–79.

CHAPTER ONE

The Beginning of Reflection

Glimpses of Light: Ancient Philosophy

According to one account, philosophy began on May 28, 585 BCE, at 3:15 in the afternoon. To be that precise about something so abstract seems absurd, but at that time an ancient Greek thinker named Thales confirmed his theory of a solar eclipse. He had observed the movements of the heavens and noticed a regularity that allowed him to predict that darkness would cover the earth at midday. Instead of simply accepting the world as a jumble of unrelated events, he tried to make sense of it all, to understand the underlying principles. He felt the need to find a reason why things happened as they did, and that search for hidden order was vindicated by the eclipse. In this sense, the account is true. Philosophy does begin where acceptance ends, when we try to understand life more deeply and ask why things are the way they are. Beyond eclipses, we wonder where we fit in the scheme of things, both as human beings and as individuals, whether there is any meaning or value to our lives. Did the world and everything in it come about by chance, or is there an underlying purpose to our being?

We wonder whether there is a God who created life in accordance with a grand cosmic plan, so that everything happens for a reason, including the death of those we love. We ask ourselves how we should live, what would be fulfilling, and what obligations we have to other people. Is there life beyond the grave where we will receive our just reward, or should we make the most of our time on earth because there is nothing more?

Figure 1.1. Bust of Socrates (National Archaeological Museum in Athens).

Whenever we speculate about such fundamental questions, and try to find answers by deep and careful thought, then we are engaged in philosophy. And it was the ancient Greeks who first raised such issues, reflecting on them in a systematic way; they took the first steps in philosophic thinking, asking the questions we still debate today.

None of the information we have about the early Greeks is certain, of course, because we have to piece together their story from fragments of writings that have survived. For example, we have 150 lines of the philosopher Parmenides, 340 of Empedocles, and about 300 fragments of Democritus. We also have to rely on summaries written by ancient historians, such as Plutarch, Iambichus, and Herodotus, and commentaries of later philosophers, such as Plato, Aristotle, and Seneca. What's more, some of the accounts are contradictory and no source has been judged completely reliable. Nevertheless, we do know enough for an approximation to be made, and we have to celebrate what was saved instead of regretting what has been lost.

Thales

The philosopher Thales, who lived in the sixth century BCE, is classified as one of the "pre-Socratics" because he preceded (the better-known) Socrates a century earlier. His home was in Ionia, on the west coast of Asia Minor, a region the Greeks had colonized. More specifically, he was a resident of the city-state of Miletus, a small Greek seaport, and his philosophic ideas are therefore part of the Milesian school. He probably visited Egypt at one time, studying their astronomy and mathematics, and he may have developed a theory for the rise and fall of the Nile, as well as a method for calculating the height of pyramids. We know he measured the distance of ships at sea and taught sailors to navigate by the Big Bear constellation. In fact, he compiled whole star charts, which meant that he had celestial records from Babylonia.

We also know that he split the waters of a river to make it shallow enough for an army to cross:

> Beginning upwards of the army he dug a deep channel, giving it a crescent shape, so that it should flow round the back of where the army was encamped. . . . The result was that as soon as the river was divided it became fordable in both of its parts.

On another occasion he made a fortune by predicting a bumper crop of olives.

> When he was reproached because of his poverty, as though philosophers were no use, it is said that, having observed through his study of the heavenly bodies

that there would be a large olive crop, he raised a little capital while it was still winter and paid deposits on all the olive presses in Miletus and Chios, hiring them cheaply because no one bid against him. When the appropriate time came, there was a sudden rush of requests for the presses; he then hired them out on his own terms and so made a large profit, thus demonstrating that it was easy for philosophers to be rich, if they wished, but it was not in this that they were interested.

Despite this evidence of practicality, Thales had the reputation of being absentminded. According to one story, "[a] witty and attractive Thracian servant-girl mocked Thales for falling into a well while he was gazing upwards at the stars; she said that he was eager to know the things in the sky, but what was behind him and just by his feet escaped his notice." Although astronomy had made Thales rich, this has remained the stereotype of the philosopher—lost in the stars rather than having his feet on the ground.

Thales did engage in more serious speculation, specifically on what might be the fundamental "stuff" of the universe. At the time, the Greeks thought that air, earth, fire, and water were the basic elements, and that they could not be reduced to anything simpler. That did not satisfy Thales, who wanted to find a single world-stuff that would account for every other material thing. He wanted an element that was ultimate, lying at the heart of reality and responsible for the variety of natural forms.

Strangely enough, Thales chose water as the basic element, and evidence suggests that he devised an ingenious system of thought to justify his claim. Water gives rise to air through the process of evaporation, first transforming itself into mist or vapor. In that same process, water produces earth, because soil is left in dried-up pools, first in the form of mud. Thales must also have seen silt deposited at the mouth of rivers, especially the delta of rivers, and he thought underground springs showed earth becoming water once again. What's more, in volcanic eruptions we see liquid become solid as the molten lava cools, and when water freezes, of course, it becomes hard as rock.

The connection between water and fire must have been more difficult to explain because the two seem to be opposites. However, Thales pointed out that the sun bakes the earth, drawing the liquid into itself so that water becomes fire. Furthermore, there is a connection between water and fire in thunderstorms: the rain causes the lightning—fire in a liquid sky. The sun's rays produce drops of water on cold objects, and lightning has an attraction for water as we can see when it strikes lakes or oceans.

Not only can water account for air, earth, and fire, but Thales believed the earth originated from water and now floated upon it like a raft; if you dig deep enough, you can find the water underneath the soil and build a well.

Storms at sea make the land move because "the world is held up by water and rides like a ship, and when it is said to 'quake' it is actually rocking because of the water's movement." He might have added that earthquakes can make the oceans move, forcing tsunamis onto the land.

Thales probably observed that the seeds of animals are wet and that wriggling organisms are left in mud pools, so that life might have begun in water. Today we know that life did first appear as specks of protoplasm in the scum of tides, acted on by the sun's rays, the "primal soup." We have also learned that all plants and animals need water to survive, so when we search for life on other planets, we first look for signs of water. The human body itself is largely made up of water: up to 60 percent for men, 65 percent for women, and 70 percent for infants.

All parts of the earth were watery to Thales, which meant to his mind that they were permeated with a life principle that made them divine. In one fragment he wrote, "All things are full of gods." This identification of water and spirits might have come from the Egyptian notion that the world was created by Nun, the goddess of primeval waters. As the Nile flooded and receded each year, the land miraculously reappeared. Thales does refer to gods, but at bottom he did not think of the world as spiritual but material. The gods were impersonal to him, and the divinity of the universe consisted in its agelessness, power, and freedom from human limitations. This reality was understood through observation and hypotheses, not from scripture or revelation.

Obviously, many of Thales' ideas were mistaken, even though they were imaginative and consistent. Water may be vital but it is not fundamental. But the important point is not whether he got it right, but that he was searching for a comprehensive explanation for the world of experience. Rather than taking life at face value, he attempted to understand the underlying essence of things, the structure and development of physical reality. For that reason Thales is considered the first philosopher, and to neglect his thought or that of the other pre-Socratics is like entering into the middle of a conversation.

Thales' assumptions are certainly not outmoded, for today we also assume we can discover a single explanation for all of creation. To some this ultimate reality is the atom and molecular structure, to others energy and field of force, and to still others a unified field theory that will reconcile alternative models in physics. We also have the spiritual idea that love is basic, or that a divine being is the ultimate reality, creating everything we see and that which lies beyond our vision. Technically, this study of the nature of reality is called metaphysics.

Following Thales, other pre-Socratics offered alternative explanations of reality, motivated by the same desire for understanding. A fellow Milesian named Anaximander speculated about a cosmic stuff that he called "the Infinite" or "Indefinite," a material that was eternal and imperishable. Creation occurred when fire and dark mist separated from this "boundless." Democritus, a surprisingly modern thinker, postulated that atoms were the basic building blocks of matter—indivisible and imperceptible particles that combined to form the variety of objects, and Empedocles suggested that human beings evolved from lower forms of life, the first theory of evolution. Another pre-Socratic, Pythagoras, is considered "the father of numbers," even though he never wrote a mathematical equation.

Anaximenes named air or mist the basic element. The earth floated on air (we call it space now), and the variety of natural forms came about through rarefaction and condensation. If you breathe out with your mouth open, you produce warm air; purse your lips, and your breath is cool. That is why we blow on our hands to warm them in winter and blow on our soup to make it cooler. Medicine, too, has a quaint history of applying heat or cold, wet or dry, some of which is practiced today.

Heraclitus
One of the most interesting of the early Greek philosophers was a man named Heraclitus, who offered a very different model of reality. Instead of trying to identify some physical element as basic, he wondered what *process* characterized the natural world. That is, rather than asking whether air, earth, fire, or water was the most fundamental stuff, Heraclitus looked for a governing principle underlying them all.

A citizen of the Greek city of Ephesus (ca. 520–480 BCE), Heraclitus came from an aristocratic family but did not assume his traditional place in government. Rather, he withdrew from society and became a critic, ridiculing people for their stupidity. He detested philosophers in particular, which was a type of self-loathing. In both his life and his thought he appears to have been a self-styled curmudgeon. In his crabbed and cranky way he wrote, "The majority are contented like well-fed cattle, and asses (who) prefer chaff to gold." He was even eccentric enough to dismiss Hesiod and Homer as poor writers.

We know he had little regard for the religious practices of his day, including prayers to images and rites of atonement, and he especially ridiculed a cult called the Orphic Brotherhood. Here the worship centered round Orpheus, a legendary singer in Greek mythology who could charm even the animals, stones, and trees by the sweetness of his voice. In one tale, Orpheus rescued his wife, Eurydice, from the Underworld with his singing. As a mystery religion, the cult promised life after death, symbolized by a cosmic egg with a serpent coiled around it. The soul could break the shell and ascend along the serpent spirals to live forever with the gods; it could be released from the prison of the body only through abstinence and rites of purification. To Heraclitus, such beliefs were unfounded, fostered by ignorance, desperation, and madness.

Heraclitus also appears to have been rather condescending and impatient with his countrymen. When his city-state banished someone he considered an outstanding citizen, he wrote sarcastically, "The Ephesians would do well to hang themselves, every adult man, and leave their city to adolescents, since they expelled Hermodorus, the worthiest man among them." Clearly, he never suffered fools gladly.

We have a number of writings of Heraclitus, or rather fragments of them, mostly in the form of epigrams—witty, pointed, condensed sayings that offer a glimpse into the workings of his mind. Because of the way in which they are written, we can identify with his personality and his thoughts twenty-five centuries later. He liked to hide his meanings, though, and some of his sayings are so obscure that they earned him the title of "the dark philosopher." Nevertheless, he wrote a book called *On Nature* that was clear and persuasive enough to win disciples.

When Heraclitus began his speculations, looking not for a material substance but a principle that applied to matter, he hit upon the idea of change. To his mind, motion and mutability characterized the earth. "All things flow" he wrote, meaning that nothing remains constant, that everything is mutable. Only the law of change does not change, because if it changed, then it would no longer be true that everything changes. But with that one exception, we live in a world that is transitory, dynamic, and ephemeral, and the only thing we can count on is that nothing stays the same or lasts forever.

There is something of Heraclitus in contemporary "chaos theory," which claims we cannot predict when changes, even small ones, will have extreme impact. This is the assumption behind the "Cleopatra's nose" theory of history of Blaise Pascal—"had it been shorter, the whole face of the world would have been changed"—as well as the "butterfly effect," first articulated by Edward Lorenz: that the flap of a butterfly's wings in China can set off a tornado in Texas. Chaos theory, though, looks for order in apparent randomness so that cascading events can be predicted, such as avalanches and earthquakes.

In any case, to Heraclitus the process of change took the form of development, maturity, and decay, and it applied to all things—plants and animals, houses and temples, monuments, theories, and civilizations. The bud on an apple tree turns into a blossom, the flower then becomes fruit, which is eaten by worms, and the worms are transformed into baby birds. Mountains are scoured by wind, water, and ice until they become the soil of valleys, just as human beings die and become one with dust. All animals perish and fertilize the soil, which grows plants for animals to eat, in an endless cycle of death and rebirth.

Water represents this process of change, not as the basic element, the way Thales imagined, but as a metaphor for change. The flow of water is like the flux of life, continuously in motion and constantly renewing itself. "It is not possible to step twice in the same river," Heraclitus wrote. "Different waters flow." That is, the second time one steps into the river, new water will have flowed from the source, so that it is no longer the same river. According to legend, one of his disciples went one better and said, "You cannot step *once* in the same river," because the river changes between the intention and the act, and because you will have changed before your foot ever reaches the water. Between the thought and the deed lies an eternity.

Fire also symbolizes change, because it represents the flickering, waxing, and waning of things, comparable to the tide's ebb and flow. Fire needs air to burn, steams water from wood, and leaves a residue of embers and smoke. People are fascinated by the way it transforms even hard coal into ashes while still remaining itself. We gaze at fire and watch it keep its identity while changing everything it touches.

In a deeper sense, Heraclitus did not think that every object changes, because something persists that survives change. He calls this underlying principle *logos*, which can be interpreted as balance, measure, or proportion. "In the beginning was the logos," the book of Genesis states, which is usually translated as "word." To Heraclitus, logos is the identity in difference that holds things together, keeps them from flying apart. It means that which maintains the unity of all objects despite continual change.

Sometimes the tree has leafy branches, sometimes bare ones, but it is still a tree; we renovate a house, but it is nothing other than that house; and people change throughout their lifetime, but they are still the same person from birth to death. Logos is that which maintains the interaction of opposites and continuity through change.

Heraclitus, in fact, saw life as a perpetual struggle between opposing forces: love and hate, selfishness and generosity, emotion and reason, will and imagination. "It is the forward and backward pull on the bow that makes the arrow fly," he wrote. "War is the father of all, the king of all." The absence of tension means death, so we should welcome strife, depending on logos to hold contrary forces in a creative tension.

In an enigmatic way, Heraclitus claimed that everything is identical when viewed in the right light. "Immortals are mortal, mortals are immortal," "the path up and down are one and the same," and "day and night: they are one." More clearly, he wrote, "What is in opposition is in concert, and from what differs comes the most beautiful harmony." Perhaps he meant that even opposites can be considered the same because they are part of a cosmic equilibrium. Either/or has a Janus face.

As a mystical idea, Heraclitus's "unity of opposites" may be profound or simply nonsense—perhaps the type of irrationality he condemned in the Orphic Brotherhood. Death is not life, up is not down, and day is not night. We might doubt that "all things are one" even while we accept the notion that something binds the opposite parts of the universe together. What is apparent is that Heraclitus believed he had discovered an idea that no one else had the sense to grasp, and he complained bitterly that his originality was not recognized by his contemporaries. Arthur Schopenhauer, a nineteenth-century German philosopher, once said, "When modesty was invented it must have been a great day for fools, because everyone is supposed to behave as if he were one." Heraclitus, at least, did not suffer from that vice.

According to historical records (or legend), his death was very odd. To cure his dropsy, he asked to be covered in dung to draw the bad humors out of his body. "In one version the cow dung is wet and the philosopher drowns; in the second, it is dry and he is baked to death in the Ionian sun." This is as bizarre as the fate of Aeschylus, who was killed when an eagle dropped a tortoise on him, mistaking his bald head for a stone.

Parmenides

The cosmic picture painted by Heraclitus is one of continual movement, a restless and fleeting universe, continually *becoming* rather than being. He also thought, as Thales did, that reality was known through our senses, that we could access the truth through observation. However, another pre-Socratic, named Parmenides, disputed both ideas. He believed reality was fixed and unmoving, and rather than being perceived by our senses, it had to be understood by our mind. Technically, the controversy is called the many and the one.

Parmenides was a citizen of Elea, a Greek colony on the west coast of Italy, south of present-day Naples, and was born about 510–515 BCE, thirty years after Heraclitus. We have evidence that he was involved in business and politics, and might have been responsible for some of the prosperity of the city. Not much is known about his personal life, but apparently he traveled to various parts of the Greek world and at age sixty-five met Socrates in Athens. Socrates wrote of him,

> Parmenides seemed to me, in the words of Homer, a man to be reverenced and at the same time feared. For when I was a mere youth and he a very old man, I conversed with him, and he seemed to me to have an exceedingly wonderful depth of mind.

He appears to have been generally admired, because "a Parmenidean life" became a proverbial saying among the Greeks, meaning "something fine and noble."

Parmenides, coming from Elea, is part of the Eleatic school of philosophy; in fact, he is the chief figure. He enjoyed an almost mythical reputation in the ancient world, based largely on his philosophical poem, *On Nature*. The style of the poem is rather lofty, apparently following the model of Hesiod, "father of Greek didactic poetry," with stilted writing at odds with its content. Nevertheless, the ideas are rich and intriguing.

In the prologue Parmenides pretends he ascended in a chariot, guided by Sun maidens, to the home of a goddess; she then dictated verses to him, revealing the secrets of the universe:

> 'Tis necessary for thee to learn all things, both the abiding essence of persuasive truth, and men's opinions in which rests no true belief. . . . Come now I will tell thee—and do thou hear my word and heed it—what are the only ways of inquiry that lead to knowledge.

Parmenides then expounds his philosophy in hexameter verse, offering a combination of airy speculation and systematic, rational argument. On the more fanciful side he tells us that the mixture of dense and thin gives a white appearance to the Milky Way; that the earth is equally distant on all sides from other bodies, thereby resting in equilibrium; and that god is an orb of light with continuous heat, arching the sky. However, he also presents a clever theory of reality that philosophers have taken more seriously.

Parmenides was primarily concerned with attacking the Heraclitean theory that "all things flow," not because he wanted to distinguish himself from his predecessor, but because he was sincerely convinced that motion is impossible. Strange as it seems, reality for him was a changeless, timeless, compact, indivisible ball of homogeneous world stuff, without movement, gaps, or parts: "all is one."

Obviously, this is an extreme position, contrary to common sense. Nothing could be more obvious than that things change, and that objects are different from one another. Our senses tell us that movement happens all the time, but Parmenides rejected the validity of sense experience and argued that reason could prove the oneness of things, despite all appearances.

Essentially, he argued that a thing must either be or not be. But being cannot come from nonbeing, since something cannot come from nothing; nor can it change into nonbeing, since, by definition, nonbeing does not exist. Therefore, everything that is has always been, and cannot not be.

The implication is that we live in a fixed and frozen world, because in order for something to change, it would have to change into nothing. But nothing is not another thing; rather, it is no thing. It is an absence rather than a presence, and objects cannot change into that which is not.

Parmenides' logic is extremely abstract, and his conclusion counterintuitive: that there is no motion or change, no alteration or variety. "All these things are but names which mortals have given, believing them to be true—coming into being and passing away, being and not-being, change of place and alteration of bright color." Although most people feel certain that we live in a world of change, to Parmenides that belief is an illusion. Logically, whatever *is* exists as an eternal, immovable whole, a bloc universe "all together, one."

These ideas seemed far-fetched, requiring much more proof before anyone could accept them. That task was undertaken by Zeno of Elea (490–430 BCE), the prize pupil of Parmenides, who defended his master's ideas in a singular and startling way. He was a flamboyant character, and according to tradition, when a Sicilian tyrant tortured him to disclose the names of his political associates, he bit off his tongue with his teeth and spit it in the face of his torturer.

Zeno's defense of Parmenides took the form of paradoxes, all of which were designed to show that motion is impossible. These paradoxes have been given names such as "the flying arrow," "Achilles and the tortoise," "the dichotomy," and so forth. Each puzzle reduces the idea of change to absurdity, implying that if we analyze events rationally, all motion is seen to be impossible, and without motion there is no change.

The "flying arrow" is typical of Zeno's paradoxes. He reasons that for an arrow to move, it must go from where it is to where it is not, but if you think about it, nothing can ever be where it is not. Therefore the arrow, as well as everything else, will always remain where it is, fixed and stationary for all eternity.

If it is argued that the arrow was or will be where it is not, the same objection applies. Things cannot have been in any other place, since the only other place they could have been is where they are not, and there is no future place where they will be, since that could only be the place where they are not. Nothing can ever be where it is not, whether in the past or the future, so motion is impossible. In fact, since things are always where they are, there is no yesterday or tomorrow, but only a timeless instant of now.

This is the kind of argument that makes your head spin and gives philosophy a bad name. You can't accept it, but it's hard to fault the logic. In this particular case, however, the reasoning does seem flawed. Zeno's argument would be like claiming that tomorrow never comes, because it is always today. However, if today is Tuesday, we know that Wednesday will arrive, and then that will be today. In other words, although it is always today, the day that is today can change.

In the same way, it appears sensible to argue that you can't cut off the top of a tree. because, insofar as it is a tree, it will always have a top. But we know we can do that, so there must be something wrong with the thinking. The answer seems to be that, in a relative sense, a tree will always have a top, but in an absolute sense, we can cut off those topmost branches—the ones that have forked twigs and that discolored bark. Looking back, we see the tree still has a top, but we can still cut away that particular top. "Top of the tree" is an ambiguous phrase.

Another paradox, "Achilles and the tortoise," is more difficult to solve. Zeno argued that although Achilles was a swift runner, he could never win a race against a tortoise if the tortoise had a head start. For by the time Achilles reached the point where the tortoise began, the tortoise would have advanced a little bit farther, and by the time Achilles had covered that ground, the tortoise would have lurched forward a bit more. This process continues to infinity, of course, because Achilles must first reach the last place the tortoise has been. Therefore, he can never overtake the tortoise, much less win the race.

Zeno's argument "the dichotomy" is similar and easier to follow, although just as puzzling. In order to travel from one point to another, we must first go half the distance, but before we get to that halfway point, we have to go halfway first. This continues infinitely because there is always a half distance to go before we begin, which means we can never start.

Although this is a more subtle argument, modern physics and mathematics have shown where Zeno went wrong. The flaw seems to lie in regarding space as discrete, when in fact it is continuous. That is, from a mathematical standpoint, space is infinitely divisible, but that numerical infinity can still be physically traversed.

What has the tortoise taught us? By means of flying arrows, races, and dichotomies, we are made to question what we see and take to be true. In true philosophic fashion, Zeno advises us to be skeptical of the world of seeming and appearing, and to search for the underlying reality. He may be wrong in what he claims, but he displays a genuine philosophic mentality in questioning the conventional view of reality.

This philosophic approach has been reinforced by contemporary science, which tells us that what we perceive is not always so. For example, we think the earth is standing still, but in truth it rotates on its axis, and the ground that we consider to be steady is constantly moving beneath our feet. We would swear the sun rises and sets, but it is the earth that turns, without our sensing it. In the same way, nothing seems more obvious than the solidity of things, especially dense rock, steel, and concrete, but according to physics, all objects are mainly space. And rather than their being stationary, as common sense tells us, everything is a whirling maelstrom of atoms.

We see purple mountains that are really green, a bent stick in the water that is actually straight, and railroad tracks merging in the distance, when in fact parallel lines never meet. And we would swear that we see the stars at night, but we never do. All we see is light emanating from the stars, and because of the vast distances of space, the stars we think we see may have ceased to exist by the time we see them. At best, we are looking at a ghostly image from the past, seeing what used to be.

Astronomers calculate there are five hundred billion stars in our galaxy alone, with orbiting planets that could sustain life, and there are one hundred billion galaxies. We see only a few of these, including the star we call the sun. But because it is ninety-three million miles away, its rays do not reach us for eight minutes, even though light travels at 186,281 miles per second. We certainly never see the sunrise or the sunset, but only the earth turn.

Sense experience, then, may not be enough; reality may not conform to our ordinary perception. If we are to grasp what is real, we need to question our customary beliefs. As Plato noted, part of the purpose of philosophy is to make people less sure about things and, at the same time, to expand their vision of possibilities. Or as Bertrand Russell (1872–1970) said, "The point of philosophy is to start with something so simple as not to be worth stating, and to end up with something so paradoxical that no one will believe it." Then the hard work begins of examining ideas in a rational way, trying to figure out what is so, even if it seems absurd. Of course, if you do not care what is real and would just as soon believe in illusions, you can always gaze at the stars and think you are seeing them.

The Unexamined Life Is Not Worth Living: Socrates

Christianity has numerous martyrs, from Rudolf, broken on the wheel, to Ignatius, eaten by wild animals, to St. Sebastian, who was shot to death with arrows. Philosophy has essentially one—the ancient philosopher Socrates (470–399 BCE), who was condemned to die by drinking hemlock. According to a work called the *Phaedo*, he drank the poison cheerfully, discoursing about philosophy until the cold reached his heart. He was an old man by the standards of his time, and he seemed to think this was an honorable end—a fitting death for the way he had lived his life.

We know a great deal more about Socrates than we do about his predecessors, thanks largely to his celebrated pupil Plato and to the historian Xenophon. Born in fifth-century Athens, he was the son of Phaenarete, a midwife, and Sophroniscus, a sculptor or stonemason. This parentage prompted a number of comparisons in his later life. For example, his supporters said he brought ideas to birth, while his opponents thought he descended from Daedalus, the mythological image maker. Just as the sculptures of Daedalus ran away once they were completed, their arguments seemed to vanish in the face of Socratic questions.

We also know that Socrates received a typical education for his time in literature, music, and gymnastics, and studied under Archelaus, a native Athenian philosopher. He was also familiar with the Sophists, a group of pragmatic, itinerant teachers who gave instruction for worldly success, although they seemed more interested in the fees than the education. What's more, the Sophists used their rational skills to win arguments rather than gain understanding, so they came to represent the embodiment of distorted, dishonest thinking.

Apparently, Socrates was not an attractive-looking man: he was squat and stocky, with a round face, bulbous nose, and protruding eyes, which he rolled when he spoke. In Aristophanes' comic play *The Clouds*, he is shown descending from the sky in a basket and strutting about with splayed feet like a waterfowl. Aristophanes, in fact, portrays him as a ludicrous figure, operating a "thinking-shop" for young men who want to learn the "unjust logic."

On the other hand, Socrates is positively described in a Platonic dialogue called the *Symposium*. A man named Alcibiades compares him to a Silenus figure sold in the shops. The exterior was made of coarse clay, but the inside contained gold, which shone through openings in the surface.

Physically, Socrates seems to have been quite hardy, with great powers of endurance, wearing a thin garment in winter and summer and going barefoot, even in the winter campaigns. During the Peloponnesian War with Sparta, he served as a hoplite, or foot soldier, distinguishing himself for bravery at the battles of Potidaea, Delium, and Amphipolis. In two political disputes in Athens, according to Thucydides, he risked his life by refusing to sanction a mass trial of generals and by rejecting an illegal order by the Thirty Tyrants.

But rather than choosing a military career, with its austerity and discipline, it was the intellectual excitement of the city that appealed to Socrates. In conversations at the agora, or marketplace, he displayed a wonderful spirit and an ironic wit, softened by humaneness and generosity. He found the social life and the interplay of ideas exhilarating, and although he was moderate in food and wine, he could drink a great deal, continuing to philosophize as his companions slowly slipped under the table. By all accounts, he loved life, dining and talking in an urbane and genial way.

The Athenian city-state was not an ideal society in terms of justice and equality. Slavery was accepted as routine—in fact, it supported the economy—and women played a very subservient role. The highest aspiration for a woman was to be a wife rather than a slave or prostitute, and she had no political rights, first controlled by her father, then her husband. However, although parts of the population were clearly oppressed, Athens was a remarkably advanced culture, one of the first societies to establish democracy (in 508 BCE) and to stress the values of individuality, freedom, and the achievement of excellence. The Athenian city-state was considered the intellectual and cultural center of the ancient world, contributing immeasurably to Western civilization in astronomy, biology, mathematics, physics, government, politics, architecture, painting, literature, theater, and philosophy. It was this play of ideas that Socrates cherished, a city dedicated to the spirit of Athena, the goddess of wisdom.

The statesman Pericles (496–429 BCE) in his famous "Funeral Oration" describes, in idealized terms, the Athenian city-state:

> Our constitution is named a democracy, because it is not in the hands of the few but of the many. But our laws secure equal justice for all in their private disputes, and our public opinion welcomes and honors talent in every branch of achievement, not as a matter of privilege but on grounds of excellence alone. And as we give free play to all in our public life, so we carry the same spirit into our daily relations with one another. We have no black looks or angry words for our neighbor if he enjoys himself in his own way, and we abstain from the little acts of churlishness which, though they leave no mark, yet cause annoyance to who so notes them. Open and friendly in our private intercourse, in our public acts we keep strictly within the control of law. We acknowledge the restraint of reverence; we are obedient to whomsoever is set in authority, and to the laws, more especially to those which offer protection to the oppressed and those unwritten ordinances whose transgression brings shame.
>
> Yet ours is no work-a-day city only. No other provides so many recreations for the spirit—contests and sacrifices all the year round, and beauty in our public buildings to cheer the heart and delight the eye day by day.

Socrates' dedication to city life and philosophy must have been hard on his wife, Xanthippe, although she is sometimes described as a shrew. Socrates himself stated that having learned to live with Xanthippe, he would be able to cope with any other human being—like a horse trainer who has worked with wild horses. To bring in money, Socrates followed in his father's footsteps for a time, producing elegant statues, such as *The Three Graces*, which stood near the entrance to the Acropolis, but later he lived on a modest inheritance. He had three sons, perhaps by Xanthippe and by another wife, but he probably spent little time at home.

Early on he began to exhibit some psychic peculiarities. He would fall into trances, once standing in a fit of abstraction for a day, and throughout his life he heard a voice directing him. This daimon, or divine sign, told him what *not* to do, and it has been interpreted as either a spiritual force or a highly developed sense of morality. Some people have such a strong conscience that they experience it as a voice speaking from outside of themselves.

In a somewhat mystical sense, too, Socrates felt that he had a mission to perform for Apollo, a mission requiring philosophic thinking, and that it should be pursued not through writing, but through conversations with his fellow citizens. Writing was static, not the dynamic interaction he craved. He believed that he ought to devote his life to making the Athenians aware of their basic assumptions. He wanted people to reflect on the ideas they had accepted without thinking, to reason clearly about their actions and beliefs. "The unexamined life is not worth living," he stated, and he tried to make that credo part of Greek life. To believe only what is familiar and comfortable may be the line of least resistance but not the path of greatest advantage.

To pursue his philosophic calling, Socrates would corner prominent citizens and members of the government and ask them provocative questions: "What is the nature of justice?" "Do you think virtue can be taught?" "How would you define courage?" Conventional replies were usually given, and Socrates would then press further, asking for more adequate answers, sometimes forcing his opponents into self-contradictions. He was not looking for the definition of a word, but the meaning of the idea that the word represented.

Practicing this dialectic process of question and answer, known as the Socratic method, Socrates gathered round him a crowd of young men who enjoyed seeing powerful people challenged. They wanted the pompous deflated and took delight in being in on the kill. Furthermore, they imitated his method and asked questions of officials on their own. Of course, the people who were interrogated did not enjoy being publicly humiliated, and since they held positions of power, they became dangerous enemies.

This animosity did not deter Socrates, partly because he believed he had a divine calling to promote reflection. In fact, engraved on the great shrine at

Delphi were the words "Know Thyself." But people do not thank you for exposing their ignorance, and at the same time that he gained disciples among the young, he became increasingly unpopular with the authorities.

Socrates thought of himself as the "gadfly" (horsefly) of Athens, a necessary irritant, making the society self-aware.

> The State is like a great and noble steed who is tardy in his motions owing to his very size, and requires to be stirred into life. I am that gadfly which God has given to the State and all day long and in all places am always fastening upon you, arousing and persuading and reproaching you.

Just as the gadfly stings the sluggish horse into activity, the Socratic mission was to make the state conscious of its underlying beliefs.

By the time he was in his thirties, Socrates had acquired a mixed reputation, as a troublemaker but a wise man. The latter label probably made him more uncomfortable. Even though the Delphic oracle had told one of his admirers, Charephon, that no one was wiser than he, Socrates was acutely conscious of his shortcomings. Therefore, he interpreted this declaration to mean that although he was as ignorant as other people, at least he was aware of his ignorance. In that respect, in knowing how little he knew, he possessed a certain advantage. The moral seems to be that wisdom consists in realizing your limitations, and not pretending to know more than you do—especially to yourself.

Plato (428–347 BCE) was Socrates' principal disciple, and he undertook to record a number of the philosophic conversations between Socrates and other thinkers. Hence we have a series of books known as the Platonic dialogues. Usually they are named for the person with whom Socrates is speaking, so we have the *Euthyphro*, *Protagoras*, *Meno*, *Parmenides*, and so forth. Sometimes they are named for topics, such as the *Apology* and, most importantly, the *Republic*. The dialogue called the *Symposium* is a beautiful blend of poetry and philosophy, and shows Plato's literary powers at their finest.

However, a problem exists with regard to the authorship of the ideas the books contain. Rather than faithfully recording his teacher's thoughts, Plato inserted many of his own ideas into the dialogues, using Socrates as his spokesman. This is called the "problem of Socrates"—the difficulty of knowing where one man leaves off and the other begins. The problem is exacerbated because Plato himself never speaks directly. To differentiate between the two, some commentators use the subject matter, and others use chronology, identifying early and late dialogues. Generally, dialogues such as the *Apology*, *Euthyphro*, and *Crito* seem more faithful to Socrates, whereas the later ones, such as the *Sophist*, *Timaeus*, and *Protagoras*, are more Platonic.

However, most commentators agree that Plato provided the main ideas while Socrates furnished the spirit, method, and style of the dialogues.

In any case, we know that animosity built up against Socrates among influential Athenians. He was widely considered a disruptive force, not just a nuisance, but a threat to the well-being of the society. By the fourth century BCE the Athenians were in an ugly mood, anyway, having suffered a bitter and protracted war with Sparta. They wanted a stable government, the traditional state religion, political harmony, and a quiet citizenry. But Socrates kept challenging the status quo, fighting complacency and fomenting discord rather than allowing peace.

As a result, a plot was hatched against him, and Socrates was charged with crimes of "corrupting the youth and believing in strange gods." He was subsequently brought to trial, where he defended himself with philosophic arguments, but he was ultimately convicted of being a harmful influence on the society. The Platonic dialogue, the *Apology*, presents the account of that trial, and it seems a faithful record of what Socrates said in his defense. In this context, "apology" does not mean contrition, but a justification for one's life.

In addition to the formal charges against him, several informal ones were also raised during the trial, such as "making the worse appear the better cause," which amounted to a charge of sophistry, and "believing in things above and below the earth." As to sophistry, that was clearly false, since Socrates had not used his rationality to seek the appearance of truth and he had not charged for his teaching. The other accusation referred to speculation about metaphysics, the study of reality, but Socrates had abandoned that pursuit when he was very young; most of his life was devoted to moral matters.

The Greeks were sometimes opposed to the study of metaphysics because they believed some knowledge was forbidden, that sacred ground should not be violated by one's desire to know. Christianity has a similar notion, as seen in Genesis: Adam and Eve were expelled from the Garden of Eden for eating of the tree of knowledge. The underlying theme is that certain things are prohibited to humankind, and to seek understanding beyond one's realm is to commit the sin of hubris, excessive pride.

The Apology

In trying to refute the formal charges, Socrates faced three accusers, Meletus, Anytus, and Lycon, and he was able to challenge Meletus directly in the courtroom. Apparently, these men were fronting for more powerful interests—members of the establishment who wanted to rid the state of dissenters.

He began by questioning Meletus with regard to the charge of being "a villainous misleader of youth," first begging the indulgence of the court for proceeding in his usual manner:

> Come hither, Meletus, and let me ask a question of you. You think a great deal about the improvement of youth?
> Yes, I do.
> Tell the judges, then, who is their improver; for you must know, as you have taken pains to discover their corrupter, and are citing and accusing me before them. Speak, then, and tell the judges who their improver is . . . [t]he laws. But that, my good sir, is not my meaning. I want to know who the person is, who in the first place, knows the laws.
> The judges, Socrates, who are present in court.
> What do you mean to say, Meletus, that they are able to instruct and improve youth?
> Certainly they are.
> What, all of them, or only some and not others?
> All of them.
> By the goddess Hera, that is good news! There are plenty of improvers, then. And what do you say of the audience—do they improve them?
> Yes, they do.
> And the Senators?
> Yes, the Senators improve them.
> But perhaps the ecclesiasts corrupt them?—or do they too improve them?
> They improve them.
> Then every Athenian improves and elevates them; all with the exception of myself; and I alone am their corrupter? Is that what you affirm?
> That is what I stoutly affirm.
> I am very unfortunate if that is true. . . .

In trying to flatter the court, Meletus has placed himself in an impossible position, and his claim is reduced to an *argumentum ad absurdum*; surely Socrates cannot be the only person in Athens who harms the youth. Socrates then uses a comparison with horse training to weaken the case further. He points out that, with regard to horse training, only a few specialists will improve horses, while most will do them harm. In the same way, the few will improve the youth, and most will harm them—just the opposite of Meletus's claim. In this way Socrates discredits Meletus's authority, showing that he has not thought very deeply about such matters.

But Socrates then poses another question:

> Which is better, to live among bad citizens, or among good ones? . . . Do not the good do their neighbors good, and the bad do them evil?

> Certainly.
> And is there anyone who would rather be injured than benefited by those who live with him? Answer, my good friend; the law requires you to answer—does anyone like to be injured?
> Certainly not.
> And when you accuse me of corrupting and deteriorating the youth, do you allege that I corrupt them intentionally or unintentionally?
> Intentionally, I say.
> But you have just admitted that the good do their neighbors good, and the evil do them evil . . . (so) if a man with whom I have to live is corrupted by me, I am very likely to be harmed by him, and intentionally too? [T]hat is what you are saying, and of that you will never persuade me or any other human being.

In other words, Socrates would never intentionally corrupt people, because, by definition, bad people harm their neighbors, including Socrates himself. He would not want to be harmed; therefore he would never corrupt anyone.

Of course, that means no one would ever harm another intentionally, which is a questionable position. Nevertheless, Socrates believed it to be true. He maintained that if we knew what was good for us, and for the city-state as a whole, we would never hurt other people. We do harm only out of ignorance, not realizing that it will rebound against us. Once we understand where our interest lies, we will do unto others as we would have them do unto us; that will ensure that we will be treated the same way. We should help others, not for their sake, but for our sake.

This is the meaning of the Platonic dictum "Virtue is knowledge." Once we know what is good, we will behave in accordance with the good. In other words, knowledge guarantees virtuous conduct, which means the Socratic mission has even greater implications than it seems originally. Socrates is trying to make his society more aware and, by doing so, more moral.

As for the charge of believing in strange gods, Socrates maneuvers Meletus into claiming that he does not believe in any gods. In order to make him look as bad as possible, Meletus declares Socrates to be a complete atheist. That enables Socrates to spring a trap:

> Did ever any man believe in horsemanship, and not in horses? Or in flute playing and not in flute-players? No, my friend; I will answer to you and to the court, as you refuse to answer for yourself. There is no man who ever did. But now please to answer the next question: can a man believe in spiritual and divine agencies, and not in spirits and demigods?
> He cannot.

> Nevertheless you swear in the indictment that I believe in divine or spiritual agencies . . . (so) I must believe in spirits.

Socrates is referring to the well-known fact that he hears a divine voice, which means that he must believe in divinities. Receiving spiritual messages might indicate a belief in strange gods, but not the rejection of all gods.

Despite these arguments, the jury of 501 Athenians finds him guilty, although by a surprising margin of only sixty votes, and Meletus calls for the death penalty. As was customary, Socrates was then asked to suggest a fine for himself as an alternative. His response was as follows:

> And what shall I propose on my part, O men of Athens? Clearly that which is my due. And what is that which I ought to pay or receive? What shall be done to the man who has never had the wit to be idle during his whole life; but has been careless of what the many care about—wealth and family interests, and military offices, and speaking in the assembly, and magistracies, and plots, and parties. Reflecting that I was really too honest a man to follow in this way and live, I did not go where I could do no good to you or to myself; but where I could do the greatest good privately to everyone of you, thither I went, and sought to persuade every man among you that he must look to himself, and seek virtue and wisdom before he looks to his private interests. . . . What would be a reward suitable to a poor man who is your benefactor, who desires leisure that he may instruct you? There can be no more fitting reward than maintenance in the Prytaneum. . . .

This speech, proposing that he should be maintained at state expense in a public residence, did not endear Socrates to the members of the court. At the urging of his friends he proposed a small fine, but in the end the jury voted for the death penalty.

The arguments that Socrates offered at his trial are illustrative of his philosophic method, but they are hardly the best defense he could have mounted. For example, the analogy with horses may not be applicable to educating the young. When it comes to raising children, most people do it quite well; experts are not needed, because it is a general ability, not a specialized skill.

At age seventy, perhaps he was ready to die, or maybe he knew he would be condemned no matter how he defended himself. If he lost the arguments, he would be convicted, and if he won, that showed what a dangerously clever man he was, and he would be convicted. For whatever reason, he did not try very hard to acquit himself. In a sense, he was put to death not for what he did, but for what he was, and that could not be changed. He was also put to death for not groveling, for not bringing his family before the court to elicit sympathy:

> You think that I was convicted through deficiency of words—I mean, that if I had thought fit to leave nothing undone, nothing unsaid, I might have gained an acquittal. Not so; the deficiency that led to my conviction was not of words—certainly not. But I had not the boldness or impudence or inclination to address you as you would have liked me to address you, weeping and wailing and lamenting, and saying and doing many things which you have been accustomed to hear from others, and which, as I say, are unworthy of me. But I thought that I ought not to do anything common or mean in the hour of danger: nor do I now repent of the manner of my defense, and I would rather die having spoken after my manner, than speak in your manner and live. . . . The difficulty, my friends, is not in avoiding death but in avoiding unrighteousness.

At the end of the *Apology*, Socrates makes a final statement, referring to his sons and, more generally, to the importance of philosophic reflection over wealth, fame, or power.

> When my sons are grown up, I would ask you, O my friends, to . . . trouble them, as I have troubled you, if they seem to care about riches, or anything, more than about virtue; or if they pretend to be something when they are really nothing—then reprove them, as I have reproved you, for not caring about that for which they ought to care. . . . And if you do this, I and my sons will have received justice at your hands.
>
> The hour of departure has arrived, and we go our ways—I to die and you to live. Which is better, God only knows.

Two months later Socrates was put to death. In the account of the *Crito* he is offered a chance to escape, but he argues that it would be wrong to disobey the state, even when the law is unjust. As reported in the *Phaedo*, his final hours were spent with friends, discoursing calmly about immortality. At the very end he said, "I owe a cock to Asclepius, see that it is paid." He might have remembered a debt to a friend, or maybe he was referring to Asclepius, the god of healing; perhaps he thought he had been cured of the disease of life.

On the political level, the execution of Socrates makes us wonder how much criticism a state can tolerate before it acts to safeguard its welfare. In other words, to what extent should government limit the opposition of people like Socrates in order to function in a stable way? In a liberal democracy we support civil liberties, such as free speech, although we do impose limitations for the public good. We will prosecute slander and libel, hate speech and incendiary speech that cause a riot, but in general we assume that a free society is fundamentally strong and can withstand verbal attacks. In ridding itself of Socrates, the Athenian city-state revealed its own weakness, as well as betraying the democratic ideals expressed by Pericles. Only the unhealthy horse is bothered by the gadfly.

As for Socrates, he remained faithful to rational inquiry, which is the hallmark of philosophy, even at the cost of his life. Integrity and courage in the pursuit of truth seems to be his legacy.

CHAPTER TWO

Being Governed By the Mind: Rational Thought

Learning Is Recollection: Plato

Socrates' star pupil was Plato (427–347 BCE), a man often regarded as the most important figure in philosophic history, although Aristotle sometimes shares that honor with him. According to one well-known characterization, Plato was the first to raise every fundamental problem in philosophy, and all subsequent philosophy is merely "a series of footnotes to Plato." As we have seen, Socrates is renowned for his life of sincere and profound inquiry, but Plato is known for his philosophic ideas—ideas that have significantly shaped politics, ethics, mathematics, and intellectual thought up to the present day.

Originally given the name Aristocles, he was called Plato ("the broad") because of the width of his shoulders, a consequence of wrestling, or because of the breadth of his forehead, or perhaps his outlook. He was the youngest son of Ariston and Perictione but was raised by his stepfather, Pyrilampes, when his father died at an early age. Allegedly, he could trace his ancestry back to the first kings of Athens, and his patrician family intended him to enter government. However, Plato had a speculative mind rather than a practical one, so he was drawn to philosophic reflection instead.

Figure 2.1. *School of Athens*, by Raphael, 1509 (Vatican).

Plato fell under the spell of the charismatic Socrates when he was about eighteen, after studying briefly with Cratylus, a follower of Heraclitus, and he remained Socrates' main disciple for ten years. He was present at the trial, and the execution of Socrates had a profound effect on him, confirming his decision to avoid the intrigue and duplicity of politics. It also made him bitter toward democracy, for it was under that political system that Socrates was condemned to death. He came to believe that to be ruled by a few excellent men, an aristocracy of merit, would be the best form of government; democracy could degenerate into a tyranny of the majority, even mob rule. "Dictatorship naturally arises out of democracy," he wrote, "and the most aggravated form of tyranny and slavery out of the most extreme liberty."

Shortly after Socrates' execution took place in 399 BCE, Plato joined a group of his disciples under the leadership of Euclid, then left Athens for a time, traveling to Egypt, Sicily, Italy, and the Greek cities of Africa. He seems to have been impressed with Egyptian civilization, and brought back various inventions, including a water clock, which the Greeks had never seen. According to one account, he was captured by pirates and held for ransom, but the story is probably a colorful invention. In Italy his discussions with students of Pythagoras increased his interest in mathematics. This is apparent in various contexts, including the dialogue called the *Meno*, where a slave boy is made to educe the Pythagorean theory. By the end of the dialogue the boy articulates that the square of the hypotenuse of a right triangle is equal to the sum of the square of the other two sides.

We are sure that Plato performed military service, especially in the Peloponnesian War between Athens and Sparta. Like Socrates, he was decorated for bravery, and his writings show that he valued courage very highly, not just as a manly virtue, but as a human one.

In Plato's letter number seven, and in the biographical work by Diogenes Laertius, some other major events in Plato's life are recorded. Apparently, he traveled to Syracuse in 367 BCE at the invitation of Dionysus I, to educate his son, Dionysus II, in science and philosophy. However, the experiment was not a success; neither were subsequent trips to Syracuse. The politics and warfare in Sicily proved impossible to resolve, and Plato may have been imprisoned and sold into slavery for a time. In any case, he returned to Athens after some difficulty and remained there for the rest of his life.

In 387 BCE Plato founded a school in Athens called the Academy, which is considered the first university in the world. In fact, it has been a name for schools ever since, with academic subjects and teachers who are called academics. The Academy was designed to perpetuate the spirit of Socrates and his dialectic method, guiding students by careful increments in their philosophic education. It was also designed to educate statesmen who could rule Athens in a fair-minded way. If rulers understood the principles of justice, they could then rule justly; the application would naturally follow from the theory.

The curriculum must have included the Platonic dialogues, which were ostensibly a record of Socrates' conversations with various Athenians. However, as mentioned in the discussion of "the problem of Socrates" in chapter 1, the main ideas seem to be those of Plato, using Socrates as a spokesman. We do not know to what extent Socrates was turned into a Platonist.

Before becoming a philosopher, Plato was an accomplished poet and playwright, so it was natural for him to express his ideas in dramatic form. He even invented the myth of Atlantis, the lost continent, which inspired countless and fruitless underwater searches. However, after absorbing the influence of Socrates, he began to distrust art as "a watering of the passions," and he burned a tragedy he intended to enter in a competition. The artist has a "divine madness" about him, he thought, but lacked genuine knowledge. By stimulating people's emotions, he drew them further and further away from the truth. It is a curious paradox, therefore, that Plato used the dramatic dialogue as the vehicle for his philosophy.

Nevertheless, Plato affirmed the prime importance of rationality. The Greeks had just emerged from barbarism, and they knew what primitive emotions could do. They could produce war and slaughter, homicide and suicide. In order to be civilized, reason should govern our lives. We now know, of course, that reason, too, can lead to horrors, such as the systematic extermination of Jews by the Nazis, "the Final Solution." But perhaps an irrational hatred lay behind the rational system, and reflection would never have allowed it. The Holocaust, widespread atrocities carried out by an educated, highly cultured people, remains an enigma of history.

Plato headed the Academy for some forty years, and the school itself lasted over nine hundred years. It was closed only in the Roman era, by the emperor Constantine in 529 AD, as it was a pagan institution in an otherwise Christian world. To some extent, the Academy was intended to restore decent government so that men like Socrates would never suffer injustice. But mainly, the school fostered the most abstract level of thought. This was due to Plato's commitment to the good of the soul and the intellect, rather than to the well-being of the body. A famous story, probably apocryphal, is that a student once asked Plato what use his ideas had, at which point Plato gave him a coin so that he would not think his studies had been for nothing. The student was then dismissed from the school for presuming that knowledge should be useful rather than having theoretical value.

Mathematics was an essential part of the instruction—not applied, of course, but theoretical. Inscribed above the gates in Dante's Purgatorio were the words, "Abandon hope, all ye who enter here." Above the doorway of the Academy was written, "Let no one ignorant of mathematics enter here." Mathematics appealed to Plato as pure, abstract reasoning, and it had its representation in the heavens. In this realm alone there existed perfect geometric forms.

Plato taught that the heavens contained five "solids" of ideal shape. There were also heavenly bodies that rotated on their axes endlessly in perfect curves—the ideal circles of geometry. This notion gave rise to the idea that the planets created sound as they spun, "the music of the spheres," and in this way mathematics was linked with music. What's more, the positions of the planets, at various distances from each other, made up musical relations. For just as the tones on a stringed instrument depend on where the string is stopped, the distances between the planets create different tones in space. In this way celestial music is created, and the whole of the universe combines in a divine harmony.

Music was part of the curriculum as a whole, according to the principle of "music for the mind" and "gymnastics for the body." The Greeks also prized athletic achievement, as evidenced in the Olympic Games, and took as their overall ideal the notion of "a sound mind in a healthy body," or to quote the Latin, *mens sana in corpore sano*.

Religion and Ethics

Plato's references to the heavens and the good of the soul suggest that he was a religious thinker, and he has been identified that way by several theologians. However, in one of his important works, the *Euthyphro*, he separates religion from ethics, treating them as belonging in different realms, and he places "the good" in a higher category.

In this dialogue Socrates meets Euthyphro, a rather arrogant young man, in the anteroom of a court called the King Archon. In a short time Socrates will have to defend himself there against charges of impiety and corrupting the youth. Euthyphro is at the court to prosecute his father for impiety, specifically for causing the death of a slave boy. As punishment for some offense, the father had bound the boy and thrown him into a ditch and he had died there overnight of exposure.

With barely concealed irony, Socrates asks Euthyphro to explain the nature of piety so that he would be able to defend himself against the indictment facing him. Euthyphro must know, Socrates remarks, otherwise he could not bring his own father into court on charges of impiety.

Euthyphro rises to the bait and declares, "Piety is as I am doing, that is to say, prosecuting anyone who is guilty of murder, sacrilege, or of any similar crime—whether he be your father or mother, or whoever he may be."

However, Socrates rejects this definition, saying that he does not want an example of piety but an explanation of what it means to be pious. It would be like wanting the definition of *dog* and being given a poodle, a golden retriever, and a Chihuahua. Euthyphro then tries again, declaring that piety is "that which is dear to the gods, and impiety is that which is not dear to them." But Socrates points out that the gods often disagree: ". . . in thus chastising your father you may very likely be doing what is agreeable to Zeus but disagreeable to Cronus or Uranus, and what is acceptable to Hephaestus but unacceptable to Hera."

At this point, the dialogue takes a different turn. Leaving aside the matter of disagreements among the gods, Socrates poses a key question:

> The point which I should first wish to understand is whether the pious or holy is beloved by the gods because it is holy, or holy because it is beloved of the gods.

This sounds like double-talk, but cast in modern terms, Socrates is asking, "Is an act right because God wills it, or does God will it because it is right?" For in the first case, things such as murder, adultery, and stealing are wrong because God said so, whereas in the second case, God recognizes that murder, adultery, and stealing are wrong in themselves and, for that reason, said so.

This distinction may seem trivial, but it has enormous consequences. For if God makes actions right or wrong, then ethics is derived from religion. However, if God identifies right and wrong, then ethics is independent of religion. People could then be ethical without being religious, for ethics is not based on God's will to begin with.

Socrates chooses the latter option, declaring that the holy "is loved because it is holy, not holy because it is loved." He argues that the gods would not arbitrarily declare an action pious but would recognize its inherent piousness and therefore approve of it. Besides, the gods cannot make the wrong right, or the right wrong, by willing it; rather, they must acknowledge the rightness of actions and will them for that reason.

Ethics, therefore, does not depend on there being a God, for principles would have value even if God did not exist, and a decline in religion need not entail a decline in ethics. There may be a psychological connection between the two but not a logical one. Dostoevsky declared that if there is no

God, then everything is permissible, but an atheist could still acknowledge principles and live morally.

The Theory of Forms
Ages are known by the questions they ask even more than the answers they give, and as we have seen, the issue of change in the physical world preoccupied the early philosophers. Heraclitus declared that the whirl is king, that nothing is certain except change, while Parmenides and Zeno argued for an unchanging universe of unity, stability, and perfection. Against this background Plato proposed a radical theory about constancy and mutability that reverberated throughout the Middle Ages and to the present day.

Plato claimed that reality consists of two realms: physical objects and the ideas of those objects. That is, we have things on earth, like horses and trees, which we know about through our senses, and then the concepts of horse and tree, known by our rational understanding. We perceive horses of various colors, types, and sizes, but beyond that, we have the idea of what a horse is. In the same way, there are various kinds of trees, but there's also the general notion of a tree, i.e., the characteristics that something must have in order to be called a tree.

When we think about it, there have to be ideas behind every group of things, otherwise we could not classify them, and just as the sum of physical objects makes up a world of sense, the totality of ideas behind objects make up a virtual world of ideas. The latter are sometimes called "forms" or "universals," and not only does Plato believe them to be real, but he also claims they are more real than things.

Now, we might agree with Plato that ideas have a type of reality, the way that memories, dreams, or thoughts do, but Plato goes further, insisting that ideas are the fundamental reality. He bases this claim on two considerations: that ideas last forever, while things are ephemeral, and that ideas are perfect, whereas their physical representations are always flawed.

Let's take the previous examples of horses and trees. A horse is born, matures, and dies, but the idea of a horse continues on, surviving the death of any particular example of it. The same applies to a tree, which grows, then collapses, while the idea of a tree remains. We know that dinosaurs and dodo birds have become extinct, but we still have an idea of them. Furthermore, ideas precede as well as succeed things. In order to identify something as a horse, we must already have an idea of horse in our minds, otherwise how could we recognize it as a thing? This shows that the idea existed before its physical manifestation. The particular label does not matter—it could be called a horse, *chevalle, caballo,* or what have you—but we could not realize that something is a horse without prior knowledge of the nature of horses. All ideas, therefore, are eternal, and whatever is eternal is more real than that which is transitory, passing in and out of being.

As for the perfection of ideas, Plato argues that the idea of something is always an ideal form of it. The idea of a horse has perfect lines, grace, proportions, balance, confirmation, movement, and so forth; the idea of a tree is one of ideal shape, height, solidity, color, and texture. In fact, we measure a particular thing against the perfect idea that it exemplifies. One horse might have a swayback; another, a ragged trot; and still another, legs too thin for its body. A tree might have missing branches or mottled bark, and be stunted and scraggly. But how could we judge these as deficiencies unless we knew what a perfect horse or tree was?

And just as the eternal is more real than the finite, the perfect is more real than the imperfect. The intelligible world of ideas, therefore, is the basic reality, and the world of sense has a lesser reality.

Because of this theory, Plato largely rejected art. A painting of a horse or tree is two steps removed from ultimate reality, a copy of a copy. We should therefore avoid art, for it excites our senses, instead of allowing the cool contemplation of ideas. At one point Plato states that in his ideal society he would crown artists with laurels, give them every honor, then conduct them to the borders of the country, saying, "We do not allow artists in our republic." In a sense, he feared that art would seduce people into a sensual world, which is a left-handed compliment to the power of art.

Plato was not just concerned with horses and trees, but more importantly, with the abstract ideas of virtue, beauty, knowledge, justice, and so forth. For example, there is a form of the beautiful that is perfect and eternal, exemplified by particular beautiful things. A multicolored sunset, a rose or orchid, moonlight on the water, snowcapped mountains—all are manifestations of the idea of beauty, while being imperfect copies of it. They participate in the nature of beauty, although never measuring up to ideal beauty itself.

The same holds true for justice. Various forms of government will be closer or further away from the idea of a just state. That means there is an abstract ideal of justice that we use as a measuring rod in judging which government is best. If there were no concept of justice per se, that is, an objective standard of justice, we could not criticize our own society or others for falling short of the ideal.

In the *Republic* Plato illustrates his theory in the celebrated "Allegory of the Cave." Here he writes,

> Imagine human beings living in an underground den which has a mouth open towards the light and reaching all along the den; here they have been from their childhood, and have their legs and necks chained so that they cannot move, and can only see before them, being prevented by the chains from turning round their heads. Above and behind them a fire is blazing at a distance, and between the fire and the prisoners there is a raised way, and you will see, if you look, a low wall built along the way, like the screen which marionette players have in front of them, over which they show the puppets....
> And do you see, I said, men passing along the wall carrying all sorts of vessels, and statues and figures of animals made of wood and stone and various materials, which appear over the wall? Some of them are talking, others silent. ... [The prisoners] see only their own shadows, or the shadows of one another, which the fire throws on the opposite wall of the cave? And of the objects which are being carried in like manner they would only see the shadows?

Glaucon, the person to whom Socrates is speaking, remarks, "You have shown me a strange image, and they are strange prisoners," to which Socrates replies, "Like ourselves." In other words, we are like prisoners chained in a cave, seeing only shadows, which we mistake for reality. But the truth lies beyond us, accessible not to the senses, which capture only illusions, but to the mind—"the talking of the soul with itself." Plato continues,

> And now look again as the prisoners are released and disabused of their error. At first, when any of them is liberated and compelled suddenly to stand up and turn his neck round and walk and look towards the light, he will suffer sharp pains; the glare will distress him, and he will be unable to see the realities of which in his former state he had seen the shadows; and then conceive some one saying to him, that what he saw before was an illusion, but that now, when he is approaching nearer to being and his eye is turned towards more real existence, he has a clearer vision,—what will be his reply? And you may further imagine that his instructor is pointing to the objects as they pass and requiring him to name them,—will he not be perplexed? Will he not fancy that the shadows which he formerly saw are truer than the objects which are now shown to him?
> And suppose once more, that he is reluctantly dragged up a steep and rugged ascent, and held fast until he is forced into the presence of the sun himself, is he not likely to be pained and irritated? When he approaches the light his eyes will be dazzled, and he will not be able to see anything at all of what are now called realities....
> He will require to grow accustomed to the sight of the upper world. And first he will see the shadows best, next the reflections of men and other objects in the water, and then the objects themselves; then he will gaze upon the light of

the moon and the stars and the spangled heaven; and he will see the sky and the stars by night better than the sun or the light of the sun by day?

Last of all he will be able to see the sun, and not mere reflections of him in the water, but he will see him in his own proper place, and not in another; and he will contemplate him as he is. . . .

The prison-house is the world of sight, the light of the fire is the sun, and you will not misapprehend me if you interpret the journey upwards to be the ascent of the soul into the intellectual world . . . the idea of good appears last of all, and is seen only with an effort; and, when seen, is also inferred to be the universal author of all things beautiful and right, parent of light and of the lord of light in this visible world.

The light of the sun illuminates the perceptual world, a "visible god," and the form of the good corresponds to the sun, the supreme idea in the conceptual world. The good sheds light on all other ideas, like a benediction. The person with a philosophic mind can escape the ignorance of the cave and, after a demanding intellectual journey, accompanied by ridicule from others, can discover a higher realm of perfect and eternal goodness.

What's more, all human souls once dwelt in this ideal realm and therefore can recognize the ideas they once contemplated; they are, in fact, contained within us. When we see the shadows, we are reminded of the higher ideas they represent, just as engaging in philosophic debate enables us to understand the reality behind appearances. Learning, therefore, is recollection. We never learn anything new but only remember the truths we already know, dredging them to the light of consciousness. This notion, that truth is embedded in our minds and can be drawn out by reasoning, influenced theories of knowledge for centuries.

Of course, opponents point out that to know things, we need not have prior knowledge of them. We can abstract common qualities of objects that we have experienced through the senses, and build categories or forms labeled *horses* or *trees*.

The Ideal State
Plato's political philosophy follows naturally from his theory of reality. Those individuals who understand the ideas, especially the idea of justice, are best suited to rule the state. Once the rulers know what is right, they will do what is right. They will strive to bring fairness, honesty, equality, freedom, and other virtues down to earth so that people are governed justly. Those who live everyday lives in the material world see only distortions of justice and have no ideal model to guide them. In other words, the reflective people

must command the ship of state, navigating by the light of heavenly forms. In the *Republic* Plato writes, "There will be no end to the troubles of humanity itself, till philosophers become kings in this world . . . and rulers really and truly become philosophers."

In saying this, Plato is not just favoring his own profession because the rulers do not derive any benefits from their position. Rather than having special privileges, they are forbidden gold or silver, and they cannot become wealthy or famous, purchase homes, marry, or establish families. They live in barracks and eat plain food, with a bit of wine on feast days, and their sexual relations are severely regulated: only outstanding men can mate with outstanding women in order to ensure genetic excellence in their children. It has been described as monasticism without celibacy. All children are raised in common and never know who their parents are. Mothers are to be between twenty and forty, and men twenty-five to fifty-five; outside these ages sex is free but abortion is compulsory, and deformed children are "put away in some mysterious unknown place." Since there is no luxurious living, the only motivation for becoming a guardian is to serve society, and the only qualifications are an intelligent mind and the desire for social justice.

Plato in fact divided people based on their predominant characteristics. Those who function primarily in terms of their appetites are suited to become farmers, merchants, builders, and so forth, because they will work hard to become rich and enjoy their creature comforts. Their virtue is to be *temperate*. Those who are strong, spirited, and courageous are suited to protect the state as police or soldiers, what Plato terms "auxiliaries." Their virtue is to be *courageous*. And those who are bright, dedicated, and reflective should govern the state, thus creating an aristocracy or rule of excellence. Plato calls these individuals the "guardians," and both men and women can perform this function. Their purpose is to direct the state with the virtue of *wisdom*. One "royal lie" to be foisted on society is that God made the guardians of gold, the military of silver, and common men of brass and iron.

Every person in this utopia is placed in one of these three classes of occupations, depending on their aptitude. People are not given any freedom of choice in the matter, but freedom is not always a blessing. It can be disastrous, both for the individual and for the state. Human beings are happiest when they express their dominant talents, interests, and capabilities, and society benefits most when people give what they are best able to give. Therefore citizens should know their place and not try to be something they're not. If someone who is primarily equipped to be a worker should want to be a soldier, that would only make the person miserable, as well as being a disservice to the state. The same holds true for a soldier who wants to be a ruler. They would have to be told, "I'm sorry. You just aren't fit for it."

Obviously, this is highly undemocratic, but Plato believed that people should accept their strengths and weaknesses, and that only those who have philosophic minds and strive for ideal justice are qualified to be leaders. Reason should control the state, as well as govern the appetites and the will within the individual. Of course, such a government would be vulnerable to coups and revolutions by the military, which has the arms, and by the economic producers, who have the financial power. Nevertheless, having the most intellectual and moral people in charge is the finest form of government.

Such was Plato's vision, a mix of authoritarianism and humanism, rationalism and mysticism, a concern with excellence combined with a passion for justice. Cicero, the Roman orator, tells us that Plato died in the midst of his intellectual labors, still trying to fathom the truly good, beating back ignorance. "We can easily forgive a child who is afraid of the dark," Plato wrote. "The real tragedy of life is when men are afraid of the light."

Some critics, however, wonder whether the ideal of reasonableness is being overemphasized to the detriment of the full human being. The love of forms is a cold love of abstractions, of metaphysical structures that have both the correctness and the remoteness of mathematics. The self-mastery Plato respected so highly leaves no room for endearing weaknesses, indulgence in natural desires, spontaneous action. He wants us to temper our impulses, express our desires moderately, and lead a decorous, rational life. Our vision must be directed inward to the idea of the good impressed on our souls, not outward to the people of flesh and blood surrounding us. In Plato's scheme, feelings are emasculated, and comfort and sensuality are relegated to the lowest level. The intellectual elite who rule the state have an ascetic existence, living without families so that they are not distracted from the contemplation of pure ideas. All this seems far too severe, depriving life of its resonance, mystery, and savor. When someone suggested the good might be pleasure, Socrates exclaimed, "Heaven forbid."

In the same way, art, poetry, and drama are banned or censored if they interfere with contemplation, and modes of music are allowed only if they are uplifting. Even the lyrical Homeric myths are criticized, because the gods are sometimes pictured as quarreling among themselves or seducing mortals. Homer referred to the "inextinguishable laughter" of the gods, which Plato considered undignified and a bad example for the young.

Such an astringent life of reason, so completely disciplined and virtuous, neglects the basic joy in living. To feel contempt for the physical world and for the gratifications of our senses seems to exclude too much. We come away from Plato's system wanting immediate human experience more than a frozen world of pure ideas.

The Path of Moderation: Aristotle

Just as Socrates was Plato's teacher, Aristotle was a disciple of Plato's; he in turn became tutor to Alexander the Great. Aristotle's dates are 384–322 BCE; his birthplace is Stagirus, in Macedonia. His father, Nicomachus, was the latest in a line of physicians to Macedonian kings, and Aristotle maintained his ties to the court throughout his life. Despite his Macedonian heritage, he is widely considered a Greek philosopher.

Nicomachus died when Aristotle was ten, and his mother, Phaestis, died a few years later, and for the rest of his boyhood, he was raised by a guardian, who sent him to study in Athens when he was seventeen. Aristotle soon joined the Academy and remained there for twenty years, first sitting at the feet of Plato, then becoming a teacher in his own right. When Plato died in 347 BCE, Aristotle was the heir apparent, but the leadership of the Academy passed into the hands of Plato's nephew Speusippus. Apparently, there was some bad blood at the school, and Aristotle's ideas had diverged too radically from that of the master. According to some scholars, Plato felt that Aristotle needed more restraint than encouragement, "the curb not the spur."

Probably because of this disappointment, Aristotle left Athens and spent three years at the court of Hermias, ruler of Atarneus, where he married Pythias, a niece or sister of the king. She gave birth to a daughter, who was named after her mother. When Hermias was killed in a rebellion, Aristotle traveled with his family to Mytilene, stopping at the island of Lesbos to do biological research. At that point, King Philip II of Macedonia invited him to tutor his son, Alexander, then a thirteen-year-old boy.

The relationship between Aristotle and Alexander is the stuff of legends, the one conquering the world with ideas, the other with a sword. Alexander swept through most of what was then the civilized world, never losing a battle. According to Plutarch, Alexander learned ethics, politics, and rhetoric from Aristotle, who also stimulated his interest in science, medicine, and mathematics. Alexander, in fact, carried a variety of books with him on his military campaigns, the *Iliad* in particular. As for Aristotle, he was probably given an extensive library for his biological research, and the hunters, fishermen, fowlers, and gamekeepers supplied him with specimens of animals. Aristotle was fascinated with biology, so these specimens were carefully examined and their features meticulously catalogued. All the records were placed in a hidden vault and might have been lost forever except for an accidental discovery in about 70 BCE. The pages were badly damaged by dampness and worms, but a wealthy Athenian named Appelicon restored them to legible condition.

When Alexander left on his Asiatic campaign, his education completed, Aristotle returned to Athens and opened a school called the Lyceum—an institution of higher learning that rivaled the Academy. The students would follow Aristotle in a cloud as he paced the shady paths of the school, discoursing about philosophy. They therefore were known as peripatetics, or "walk abouts," which became the name for all of Aristotle's followers.

For thirteen years Aristotle headed the Lyceum, engaged in research, teaching, and writing, giving more advanced classes in the mornings and lectures for the general public in the afternoon. However, upon the death of Alexander in 323 BCE a wave of anti-Macedonian feeling swept through Athens, and Aristotle suddenly became persona non grata. Faced with trumped-up charges of impiety, he retreated to his country house in Chalcis, in Euboea, lest "the Athenians sin twice against philosophy." He died there a year later, presumably of a stomach disease. A more colorful legend has it that he threw himself into the sea because he could not explain the tides.

The various statues and busts of Aristotle seem to be accurate, depicting a handsome man with sharp, even features, somewhat below average height, imposing and self-confident. According to accounts of his character, he was a man of integrity, practicing the ideals he preached, a calm and noble person, generous, evenhanded, and high-minded.

When we read Aristotle, he seems to lack the liveliness or panache of some Hellenic philosophers. The image is of a dry and pedantic individual, whose works are carefully fashioned and tightly woven. Bertrand Russell describes his writing as

> critical, careful, pedestrian, without any trace of Bacchic enthusiasm. The Orphic elements in Plato are watered down in Aristotle, and mixed with a strong dose of common sense.... [H]e is a professional teacher, not an inspired prophet.

However, that could be a false impression. In Plato we have his popular writings, whereas Aristotle's works are more technical treatises—perhaps notes from his morning lectures rather than finished books. During his time, in fact, Aristotle was praised for "a golden flow of language" (Cicero). This implies that he had a more imaginative personality than his works suggest, which may have been expressed in his personal interactions. At the end of his life he wrote in a letter, "[The] more I am by myself, and alone, the fonder I have become of myths." This indicates a poetic as well as a scholarly mind.

Aristotle's most significant works are the *Nicomachean Ethics*, named for his father and his son Nicomachus, the *Politics, Poetics, Physics*, and *De Anima (On the Soul)*. His *Metaphysics* addresses subjects ranging from ethics and logic to physics, aesthetics, and biology. In fact, Aristotle contributed to nearly every branch of knowledge and even wrote texts on peripheral subjects, such as *On Dreams, On the Gait of Animals*, and *On Memory and Reminiscence*. To the Scholastics, he was quite simply "the Philosopher," and he remains the principal theorist of the Catholic Church.

Aristotle's philosophy differs from that of Plato's principally because it is oriented toward the natural world, especially biological principles. Above all, he wanted to investigate physical laws. Plato thought of philosophy as the search for ideas, the prototype of reality, that existed apart from objects. Aristotle, while concerned with the universal, wanted to begin with particular things and through them gain insight into essences. To Plato the ideal form of an object exists in a world of forms, eternal and immutable, whereas Aristotle saw the ideal as lying within matter. This is why in "The School of Athens" Plato points upward, Aristotle to the earth.

Metaphysics: The Nature of Reality
The core of Aristotle's metaphysical thought is the idea of potentiality and actuality, and this involves the notion of the "final cause" of things. We assume a pool ball moves because it is struck by the cue stick, but all objects are drawn from in front by their final cause. It is the end for which something is made, its ultimate goal. "Thus health is the cause of walking. If we ask, 'Why is he walking?' The answer is, 'In order to be well.'"

An object realizes itself by fulfilling its inherent end, its *telos*, or what it strives to become. As the ideal craftsman, nature does nothing in vain but moves its creatures toward their goal, not one imposed from outside, but an internal, generating force. In fulfilling their purpose, all things attain the full perfection of their being.

This means, in effect, that we do not see because we have eyes, but we have eyes because we need to see. "Nature adopts the organ to the function, and not the function to the organ," Aristotle writes. The ibis does not eat fish and frogs on the tidal flats because it has a long bill, but it develops a long bill in order to eat fish and frogs. The same is true of a tiger's claws, a turtle's shell, a deer's antlers, or the chameleon's ability to camouflage itself. These forms occur because of a necessary end toward which the creatures tend, and the form that something assumes is its unique reality.

Teleologism is the name of this view, according to which form is intrinsic to matter and the virtue of anything lies in the realization of itself. In contrast, naturalism stands for the opposite view: that all creatures use their abilities in order to survive. The ibis eats fish and frogs because it has a long bill, just as a tiger tears its prey because it has claws, the turtle is protected by an armored shell, antlers enable the deer to fight, and chameleons escape detection because they are able to change colors.

This is why the Catholic Church, following in Aristotle's footsteps, declares that human life begins at conception, because at that point an unborn child is drawn toward the realization of its humanness. The naturalistic position, in contrast, is that although the embryo will become human, it is not already human, any more than an acorn is an oak tree.

Aristotle amassed a great deal of data about living things, and he is celebrated for his extensive biological classifications in terms of similarities and differences (*genus* and *differentia*), but his research also yielded this distinctive theory of nature. For him, the final cause of the seed is reached in the blossoming of the flower, which is the actualization of its potentiality, its final form. All of Aristotle's philosophy is grounded in the teleological model, largely derived from his biological research.

In later centuries theologians such as St. Thomas Aquinas identified God as the being that infused life with purpose, and this became the "teleological argument" for God's existence. In *Summa Theologica*, as the last of his "five ways," St. Thomas argued that something must have given creatures their goal in living, and that could only be God. The world and everything in it was created for a purpose, for some good reason, and is not the accidental product of mutations and natural selection.

Ethics and the Primacy of Reason
Since all things contain a purpose, we can legitimately ask, "What is the purpose of human beings?" Another way to pose the question is, "What is the human function?"

Now, the function of an object is something unique to it, or at least that which it does supremely well. For example, the function of an axe is to chop, and a good axe is one that chops well. It was, in fact, made for that purpose, and a skilled craftsman is one who makes axes that are excellent in their particular qualities. In the same way, a bird's wing enables it to fly, a house provides shelter, and a knife is made to cut. Since everything has a function, what then is the function of "man"?

We cannot say the human function consists of nourishment and growth, since that is the life of plants. We are not meant just to keep ourselves alive and reproduce. Likewise, the function of humans cannot be sensation and feeling, since animals have that mode of existence. Living in terms of our senses is beastly—even in terms of sight, which is the most ennobling; or hearing, which instructs us; or touch, which is the most rudimentary. Rather, we should live according to reason, the distinctive characteristic of human beings and therefore the human function. Reason makes the world intelligible, just as the sun makes the earth visible.

Aristotle reaches the same conclusion from a different starting point. Our purpose cannot be fame or glory, because that depends too much on the "honorers" and not on us. It cannot be moneymaking, because that consumes too much of our lifetime; wealth is not life's report card. It must therefore be the life of the mind, of thought and contemplation, which is within our control.

Rationality therefore distinguishes the human species, and our "good" must in some way involve our reasoning faculty. Humans are the rational animals, and man's good in life must be connected with the proper use of this unique ability.

In his chief ethical work, *The Nicomachean Ethics*, Aristotle defines "good" as *eudaimonia*, which has been translated as "well-being," "vital well-being" or simply "happiness." "Vital well-being" is perhaps closest to the Greek, for it implies a dynamic state of personal satisfaction, as well as health, attractiveness, material comforts, achievements, etc., which seems to be what Aristotle meant. In any case, Aristotle took *eudaimonia* to be the *summum bonum*, the "highest good" that human beings can attain.

The next question, of course, is, "How should we exercise our rational function so as to attain the good?" Aristotle specified two ways: to engage in reflective contemplation, and to make wise choices by controlling the tendencies of our passions. Although the first is considered more important, the second plays a more prominent part in his system.

Aristotle maintained that we must strive to attain the *mean between extremes* by allowing reason to adjudicate the conflicting claims of our emotions, choosing that area of moderation between excess and deficiency. What is needed is for reason to select, deliberately and objectively, the mean states and activities, and not allow the individual to go to extremes. "*Meden agan,*" Aristotle declared, "nothing in excess," and it is reason that will keep us from excessive states or actions.

Just as it can be said of a good work of art "that nothing could be taken from it or added to it," so in action we must aim at the perfection of balance. "For instance, it is possible to feel fear, confidence, desire, anger, pity, and generally to be affected pleasantly and painfully, either too much or too little, in either case wrongly; but to be thus affected at the right times, and on the right occasions, and towards the right persons, and with the right object, and in the right fashion, is the mean course and the best course." We should strive to achieve what Aristotle's followers called the *aurea mediocritas*, or the "golden mean" under the guidance of reason.

Aristotle realized that these generalizations do not help us practically in our lives, so he specified particular states and actions that his doctrine would engender; in fact, he offered a handbook of morality. With regard to feelings of fear and confidence, the mean is courage, the excess rashness, and the deficiency cowardice. With respect to pleasures and pains, the mean is temperance, the excess is profligacy (dissipation), and the deficiency, Aristotle said, has not been given a name, because it is hardly ever found (*sic!*). In money matters involving large sums, moderation is magnificence, while excess and deficiency are vulgarity and meanness, respectively. With regard to honor and disgrace, the mean is pride, the excess vanity, and the deficiency humility.

Aristotle provided us with an extensive list, including, for example, the virtue of wit as a mean between buffoonery and boorishness, modesty as a virtue between bashfulness and shamelessness, and friendliness as the path of moderation between being obsequious and quarrelsome. In all cases, following the "middle way," as the Buddha put it, constitutes virtuous behavior. Aristotle did not say that we should strike a precise midpoint but rather that we ought to find a middle range along the continuum from excess to deficiency. To forestall criticism, he wrote,

> It is not all actions nor all passions that admit of moderation; [t]here are some whose very names imply badness, as malevolence, shamelessness, envy, and, among acts, adultery, theft, murder. These and all other like things are blamed as being bad in themselves, and not merely in their excess or deficiency. It is impossible therefore to go right in them; they are always wrong: rightness and wrongness in such things [e.g., in adultery] does not depend upon whether it is the right person and occasion and manner, but the mere doing of any one of them is wrong. It would be equally absurd to look for moderation or excess or deficiency in unjust, cowardly or profligate conduct. . . . The acts are wrong however they be done.

In summation, Aristotle argued that if we use our primary function of reasoning in an excellent way, we will choose the mean between extremes and thereby bring about our vital well-being. And if we use reason for *theoria*, or theoretical understanding, this will advance our development still further. That is, reflection on timeless truths will express our highest faculty and thereby increase *eudaimonia*. In fact, we can actually achieve contemplative happiness, which is the happiness of God. Certainly Aristotle's notion of moderation has a certain commonsense appeal, because many people do seek centeredness, a harmony of feelings. If we go to extremes, our equilibrium is destroyed and our development distorted. To live in such a way that we achieve a sense of proportion through rational choices, that seems to define successful living.

A Critical Appraisal
To begin with, some philosophers have questioned Aristotle's central notion that all objects have a function or purpose in being. Tools that we make, such as axes, hammers, or saws, certainly serve a purpose, as do cars, trains, and airplanes, but do all natural objects have a purpose? For example, we may use a rock as a paperweight, or to build a wall, or to throw at someone, but is there an inherent function that rocks have on earth?

Even though trees provide lumber, cows give milk, and plants give off oxygen, that may not be why they exist, but simply capabilities they have. In fact, some philosophers maintain that there might not be a raison d'être for anything that exists, aside from the objects we create to serve some purpose. This includes human beings, who may not exist for any reason. The entire teleological approach of seeing objects, animals, or people in terms of an inherent purpose may be wrongheaded.

Besides, most things have more than one function. Fire provides light as well as heat, a way to cook food, and for early man, a means of frightening away animals. The mouth is used for eating but also for speaking, and the foot is used for walking but sometimes to kick a soccer ball. People are able to reason, although they are not unique in that respect (consider dolphins and chimpanzees), but they are also capable of moral feelings, aesthetic sensibilities, a spiritual sense, and so forth. Why claim that reason alone is our particular function, much less that whatever is special should be expressed? A man with a unique ability to steal should not fulfill himself as a pickpocket.

The weakness of this perspective is illustrated by an argument used to suppress women in their career aspirations. "A woman's purpose is to be a mother," it has been said, "for unless you have children you have failed to fulfill your unique function. In fact, you are hardly a woman, any more than we can call something an apple tree that does not bear apples." But this kind of reasoning is repugnant to our contemporary mind. Although women have the ability to bear children, that is not necessarily a woman's function in life. Women can choose whether they want to bear children or whether they want to realize other capabilities—their artistic talent, their communication skills, athletic ability, interest in science, and so forth. Instead of searching for our purpose in living, perhaps we should decide what we want out of life.

Apart from the problems surrounding the concept of function, a second criticism of Aristotle has to do with his championing of moderation. He claims that reason achieves excellence (*arête*) when it serves as a guide to the mean, but is the mean always best? In some cases, we would be right in going to extremes. A painter, for example, might be justified in indulging his passion for art, the way Gauguin did, and Christianity is based on an extreme of self-sacrifice. Should the artist, the devotee, the national leader, the explorer, or the gifted scientists live in moderation or to the limit of their abilities? We want to avoid fanaticism, but we do not want to replace it with mediocrity, being so afraid of making that mistake that we make different ones. We might prefer passion to poise, and think of the temperate life as bloodless.

It seems as though Aristotle had already decided to his own satisfaction which actions were right and then fitted them into a general scheme. He took the conventional Greek virtues and found a structure to justify them. On the Parthenon was inscribed, "Everything in moderation, nothing in excess." This was what Aristotle affirmed, stating that we should be temperate, courageous, truthful, gentle, modest, and so forth, listing a string of clichés that cannot be disputed but are also quite banal. They are the values of conservatives and conformists, the middle class, the middle-aged, and the middlebrow, the people who play it safe and never do anything drastic. Aristotle thus became a spokesman for a commonplace morality that is comforting but not very exciting. In the human oscillation between venturing and centering, he chose the tame, measured way. The rumor is not true, however, that Aristotle died of moderation.

Government and Art
A final word should be added about Aristotle's views on government and art—views that are extremely sensible. Unlike Plato, he rejected an ideal form for the state but thought various kinds of governments could be effective depending on the circumstances. Instead of a government of excellence, where kings are philosophers and philosophers are kings, Aristotle identified three positive and three negative types of rule.

A monarchy is best if a wise and good monarch can be found, but it will degenerate into tyranny if the ruler is corrupt. Then he will cut off the heads of men of spirit; Nero, for example, liked music and massacres. A second positive form is aristocracy, a rule of gifted, intelligent men, but it can lapse into oligarchy, with power vested in the hands of a wealthy class. A third form of government, polity or constitutional government, can occur when the rulers want fame, power, advantage, and prestige. This can be effective, but it can also decay into democracy, which, to Aristotle is rule by the lowest common denominator, a left-wing tyranny, as evidenced by the execution of Socrates.

In fact, there is no ideal state in the abstract, apart from a historical and social context. The best state is one that enables its citizens to thrive and flourish, to be virtuous in particular circumstances. Since man is "the political animal," life should be lived within a moral community, but we cannot identify any one as best. Today Americans believe that all nations should be democratic, but Aristotle thought that would be a mistake.

Aristotle and Plato also disagreed regarding art. Plato distrusted the emotive power of art, but Aristotle welcomed it, especially tragic drama. By portraying strong emotions, tragedies provide a "cathartic" release of pent-up, unhealthy feelings. The audience members relate to the characters onstage "through pity and fear," and they feel purged at the end of the play. That is why tragedies that contain bloodshed and horror are so enjoyable. In a well-written drama, the hero always has a "tragic flaw," which inevitably leads to his or her downfall, and as people live the events vicariously, they feel cleansed. Their own violent impulses are displaced, and they are less likely to commit awful acts themselves.

In retrospect, Aristotle's ideas have flaws, but they are well worth considering. That is why he has deeply influenced Western thought, especially his concepts of potentiality and actuality; purpose and function; moderation; appropriate forms of government; and catharsis in art. Unfortunately, we have only one-fifth of his original works and can only imagine the ideas that are gone.

Accept What You Cannot Change: The Stoics

The next major movement in Hellenic philosophy was Stoicism, which came via a circuitous route from Socrates. Unlike Plato, who taught in the Academy, and Aristotle, who gave instruction in the Lyceum, the Stoics taught in the *stoa poikile* ("painted porch"), from which the philosophy got its name. The Stoicism that has come down to us today is actually close to the original doctrine: to maintain control, detachment, and tranquility, even in the face of catastrophe.

Being Cynical

To understand the Stoics, we must begin with their immediate and colorful predecessors—a group of street philosophers called the Cynics. The Cynics did not organize themselves into a formal school of philosophy but were a disparate group of like-minded people. They were unconventional and antisocial for the most part, celebrated as much for their independence as their notions of right living. Self-sufficiency and correct conduct actually became fused, because the Cynics considered their individualistic way of life a "shortcut to virtue." In effect, their philosophic legacy lies in how they lived.

Although the Cynics were frequently referred to as "the dog philosophers" because of their slovenly appearance (people, in fact, would throw bones at them), they were actually quite disciplined, practicing *askasis*, which means "self-training." They believed in mental control rather than physical indulgence or conformity to society. They ridiculed Athenian etiquette; were abrasive, unruly, and shameless; and performed private acts in public, such as drinking and masturbating. They disdained bathing, marriage, money, and all the trappings of success. They also opposed all intellectual theory, although they did maintain that we should disregard pleasure and pain since the soul was more important than the body. On principle, they lived a life of relentless poverty.

If the Cynics had a common philosophy, it was that we should follow nature, which to their minds exhibited the qualities of freedom, self-sufficiency, and reason. Athenian conventions, on the other hand, restricted these virtues, especially personal freedom, and therefore had to be resisted. We have an obligation to be cynical about civil society, to disrupt its political and social traditions through outrageous behavior. We must also oppose the values of the culture by providing an alternative model—a virtual anarchy within which the individual can thrive. Nothing natural is corrupt or shameful, whereas civilization is evil incarnate.

Counted among the Cynics are a variety of philosophers: Diogenes of Sinope, Crates, Hipparchia of Maronea (a female Cynic), and Zeno of Citium, the founder of Stoicism. The Greek Antisthenes seems to be a transition figure, for in the ancient source *The Lives of Eminent Philosophers*, we read, "From Socrates he learned his hardihood, emulating his disregard of feelings, and thus inaugurated the Cynic way of life."

Of this group the most vivid and romantic by far was Diogenes (412–323 BCE), who became a disciple of Antisthenes. Numerous tales about him have survived, which illustrate his commitment to the ascetic ideal, as well as his contempt for all vanities. Most of the stories are inventions, but with some slight basis in fact.

Diogenes is reputed to have lived in a barrel or tub that belonged to the temple of Cybele, with few possessions besides a robe, a walking stick, and a wooden bowl. When he saw a boy drink from his hand, he threw the bowl away as vanity and affectation. He is reputed to have lit a lantern during daylight and to have declared, "I am just looking for an honest man." When he heard that Plato had defined the word *man* as "a featherless biped," he plucked a bird and announced, "Here is Plato's man." (The definition was then amended to "a featherless biped with broad, flat nails.")

In one famous incident Alexander the Great visited him as he was sunning himself in a field. "Are you not afraid of me?" Alexander asked. "Why? What are you?" Diogenes replied. "A good thing or a bad thing?" "A good thing," Alexander declared, to which Diogenes responded, "Who, then, is afraid of the good?" Alexander was so impressed that he said, "Ask anything of me that you like." Diogenes replied, "Then kindly move out of my sunlight." As Alexander left, he is reputed to have remarked, "Had I not been Alexander, I should have liked to be Diogenes."

Although Plato described Diogenes as "a Socrates gone mad," he remains the image of the wise, rebuking Cynic. According to the various accounts of his death, he died from a dog bite at around age ninety, or from eating raw octopus, or perhaps from holding his breath.

The Stoics

Following Cynicism, there developed the Greco-Roman philosophy of Stoicism, probably founded by Zeno of Citium. The philosophy is identified with Cleanthes (331–232 BCE), Chrysippus (280–207 BCE), and Seneca (ca. 5 BCE–65 AD), and more importantly, the Roman figures Epictetus (ca. 55 AD–ca. 135 AD) and Marcus Aurelius (121–180 AD).

Epictetus was born a slave, but he was freed by his owner, Epaphroditus, shortly after the emperor Nero died. As a result of his servitude, he was lame all his life. Since he showed intellectual promise, his master sent him to study with C. Musonius Rufus, a prominent philosopher of the time, and Epictetus became the most famous of the Roman Stoics.

His forbearance was legendary. According to one story, his master was twisting his leg one day because of some insolence, and Epictetus said, "If you twist it any more it will break." His master did twist his leg farther, and it did break. "You see, I told you so," Epictetus remarked calmly. In keeping with Stoic virtues, he thought we should practice restraint toward events we cannot control. "It is not what happens to you, but how you react that matters."

Epictetus apparently lived simply, following the model of Socrates more than the Cynics. He lived in a small house that contained a rush mat, a pallet to sleep on, and an earthenware lamp. He married late in life, and then only to have a mother for a child who was threatened with death by exposure; according to Roman law, a married man had the right to save such a child.

Toward the middle of his life Epictetus managed to offend the emperor Domitian and was exiled from Rome, along with other philosophers who, Domitian said, had the audacity to speak the truth even to Caesar. He settled in Nicopolis, Epirus, on the other side of the Adriatic, where he founded a school attended by the children of Rome's elite. He also wrote the work on which his reputation rests: the *Encheridion*, or *Manual*.

The other great Stoic was not a slave, but an emperor, Marcus Aurelius (121–180), the only philosopher king in history. He was groomed to rule, from his early education by the emperor Hadrian to the advisory role he assumed with the emperor Antoninus Pius, who adopted him as his son. He married Pius's daughter, had thirteen children, served in the Senate, and held the high offices of consul and tribune. At age forty he ascended the throne. He was succeeded by his son Commodus—an emperor regarded as the most venal and decadent in Roman history. One commentator called it a change from a golden kingdom to one of iron and rust.

Marcus Aurelius was renowned for the quality of his character; he strove to be the perfect man. Hadrian called him Verissimus, "most truthful," and he is credited with reducing corruption, banning informers, blunting the swords of the gladiators, and freeing slaves whenever he could. His sense of justice and his political skills were severely tested, however, for during his reign there were threats from the Germans in the north and the Parthians in the east, as well as famines, epidemics, and earthquakes. In the end the *pax Romana*, or Roman peace, was shattered. Nevertheless, Edward Gibbon in his definitive work *The Decline and Fall of the Roman Empire* included Marcus Aurelius as one of the "Five Good Emperors," during whose rule "the human race was most happy and prosperous."

In the ancient world a philosopher was one who lived a philosophic life, not one who professed a philosophy. (One of the existentialists disdainfully refers to a professor as someone who professes that someone else suffered.) Marcus Aurelius therefore qualifies as a genuine philosopher, because his way of being in the world reflected his convictions.

A great deal of Aurelius's time was spent campaigning against hostile tribes and nations, but he wrote notes to himself while in the field. These became *The Meditations*, a highly personal document, searching, introverted, and melancholy, but highly appealing, even by today's standards. It contains aphorisms such as "No man is free who is not master of himself," "Make the best use of what is in our power, and take the rest as it happens," and "Wealth consists not in having great possessions, but in having few wants." In an ironic vein he also wrote, "Even in a palace life may be lived well."

According to the Stoics, when the governance of the universe is understood a necessary pattern of events begins to emerge. We realize that nothing happens by chance, accident, or luck. Rather, a rigid *destiny* operates throughout the natural world; every happening is fated to occur as it does. There is an infinite chain of causes and effects to which human lives, too, are linked. In this fatalistic universe no occurrence is free. Whatever happens in the world is wholly beyond our control, despite the fact that some actions appear to be the result of our decisions. In actuality, events occur as they must, and we have no choice in the matter. Whatever befalls us is part of a necessary design, a thread in the tapestry of destiny. Some societies think of destiny as the stars ruling our lives; others refer to a book of fate in which everyone's name is inscribed. The Muslims say "Inchallah"; the French, "C'est ecrit"; the Spanish, "Que sera, sera."

Does that mean there are gods in heaven controlling life on earth, a celestial providence? The Stoic answer is curious. These forces of destiny are themselves divine; the gods and fate are one. Zeus or Jupiter and the rest of the pantheon do not exist outside of nature but are at its core. They are not spiritual but material beings. The gods are the vital energy or positive force within nature, the impulse from which things grow, and they are diffused throughout the cosmos. In the ancient typology of air, fire, earth, and water, the gods reside in fire and air as active powers, and to a lesser extent, in passive water and earth.

Furthermore, this fated, divine universe is shot throughout with rationality, and is not a being, but an orderly machine. Our own rationality has a counterpart outside ourselves in the deliberate and systematic unfolding of events. Our rational human nature has an answering call in universal nature (Logos). As Eastern philosophy maintains, the inner and the outer are one, internal and external are fundamentally the same, and the Stoic identifies this sameness as rationality. "Look to what nature leads thee . . . following thy own nature and the common nature."

As one philosopher put it, "The law of nature is god's mathematical presence." Nothing occurs in vain or by chance in this world suffused with divine reason. Therefore we must live "in harmony with nature," acting "with good reason in the selection of what is natural" and seeking to "hold fast to the things that are by nature fit to be chosen; for indeed we are born for this."

Finally, the predestined, divine, rational order is benevolent. From a cosmic perspective, everything happens for the best. Nothing that is natural can be evil in the final scheme of things. Therefore it is shortsighted of people to complain about what happens to them, because in the end the positive will triumph over the negative, the good things will throw the last stone. Ultimately, the music of the spheres is beautiful, and the symphony is richer for having dissonance.

This, after all, is the attitude of Christians toward natural evils, such as floods or tornadoes, sickness or death. According to the faith, evils are necessary for the good of the whole. Despite our suffering, we must have faith that God is loving and that apparent evils are blessings in disguise.

But if everything is fated, how can we agree or disagree with what happens? Isn't our attitude also predetermined? Here the Stoic draws the line. We are not only physical beings; we also have an inner self capable of reacting to the inevitable. All events are fixed, but our attitude toward them is not. Our response to fate lies within our own power.

Philosophers distinguish between *free will*, the ability to decide what to do, and *freedom*, the ability to do what we decide. In Stoic terms, we do not have freedom and cannot shape the world to our heart's desires, but we do possess free will and can react positively or negatively to the inevitable. Here we are our own masters, stronger than the fate that surrounds us.

Now, if we are wise, our response will be positive. We can certainly rail against our fate, which we tend to do when tragedies occur, but that would be pointless and, in a sense, blasphemous. It certainly does no good. We cannot do anything about the diseases or disasters that afflict us, neither to prevent them nor to avoid them, so we might as well be cheerful about everything. And since destiny is ultimately good, we should not oppose it in any case. Everything is for the best in a world governed by divine nature.

The only rational response to unavoidable events, then, is to actively approve of whatever happens. Not only should we remain tranquil, even in the face of catastrophe, but we should positively endorse whatever fate ordains. The rule is to maintain an inner peace, a Stoic calm, even in the face of disaster. Although our initial reaction to catastrophes might be anxiety or frustration, curses or rebellion, we should rationally control our emotions. We must act with poise and equanimity, maintaining an attitude of *quiet approval*. "Ask not that events should happen as you will," Epictetus advises, "but let your will be that events should happen as they do, and you should have peace." Any other attitude is foolish.

If we are wise, we will distinguish that which is within our control, our mental attitude, and that which is not, namely, external events. We must realize that our well-being depends on knowing the difference, accepting what we cannot change and controlling what is within our power. Nothing can be done about a drought or a plague, but we can cultivate the right attitude toward it and achieve peace of mind. As Epictetus stated, make the best of what is in our power, and take the rest as it occurs, [separating] what is *ours*, and what is not ours, what is right, and what is wrong. I must die, and must I die groaning too? I must be fettered; must I be lamenting too? I must be exiled; and what hinders me, then, but that I may go smiling, and cheerful, and serene? 'Betray a secret.' I will not betray it, for this is in my own power. 'Then I will fetter you. What do you say, man? Fetter me? You will fetter my leg, but not Zeus himself can get the better of my free will.'

Our essential self, then, is free, which means we are capable of gaining control over our lives in a very basic way—provided we are ruled by reason. "Man is disturbed not by things, but by the views he takes of them." Rational judgment can liberate us. We must recognize which circumstances are impossible to change and, rising above them, not allow any happening to affect our peace of mind. Fear, envy, jealousy—these are the result of ignorance and false judgment. The sage has attained moral perfection, completely free of emotion and immune to misfortune. He has attained *apatheia*.

To the Stoic, then, following nature means following the rational part of our being, which corresponds to the rational spirit within nature. Then we will lead *serene and satisfying lives*. In our innermost being we will be unharmed by any catastrophe and pass through life in a tranquil manner, confident that the divine spirit moving through the natural order will inevitably bring about a good end. God is the rational soul of the world, and we must fan that inner spark from the divine fire. The goal is *apatheia*, complete emotional detachment, courage, calmness, and indifference.

This even applies to death—the ultimate symbol of an unavoidable event. Man is mortal and that seems part of being human, but our response to death lies in our hands. The Stoics do offer one thought to help us respond in the right way to the inevitable. That is, when we fear death, it is not here, and when death is here, we cannot fear it.

Stoicism Evaluated
The Stoic formula for successful living is extremely appealing at times of insecurity when people live in unsafe conditions or when the political and social order are in ferment—which was the case during the later period of the Roman Empire. During such times the tendency is to turn inward to find our well-being, rather than relying upon anything external, to concentrate on the satisfactions that are within our power and not things beyond our control. "[H]appiness should depend as little as possible on external things," the Stoics advise. We are impressed by the fact that our health or safety cannot be guaranteed any more than we can count on gaining wealth or fame, so if

we pin our hopes on such things, we may well be disappointed. But we can take the proper attitude toward anything that occurs and find contentment even in pain, poverty, or inevitable death. When people accept death as a part of life, they are evincing a Stoic attitude.

Boethius (480–525/6), the Neoplatonist, expressed this Stoic ideal in his work *The Consolation of Philosophy*. He was imprisoned after a life of public service and wrote the following words one year before he was executed:

> He who has calmly reconciled his life to fate, and set proud death beneath his feet, can look fortune in the face, unbending both to good and bad. . . . Why then stand wretched and aghast when we hear tyrants rage in impotence? Fear naught, and hope naught: thus shall you have a weak man's rage disarmed. But whoso fears with trembling, or desires aught from them, he stands not firmly rooted, but dependent: he has thrown away his shield; he can be rooted up, and he links for himself the very chain whereby he maybe dragged.

The Stoic philosophy can also be attractive when economic conditions are unstable. Then people feel they have little power over their jobs, housing, or wealth, that larger economic forces determine their fate. Working hard in school may not ensure employment, and a record of accomplishment may not bring job security in the business organization. The system might not keep its promise of rewarding those who do their part. During such times we are inclined to descend within ourselves to find satisfaction.

However, adherence to the Stoic philosophy can be problematic. In order to minimize disappointment, we may be turning away from the world too much. We might be too prone to seek safety over risk and therefore gain less than we could obtain. To avoid pain, we might not seek pleasure, making our lives smaller and more cramped than they need be. This point has often been made against the Stoic mentality, which seems too concerned with avoiding suffering, to the detriment of full living.

In this Stoicism echoes a recurrent theme in Eastern philosophy and religion (especially Buddhism and Hinduism), that attachment to this world renders us subject to pain at the loss of the things we love. If we desire nothing, then we are invulnerable. However, if we avoid suffering, we also avoid fulfillment and life becomes empty. It seems far better to get what we can out of life, even though we run the risk of disappointment. *Abstine et sustine* (abstain and endure) is a melancholy motto for living. Oscar Wilde said that unrequited love at least saves you the pain of disillusionment, but unless we try to form relationships, we will miss the beauty of love that is returned.

Furthermore, if we adopt the Stoic viewpoint, we believe that we have less control over our lives than we might actually have, resigning ourselves to our fate when we should be masters of it. We might, in fact, make the best of things when an expenditure of effort could improve our condition. In short, by following Stoicism, we would tend to underestimate our control over life, and give up before we have tested our power to change our circumstances. Many people do attain their goals and enjoy more happiness than unhappiness in their lives.

This leads to another criticism, which has to do with the Stoic belief in fate ruling all events. Obviously, there is no point in trying to improve our situation if we have no control over it. However, few people today believe in the doctrine of fate; it has lost the credibility it had in the ancient world. Even contemporary Christianity maintains a limited view of providence and holds us responsible for the choices we make.

Although fatalism has been abandoned more than disproven, the grounds offered by the Stoics for its acceptance are extremely weak. The Stoic argument is that all past events are frozen and cannot be altered by any act of will; as the English poet John Dryden wrote, "Not heaven itself upon the past has power." Also, certain future events are unalterable, such as the succession of night and day and the inevitability of our deaths. From these considerations the Stoic concludes that all events are fixed in accordance with the plan of destiny.

Obviously, from the fact that past events and some future ones are unchangeable, we cannot conclude that everything is fated. This mistake is technically referred to as the *fallacy of composition*, for it claims that what is true of the parts is true of the whole. As the joke goes, "Why do white sheep eat more than black sheep? Because there are more of them." Members of a class should not be confused with the class itself, and some does not imply all.

Another criticism of Stoicism is that predestination makes all effort pointless. This has become such a standard objection that it has acquired a name: the *lazy argument*. That is, there would be no point in doing anything if every event was fated to occur. We might decide to do nothing, confident that it was as inevitable as doing something. Furthermore, no one would be accountable for anything that happened, since events must happen as they do. No one could be judged guilty of acting badly; rather everyone would be an innocent bystander as destiny played itself out. Blame or praise would be meaningless, as would punishment or reward. Of course, if a person were imprisoned for a crime, that imprisonment could always be treated as having been predestined, but it could not be punishment for intentional wrongdoing. That, of course, leads to a tangle.

But it is hard to believe that our will has no effect on our actions, that when someone decides to throw a rock, the internal decision had nothing to do with the rock flying through the air. On the contrary, there appears to be a connection between what we decide and what then happens. We seem responsible for our actions, and stretching out on our bed is laziness, not inevitability.

Not only is the logic faulty, but we cannot say that anything in the future is inevitable, even with regard to commonsense assertions, such as "The sun will rise tomorrow" and "Man is mortal." The earth could stop rotating at some point, and if we control the telomeres of aging, then it will not be true that people must die. Certainty applies only to logical conclusions; no future event must occur.

A final criticism has to do with the impoverishment of our emotional life that comes about when we allow ourselves to respond to events only in a practical way. For example, if we feel concern for someone undergoing surgery, the Stoic would advise us to suppress our anxiety because it serves no useful purpose; it does not help and works against our peace of mind. However, we are feeling anxious not because we think it will do any good, but as a result of our attachment to the person. Our concern is not meant to be a cause of anything, but is an effect of our caring.

In fact, a great deal of our emotional life would have to be discarded because it "did no good"; it would be considered "wasted emotion." But surely we want to have the full range of emotional experiences available to human beings, including those emotions that serve no useful purpose. And the very process of controlling our emotions so completely is destructive in itself. To permit ourselves only beneficial feelings severely reduces our openness, sensitivity, and spontaneity, transforming the richness of feelings to a carefully regulated set of responses. It would be very odd if a person said, "I will feel a certain emotion if it is helpful. Otherwise I will not feel it." Our emotions should not be limited to just practical ones. Blaise Pascal (1623–1662) once remarked, "There are two equally dangerous extremes, to shut reason out, and to let nothing else in."

This attitude is characteristic of the authoritarian persona, who is highly controlled, rational, and deliberate. The authoritarian personality has such a rigid structure of responses that any genuine reactions are deeply buried within an extensive network of fortifications. To be affected by genuine emotion means to risk a crack in the foundation of the personality, threatening it with collapse. Therefore, a strict, implacable, enameled surface is presented to the world. But such strength is basically weakness. The person is most afraid of being unguarded, that is, of being vulnerable. The real person lies cowering beneath an elaborate system of defenses.

This self-protective attitude, which is supposed to provide freedom from injury, becomes the opposite of authentic freedom, for the person locks himself away from others, becoming isolated and alienated. The fortress is actually a prison, with little nourishment being delivered from outside the walls; the person feeds off himself like a snake swallowing its own tail. Such a person cannot be injured very readily but also cannot communicate with others or be touched by them. In gaining the protection of a citadel, the authoritarian personality loses his or her reality as a person. Petrified by fear, the individual becomes part of the fortress rock itself, invulnerable and less than human.

It should be added that genuine independence does not come about through self-sufficiency but by being secure enough within ourselves to risk depending on other people. Because of their insecurity, the Stoics are afraid to rely upon anyone except themselves, thereby showing that they are not in command of their lives at all. The polished sphere of Stoic philosophy leaves no room for relationships or love.

CHAPTER THREE

Religious Faith: The Philosophy of Religion

Figure 3.1. The so-called Flammarion woodcut, an anonymous wood engraving of the heavens that first appeared in the work of French astronomer Camille Flammarion, 1888.

The Glorification of God: St. Thomas Aquinas

The inheritor of the Aristotelian tradition was St. Thomas Aquinas, the *doctor angelicus* (angelic doctor), and through his writings the golden thread of philosophy continued through medieval times. Aquinas expanded and adapted Aristotle's teleology, connecting it to God as the being that imbued life with purpose. Aquinas baptized Aristotle, anointing him to Christian belief.

The Middle Ages lasted from the beginning of the fifth century, when Rome collapsed, to the end of the fifteenth century, and Aquinas lived during the High Middle Ages (1225/1227–1274). This was a dynamic period of history, when Europe was becoming more complex and creative, the age when Gothic cathedrals were constructed, the Crusades were launched to rescue the Holy Land from the infidel, and Chaucer wrote *The Canterbury Tales*, and Dante, *The Divine Comedy*.

Aquinas stands as the chief theologian of the Roman Catholic Church, which canonized him in 1323, and he remains one of the principal saints. In 1879 Pope Leo XIII declared that Thomism was the official Catholic philosophy to be used by all seminaries and universities. If Aquinas did not write on a topic, the doctrines taught should be "reconcilable with his thinking." His demonstrations in natural theology have inspired countless followers to try to prove divine truth rather than relying upon blind faith, although if reason diverged from faith, there was always revelation. To Aquinas, rationality could be trusted to support belief since both originated in spirit, but "Man needs divine help, that the intellect may be moved by God to its act."

Aquinas's parents were part of the Italian nobility, the ruling family of the Aquino region, and he was born in the castle of Roccasecca, a hilltop fortress halfway between Rome and Naples. His father was Count Landulf, his mother was Theodora, Countess of Teano, and the family was connected to the emperors Henry VI and Frederick II, as well as to the kings of Castile, Aragon, and France. Aquinas was therefore raised "on the hem of the imperial purple." According to legend, a holy hermit predicted his fame before he was born: "He will enter the Order of Friar's Preachers, and so great will be his learning and sanctity that in his day no one will be found equal to him." (This story is probably apocryphal, as is the tale that some monks once found him levitating.)

As an adult Aquinas had a large frame, a massive head with a receding hairline, and an indeterminate complexion, dark or olive or perhaps "like the color of new wheat." The theologian and novelist G. K. Chesterton describes him as "a huge heavy bull of a man, fat and slow and quiet, very

Figure 3.2. *Saint Thomas Aquinas*, by Carlo Crivelli, 1476 (National Gallery, London).

mild and magnanimous but not very sociable," "shy," "stolid," "patient," and "courteous," a "walking wine-barrel." Because he was bulky and taciturn, he was dubbed "the dumb ox," but his teacher Albertus Magnus stated, "You call him a 'dumb ox,' but I declare before you that he will yet bellow so loud in doctrine that his voice will resound throughout the world."

Perhaps because of his parentage, Aquinas developed a refined, gentle, deliberate manner, and his education gave him an impressive memory and a keen mind. In paintings by artists such as Fra Angelico or Crivelli he is portrayed before the open pages of a book, with a sacramental cap, the sun on his breast, or with a dove to signify the inspiration of the Holy Spirit. He looks out from these paintings with a serene, confident expression, assured of the doctrines of his faith.

When Aquinas was five, he was sent to the monastery at Cassino, where his uncle was the abbot, and here he excelled at the medieval trivium of grammar, rhetoric, and logic. From there he went to the University of Naples for six years, where he was influenced by the Dominicans to join their order. As a southern Italian noble he was expected to become a Benedictine, which had a higher status; the Dominicans, by contrast, were an itinerant, mendicant order that took a vow of poverty.

His family tried to dissuade him, to the point of capturing him on his way to Rome and imprisoning him at the castle of San Giovanni. Although he remained a captive for nearly two years, he did not relent, despite being assailed with prayers, threats, and temptations. According to several biographies, even a prostitute was offered to him, but he drove her from the room with a brand from the fire, thrusting it into the door and searing the sign of the cross into the wood. He then prayed for deliverance from lust. In the sleep that followed, two angels appeared to him in a dream and placed a white sash around his waist, saying, "We gird thee with the girdle of perpetual virginity," and he was never again troubled by the temptations of the flesh.

Pope Innocent IV finally intervened in the family quarrel, and Aquinas was given sanction to join the Dominican order. Because of his intellectual abilities, he was sent to Cologne to study with Albertus Magnus. At the time (1244), Magnus was a renowned figure, celebrated for the depth of his knowledge; he was called Albert the Great, the wonder and miracle of his age. Aquinas quickly became his favorite pupil, so that when Aquinas died, Magnus fell into a depression, declaring "the light of the Church" has been extinguished.

Aquinas traveled to the University of Paris with Albertus Magnus, where he earned a bachelor of theology degree and emerged victorious in several theological disputes, returning to Cologne three years later as second lecturer or *magister studentium*. He went back to Paris for his master's degree, where he was involved in another theological controversy, and later obtained a doctor of theology degree there. This enabled him to begin a career of lecturing, writing, and preaching throughout Western Europe—in Cologne, Rome, Bologna, Naples, Florence, and Paris. Aquinas also functioned as a type of ambassador for the pope, settling disputes about church doctrine and carrying out the affairs of his order. For example, he resolved a doctrinal dispute between the Averroists and the Augustinians over the relation between faith and reason.

His most productive years were between 1257 and 1273, when he wrote over fifty major treatises; he is reputed to have dictated several different works to his scribes simultaneously. However, his principal work, *Summa Theologica*, was left unfinished when he underwent a mystical experience one year before his death. As he explained, "I cannot go on. . . . All that I have written seems to me like so much straw compared to what I have seen and what has been revealed to me."

Aquinas died while on a journey for the pope at the monastery of Fossa Nuova, perhaps poisoned by Charles of Anjou, as Dante claims, but more probably of natural causes after a seven-week illness. His body now rests at the Church of St. Sernin; a bone from his left arm, at the Cathedral at Naples; and his right arm, at the Church of Santa Maria Sopra Minerva in Rome.

Theology and Philosophy

The theologian prays, "Dear God in heaven," but the philosopher says, "Dear God, if there be a God, in heaven, if there be a heaven." The one begins with a set of beliefs; the other tries to clear his mind of assumptions in the pursuit of truth. Aquinas thought that philosophy dealt with ideas that everyone understood about the world, and through logic, produced new truths as thought developed. Theology, on the other hand, assumed certain dogmas as a starting point—that God is three in one, that Jesus has both a divine and a human nature, and that our salvation depends on accepting Jesus as the Christ. Aquinas endorsed both reason and the senses, but his writing was grounded in faith. As G. K. Chesterton remarked, he believed in the sun, not because he could see it, but because it illuminated everything else.

Nevertheless, Aquinas claimed that God's existence could be proven intellectually, and that people would listen to reason along with the evidence of the senses if they were told "the fairy tale that is really true."

> I do not believe that God meant Man to exercise only that peculiar, uplifted and abstracted sort of intellect . . . [but] a middle field of facts which are given

by the senses to be the subject matter of the reason, and that in the field the reason has a right to rule, as the representative of God in Man. It is true that all of this is lower than the angels; but it is higher than the animals.

The senses are the windows of the soul, and combined with common sense, they can reconcile people to God, the way that humans are a union of body and soul. As Aquinas said, "Believing is an act of the intellect assenting to divine truth" but "moved by God through grace."

As for mysticism, the dark night of the soul, Aquinas rarely trusted it, except for dreams in which spirits appeared to him. But as philosophers have noted, it is difficult to differentiate between "[a]ngels spoke to me in a dream" and "I dreamt that angels spoke to me." And mystical experience can always be interpreted as hallucination, caused by beliefs brought to the experience rather than derived from it; it is also induced by asceticism, staring at walls or at the sun, depriving oneself of food or water. As Bertrand Russell remarked, some people drink much and see snakes, while others eat little and see saints. Perhaps, then, it was fortunate that Aquinas relied on reason and not mystical awareness.

Aquinas wrote tirelessly during most of his life, producing works that the faithful call inspired: *De Principiis Naturae* (On the Principle of Nature), *De Ente et Essentia* (On Being and Essence), and his commentaries on Aristotle's *Physics*, *Metaphysics*, *De Anima*, and *Nicomachean Ethics*. His *Summa contra Gentiles* is a work of apologetics, and his greatest work, *Summa Theologica*, presents reasoned argument in favor of faith; within Roman Catholicism it is considered a near sacred text.

The Nature of God and of Man

Aquinas operated within the limits of his creed, addressing the questions he inherited and adding new ideas, interpretations, and refinements. Thomistic philosophy is, in fact, the quintessence of the intellectual thought carried on in medieval schools, and Aquinas enlarged the concept of God and his relation to man.

Within the Western tradition God is usually defined as being the creator and sustainer of the universe, resident within us but at the same time wholly other. He is all wise (omniscient) and all knowing (omniscient), holy, personal, and almighty (omnipotent). To this list Aquinas added that God is unchanging, infinite, a unity, and simple, that is, without parts. He is the perfect being, identical with his qualities of charity and love, and his intelligence is also part of his essence. He is his own wisdom, is identical with truth, and understands himself completely, realizing everything in the same instant. His nature and his existence are one.

In brief, God is everything in being, and the opposite of being does not exist. In the same way, cold is not real; there are only degrees of heat. Darkness, too, is nonexistent; there are only varying amounts of light. Evil likewise is only the absence of good.

Insofar as possible, humanity should participate in the nature of the divine. In particular, we should follow "natural law," which is part of the eternal law of God—a divine providence that arranges all elements of creation. This natural law is intrinsic to God, as well as being resident within human beings, directing them toward the good.

In *Summa contra Gentiles* Aquinas writes, "[N]othing tends to something as its end, except insofar as this is good . . . that which is the supreme good is supremely the end of all. . . . Therefore all things are directed to the Supreme good, namely God, as their end." Echoing Aristotle, he states that this ultimate good cannot be wealth, because wealth is "not sought except for the sake of something else"; it cannot be power, because power is "unstable" and can be abused; it cannot consist of indulging the senses, since this is "common to man and other animals"; and it cannot be the goods of the body, such as health, beauty, and strength, because "the soul is better than the body." The supreme good, therefore, can be only the contemplation of God, now and in the life to come, where the soul is wholly at peace.

The Five Ways

Embedded in *Summa Theologica* are five arguments, or "ways," for the existence of God, the *quinquae viae,* which remain the most interesting and celebrated "proofs" in the philosophy of religion. The first four are classified as "cosmological" arguments based on causation; the last is an adaptation of Aristotle and is referred to as the "teleological" argument. William Paley (1743–1805) articulated the teleological argument in a more accessible way.

The first way is that of change, for anything that changes must be changed by something else, and that must be changed by something earlier. But this cannot go back and back forever in an "infinite regress." We are "forced eventually to come to a first cause of change not itself being changed by anything, and this is what everyone understands by *God.*"

With regard to the second way, Aquinas says, "[A] series of causes cannot go on forever," that is, we cannot have a prior cause and a still more ultimate cause in an endless chain of causes and effects. "So we are forced to postulate some first cause, to which everyone gives the name *God.*"

The third way is somewhat more sophisticated, making use of the philosophic distinction between contingency and necessity. A contingent event depends upon something else in order to be. For example, a tree would not exist if it were not for moisture, sunlight, and nutrients in the soil; factories would not be created unless there were bricks and mortar, land for buildings, and a demand for the product; and each of us would not have been born if our parents had not met. However, everything cannot be dependent on external factors; something must exist necessarily, carrying the reason for its being within its own nature. "So we are forced to postulate something which of itself must be, owing this to nothing outside itself, but being itself."

The fourth way stretches causation to include the existence of the *ideal*, which then produces lesser qualities in objects. That is, "there is something which is the truest and best and most excellent of things, and hence the most fully in being." In fact, we rate or grade objects according to this perfection, as when we judge the worth of a person's life relative to a human ideal. "Now when many things possess a property in common, the one most fully possessing it causes it in the others; fire, as Aristotle says, the hottest of all things, causes all other things to be hot." Aquinas therefore concludes, "So there is something that causes in all other things their being, their goodness, and whatever other perfections they have. And this is what we call *God*."

These ways are all versions of a causation argument. It seems only common sense that if everything has a cause, there must be a first cause, a *primum mobile* or prime mover, which is God. However, philosophers have not treated the argument very kindly; one remarked that no one ever doubted the existence of God until St. Thomas tried to prove it. For example, why can't there be an infinite regress of causes, just as there can be an infinite series of effects? The arrow of time could go backward as well as forward, and mathematical sequences are infinite, positively and negatively, so perhaps there is no beginning, just as there might not be an end. Besides, if there must be a start to the process, why must that start be called God? Couldn't there be a natural explanation, such as a "big bang," rather than a supernatural one, a spontaneous, physical explosion of sufficient magnitude to create the universe?

However, the main criticism of the cosmological argument is that it rests on a self-contradiction. If everything has a cause, then so does God, and if God is an exception, then the world might also be an exception, in which case we have no need for God. In other words, to call God an uncaused cause contradicts the premise of the argument that all things have a cause.

This is the child's line of questioning. If the child asks, "Where did everything come from?" and the parent answers, "God made it," the precocious child then asks, "Who made God?" And if the child is told that no one made

God, that he always was, then the truly precocious child says, "Then maybe everything always was, and God did not make it."

Aquinas's fifth way has a different character, tipping its hat to Aristotle. He asserts that all things appear to have a purpose in being. "Goal-directed behavior is observed in all bodies in nature, even those lacking awareness. . . . But nothing lacking awareness can tend to a goal except it be directed by someone with awareness and understanding . . . and this we call *God.*"

This view, that everything has an end toward which it tends, is Aristotelian teleology. In fundamental terms, the world contains an inherent design, and a design implies a designer, just as a plan requires a planner, and the architecture of the universe a divine architect. If nature is a work of art, then the landscape shows the brushstrokes of God. As Shakespeare wrote, there are "tongues in trees, books in the running brooks, sermons in stones."

William Paley (1743–1805) reinforced this argument from design with his famous watchmaker analogy, arguing that "if we found a watch upon the ground in perfect working order, with the gears properly positioned so as to interlock; the teeth, pointer, and balance all of the right shape and size to regulate the motion; the wheels made of brass to keep them from rusting; a spring of flexible steel; and glass over the face, where a transparent material is required, we would be forced to conclude "that the watch must have had a maker . . . who formed it for the purpose which we find it actually to answer." By analogy, when we encounter the intricate mechanism of the world, we must infer that it, too, had a maker; the parts could not have fallen together by chance in just the right combination to produce a perfectly functioning system. "There cannot be a design without a designer," Paley wrote, "contrivance without a contriver; order without choice; arrangement without anything capable of arranging." That is, unless we assume "the presence of intelligence and mind," the world in its orderliness is inexplicable. As even Voltaire admitted, "I cannot imagine how the clockwork of the universe exists without a clockmaker."

This teleological argument is reinforced by various startling facts, for example, that the earth is perfectly positioned in the solar system to sustain life. If it were closer to the sun, we would sizzle, and if it were farther away, we would freeze to death—a kind of Goldilocks phenomenon. In addition, human beings need to eat plants and animals, and edible plants and animals are provided. The marvelous mechanism of the human body itself points to a supreme designer, who organized our complex systems and organs, our anatomy and physiology for ideal functioning. The intricacy of the human eye alone testifies to the genius of creation.

Evidence of design has also been cited within the animal kingdom, where there is a perfect distribution of the qualities needed by various species: the hard shell of the turtle, the ability of the chameleon to camouflage itself, the giraffe's long neck, enabling it to reach the leaves at the tops of trees, and so on. Each creature had been given the exact attributes it needs to exist.

Objections to the Teleological Argument
However, even though a design and a designer seem self-evident, Charles Darwin opposed this scenario in *The Origin of Species* in 1859. In a book that changed the world, Darwin offered an alternative explanation for the orderliness that exists. He stated that if turtles had not possessed hard shells, chameleons the ability to change color, or giraffes long necks, they would not have survived as a species. These were the mutations called for in the life struggle, so it is not remarkable that the species now living possess the characteristics they need. To regard it as uncanny would be like being surprised that all Olympic winners are good athletes; if they were not good athletes, they would not be Olympic winners. Or it would be like being amazed that so many major cities are next to navigable rivers; if the rivers had not been navigable, they would not have become major cities.

In the same way, we can understand the ideal position of the earth relative to the sun, the edibleness of plants and animals, and the efficient functioning of the human body. If these factors had not been present, we would not have the world we do. All aspects of life evolved in accordance with the principle of natural selection. Our hand was once a hairy paw, and before that, a scaly fin.

In a famous debate Bishop Wilberforce asked Thomas Huxley whether it was from his grandmother or his grandfather that he claimed descent from monkeys. Huxley replied that he would not be ashamed of ape ancestors, only of arrogance and closed-mindedness. Evolutionists see a common ancestry for both human beings and the higher apes; the human species branched off from the tree of primates.

Darwin also maintained that life began well before 4004 BCE—the date claimed by some theologians; it had existed for millions of years. Contemporary biologists have confirmed this, and astronomers now estimate that the universe started with the explosion known as the big bang about 13.7 billion years ago, the sun formed 9 billion years later, the earth is 4.5 billion years old, and the genus *Homo* has existed for 1.5 to 2.4 million years. *Homo sapiens* (or *Homo*, but not very *sapien*) originated some 200,000 years ago.

In essence, Darwin offered a naturalistic explanation in place of a supernatural one, and initially that seems preferable; if we hear galloping, we should think horse before we think zebra. Although God might lie behind evolution, using it as his instrument, that addition is not strictly necessary.

As "Occam's razor" states, we should not compound explanations beyond what is required; the simplest theory is best. Since evolution can explain the order of the world, it becomes superfluous to add a God who lies behind it. When the mathematician de Laplace presented his treatise on celestial mechanics to Napoleon, the emperor remarked, "I see no mention of God here." Laplace replied, "I had no need of that hypothesis."

Furthermore, it is difficult to account for the extinction of dinosaurs using the biblical account of creation, but it can be explained in terms of the Darwinian model: when a species lacks the adaptations necessary for survival, then it becomes extinct. Hundreds of thousands of species have disappeared from the earth for this reason, and only relics remain to show that they once existed. And as some philosophers have pointed out, it would be odd for God to recall dinosaurs and to try mammals instead, to change his mind; it is more plausible to attribute the extinction of dinosaurs to catastrophic changes in the environment.

In defense of the religious view, theologians sometimes use questionable arguments, such as "God planted fossils on earth to test our faith," or "Man evolved from primates but was adopted by God." Now, it can always be argued that *for all we know*, God made the earth complete with fossils, but this sounds rather desperate. *For all we know*, oysters may be doing differential equations, and hibernating bears are dreaming of the periodic table of the elements, but *as far as we know*, they are not. In the same way, it seems more reasonable to regard fossils as preserved remains of living organisms, some of which are now extinct. Geologists debate whether fossils are bone or stone, but no one doubts they are more that 4004 years old.

Furthermore, theology plays a dangerous game if it calls "God" whatever we do not know. For then the more we know, the less room there is for God. In this way, religion is edged out of the universe. This has, in fact, been a recurrent pattern. No one knew what caused lightning, locusts, earthquakes, or the Black Death, so these events were ascribed to the power of God, but that meant that the more science understood, the less was attributed to supernatural agency. Historically, as science advanced, religion retreated, partly because the divine was used as an explanation for what we did not know. A "God of the gaps" is vulnerable.

The contemporary version of the teleological argument, called "intelligent design," has essentially the same features and suffers from the same defects; it is new wine poured into old wineskins. For example, the "irreducible complexity" of biological systems, it is argued, suggests that some intelligent force must drive the mathematics. Adherents of intelligent design claim that the chances of the universe developing as it did are incredibly small. What is remarkable is not that we have survived, but that we have arrived. Take the expansion rate—just one of the conditions that had to be right for life to develop. In *A Brief History of Time* Stephen Hawking writes, "If the rate of the universe's expansion one second after the 'big bang' had been smaller by even one part in a hundred thousand million million, the universe would have collapsed into a hot fireball." Therefore, an intelligent mind must have created the initial conditions.

Most biologists disagree, maintaining that Darwinism is sufficient to account for the complexity that exists, and that natural selection and mutations can provide the "information" needed. At a simple level, the mechanism of the eye was once a light-sensitive cell; the hand a pseudopod, protruding from protoplasm for locomotion and grasping.

Chance can imitate order if the numbers are large. It used to be said that if enough monkeys were typing on enough typewriters, they would eventually produce all the books in the British Museum. Similarly, if there were not one but millions of big bangs, it would be likely that one would have the conditions necessary for life. As Carl Sagan remarked, our universe was a winner at the cosmic slot machine, even though the odds were long. As for mathematical beauty, that need not be purposeful; some people are naturally elegant, without even trying.

Meanwhile, the biological evidence in support of evolution continues to mount and to be corroborated by anthropology, geology, paleontology, archaeology, and astronomy. Biologists now argue mainly about the exact process—whether there was "common descent" or "convergent evolution," "steady change" versus "punctuated equilibria." Sociobiologists claim that a chicken is a device used by an egg for producing another egg. Missing links are continually being found. For example, in 2005 three specimens were discovered that help fill the gap between fish and land animals, and in 2006 the skull of a child was discovered that dated back 3.3 million years and had both ape and human features. Evolution, in fact, is no longer a "theory" in the ordinary sense but virtually a scientific law, similar to the laws of gravity and electromagnetism.

Fairly recently, biologists have discovered that snakes, dolphins, and porpoises have limb buds in their early development, and whales have been found with atavistic hind limbs, some four feet long, complete with feet and digits; this suggests their descent from terrestrial creatures. All mammals, including humans, have gill pouches in the embryonic stage, reflecting that they were once aquatic vertebrates, and human embryos have webbed feet and hands and also develop tails. The last usually disappear in utero, but some children are born with tails, one to five inches long, and humans retain twice as many tail vertebrae as chimpanzees. In short, the embryo in its development goes through several stages of human evolution.

Aside from evolution, this world that was reputedly created by an omniscient, omnipotent, wholly loving God is not entirely good. In fact, it contains awful, widespread suffering. This criticism of the teleological argument is called "the problem of evil": why would a God who knows every possible model of creation, possesses the power to arrange the world as he pleases, and wants the best for his children design the earth with so much misery? There are natural disasters, such as earthquakes, hurricanes, volcanic eruptions, floods, and fires (from lightning); diseases, such as malaria, tuberculosis, smallpox, and cancer (from sunlight or radon); hostile environments, such as deserts, jungles, Arctic wastes, and oceans (and humans have no gills); as well as abnormalities, handicaps, death, and old age (when people become caricatures of themselves). Why have carnivores as well as herbivores when that means so much agony in nature? In a figurative sense, why not make roses without thorns, rainbows without rain? Why should Monet have gone blind, Beethoven have become deaf, and why, above all, should children suffer? This problem has vexed theists for generations, because the pain of human beings from natural sources seems inconsistent with a perfect God, especially a loving one.

The teleological argument, therefore, has been difficult to sustain, with evolution as the main obstacle to this fifth way of Aquinas. The conclusion seems to be that none of Aquinas's arguments are foolproof, each has debilitating defects. But does that mean God does not exist? Can we take the absence of proof as proof of absence? Some philosophers answer no. All that the objections show is that Aquinas's *arguments* for God's existence are deficient; they do not disprove the existence of God. However, other philosophers claim that, in the absence of rational arguments and empirical evidence, we ought not to believe in God, that atheism is the default position. The burden of proof is always on the affirmative, and Aquinas, at least, has not made his case.

The question, then, is whether we should believe until it is disproven, or disbelieve until it is proven. And what role does faith play in this debate? If we hear voices, should we be institutionalized or canonized, like Joan of Arc?

Love One Another: Christian Agape

The Ethics of Judaism

Christians often consider Christianity as the fulfillment of the promise of Judaism, so we should begin there, specifically with the ethics of the Old Testament.

The *Tanakh*, or Jewish Bible, consists of a series of sacred books produced by Hebrew writers over a period of four hundred years. Jewish thought is also the product of theological reflection, most notably that of Moses Maimonides, the Jewish counterpart to St. Thomas Aquinas.

Wrongdoing in the Old Testament is not the result of ignorance, but of disobedience to God's laws. To Socrates, Plato, and Aristotle, knowledge is paramount, whereas to the Hebrews it is the will that matters—a will that should be obedient to the word of "Yahweh."

Beginning with Genesis and running through the first books of the Bible, the emphasis is placed on man's duty to obey God and never to challenge his authority. In the story of the fall, for example, in which Adam and Eve were banished from the Garden of Eden, the sin they committed was to disobey the express word of God. They had been told not to eat the forbidden fruit, but they succumbed to the temptations of the devil, in the form of a snake, and they were punished accordingly. "Ye shall not eat . . . of the fruit of the tree which is in the midst of the garden," God had commanded, upon pain of death. However, "when the woman saw that the tree was good for food, and that it was pleasant to the eyes, and a tree to be desired to make one wise, she took of the fruit thereof, and did eat, and gave also unto her husband with her; and he did eat" (Genesis, 3:3–6).

Biblical criticism, or hermeneutics, has offered various interpretations as to what the fruit might symbolize. The usual reading is that it represents knowledge of good and evil, but it could also be sensual experience or private property (a Marxist view). And it matters whether Eve was tempted by the snake or by the apple; the snake could be a phallic symbol or that serpent reason. But the wrongdoing of Adam and Eve consisted of their rebellion against God's will, their defiance of his wishes. As a consequence, they lost paradise for themselves and their descendants, so now human beings must live in a world of disasters and disease, pain, suffering, and the final humiliation of death.

Some philosophers have questioned whether anything the fruit might represent, including knowledge, should be forbidden to man, and whether one should dangle forbidden fruit. We could also ask why subsequent generations of human beings should be punished for the original sin of their forebears. This, of course, would have been blasphemous to the ancient Hebrews. It would be thought presumptuous for finite man to doubt the infinite God, for people of limited understanding to do anything but obey divine commands.

Other biblical incidents reinforce the same lesson. The Flood occurred because people were living sinfully in violation of God's laws (Genesis 6:5, 7:10), and Sodom and Gomorrah were destroyed for the same reason (Genesis 19:16–28). When the Hebrew people worshiped Baals, the nature symbols of fertility, they were rebuked by the prophets Hosea, Elisha, and Elijah for disobeying God's commandment: "you shall worship no other God, for the Lord is a jealous God" (Exodus 34:14). Moses condemned the worship of the golden calf as contrary to God's will, and when Uzza tried to steady the Ark of the Covenant so it would not fall from an oxcart, he was struck dead; God had ordained that only the priests could touch the Ark (1 Chronicles 13:10). Similarly, in a war with the Amalekites, Saul violated God's instruction to destroy all men, women, children, and animals. He spared the king Agag, along with various animals that had been designated for sacrificial offerings, but he was denounced by the prophet Samuel, who said that "to obey is better than sacrifice, and to hearken than the fat of rams" (1 Samuel 1:23).

Some of these acts of the Hebrews seem justified, others appear unfair, but the common factor is disobeying God's commands. For that reason alone the people were thought to have acted wrongly and to deserve punishment.

A great deal is made within Judaism of the covenant relation with God, which it is sacrilegious to break. According to Jewish tradition, a special relationship, a solemn pact, was established between the Hebrew peoples and God. They would obey the holy laws, in return for which they were granted the privileged position of God's chosen people.

The Prophetic Tradition

Although the main tenor of the Old Testament is to define rightness in terms of formal obedience, Hebrew theology did develop beyond this stage, particularly through what is termed the *prophetic tradition*. There is a common tendency among early faiths to emphasize strict adherence to rules and rituals without understanding the reason for them. The ancient Hebrews were no exception, but they did see reason behind God's demands and followed his will not as obedient children, but because his rules were just.

In parts of the Hebrew Bible, God is viewed not as a stern, judgmental father, jealous of his authority, but as a being who commands acts because they are right. His wishes are no longer arbitrary, and he does not exact vengeance for transgressions quite so readily. Mercy and forgiveness appear more often, paternal love becomes more prominent, and his commands are seen to have a foundation in justice. Sin still consists in disobedience, but God's laws can be followed out of respect for their moral character, not just through blind obedience and fear of punishment. This advance is best seen in the development of the Ten Commandments. To be sure, God requires that we follow these commandments in a legalistic way, but they are not a mere expression of his will.

The Ten Commandments, or Decalogue, are a summary of the most important rules of behavior laid down by God; they are accepted as bedrock by Jews, Christians, and Muslims alike. There are actually three versions in Hebrew scripture—Exodus 20:2–17, Exodus 34:12–26, and Deuteronomy 5:6–21—and various denominations had different lists. Exodus 20 is most often quoted and it has sixteen commandments, although Christians and Jews reduce them to ten. The King James translation is as follows.

1. I am the Lord thy God, which has brought thee out of the land of Egypt, out of the house of bondage.
2. Thou shalt have no other gods before me.
3. Thou shalt not make unto thee any graven images, or any likeness of any thing that is in heaven above, or that is in the earth beneath, or that is in the water under the earth.
4. Thou shalt not bow down thyself to them, nor serve them: for I the Lord thy God am a jealous God, visiting the iniquity of the fathers upon the children unto the third and fourth generation of them that hate me.
5. And shewing mercy unto thousands of them that love me, and keep my commandments.
6. Thou shalt not take the name of the Lord thy God in vain; for the Lord will not hold him guiltless that taketh his name in vain.
7. Remember the Sabbath day, to keep it holy.
8. Six days shalt thou labour, and do all thy work.
9. But the seventh is the Sabbath of the Lord thy God: in it thou shalt not do any work, thou, nor thy son, nor thy daughter, thy manservant, nor thy maidservant, nor thy cattle, nor thy stranger that is within thy gates.
10. For in six days the Lord made heaven and earth, the sea, and all that in them is, and rested the seventh day: wherefore the Lord blessed the sabbath day, and hallowed it.
11. Honour thy father and thy mother: that thy days may be long upon the land which the Lord thy God giveth thee.
12. Thou shalt not kill.
13. Thou shalt not commit adultery.
14. Thou shalt not steal.
15. Thou shalt not bear false witness against thy neighbour.
16. Thy shalt not covet they neighbour's house, thou shalt not covet thy neighbour's wife, nor his manservant, nor his maidservant, nor his ox, nor his ass, nor anything that is thy neighbour's.

These commandments constitute some of our highest moral thinking and have had immeasurable influence on the ethics of Western culture.

Christian Ethics

In contrast to the emphasis on justice and obedience, the New Testament stresses the love of God more than loyalty to him. The Christian places emphasis on the spirit rather than the letter of the law, the cultivation of our hearts more than our wills. We should have the right motives, instead of performing correct actions. According to Christian teachings, God is not a lawgiver who hands down codes engraved in stone. He is a merciful being, compassionate and forgiving toward the repentant sinner. To the Christian, feelings of brotherhood, compassion, and caring are central virtues, particularly toward the poor and rejected. Having the right motive of concern toward all humankind is more significant than following principles, although social morality is important as a reflection of God's concern for humanity. The chosen-people compact is enlarged to embrace the whole of humanity as God's creatures; all souls are equally precious. To love our neighbor and forgive our enemies, rather than retaliating against them, is the worship of God through love.

In Christianity the worshipper must accept Jesus as the Christ or Son of God. He is regarded as divine, the promised Messiah sent to redeem the human race from sin. This includes both the original sin, inherited from Adam and Eve, and subsequent sins that we all commit, that is, man's inhumanity to man. Through baptism we are cleansed of original sin, washed in the blood of the lamb. Redemption and ultimate salvation must be sought through Christ.

Although we should serve God, the various sects and denominations are divided over the best way of doing this: Should it be through faith, whereby we accept certain dogmas, such as the trinity, the resurrection, and the day of judgment? Should it be through ritual, sacraments, prayer, and other acts of devotion; or perhaps through works, which means living as closely as possible to the moral example of Christ? All three ways can be thought to bring eternal life, for there are many mansions in heaven (1 John 14:2).

The debate is ongoing, and mainly a matter of how much weight to assign to each. Again, the various denominations are divided over this issue, and saints of all persuasions have been canonized in the Catholic Church.

Agape Love

Arguably, the Sermon on the Mount (Matthew 4:25) expresses the Christian approach to ethics most succinctly: love your neighbor as yourself and, in effect, above yourself. In our Western tradition, we identify various kinds of love, mainly from the distinctions made by the Greeks. They include sexual love (lust), *philia* (brotherly love), eros (possessive love), and agape, or *caritas* (selfless love).

> It is the agape type of love that is endorsed by Christian moralists, who contrast it sharply with eros. In erotic love we want the person to belong to us, to have them exclusively for ourselves; it is characterized by a desire to possess the person (or object) that is beloved. Eros is essentially a selfish form of love because we are concerned with satisfying our own desire for the other person rather than satisfying the other person's wants. We wish to embrace another person within our own being, to be enriched by them, assimilating their qualities. By making the other our own, incorporating and absorbing them, we enlarge our own being, and we do this even if it diminishes them. We do not live for someone else but rather he or she lives for us, and we maintain the relationship just so long as we continue to benefit from it. We give as long as we receive, which means we give because we receive.

In agape love, by contrast, our feelings for another person are so strong that we desire their good above our own. We are not in the relationship for what we can get but for what we can give, and our love for them impels us to act selflessly for their well-being. To the Christian, this is the only genuine love, transcending self-love by putting another above ourselves. We are even willing to allow the person we love to find happiness with someone else if that is better than the happiness we can provide.

A love relationship, then, is not a business transaction where each party comes out all right, but a commitment to the other person's welfare. And the agape love we give does not have to be earned, because it is not based on merit or deserts; in the same way, it will not be withdrawn if the person we love disappoints us. As Shakespeare wrote, "Love is not love / Which alters when it alteration finds. . . . Oh no! It is an ever-fixed mark / That looks on tempests and is never shaken." Genuine love is unconditional, like a parent's love for a child. People are loved not because of what they do, but because of who they are; it is their nature, not their accomplishments, that matters.

"Caritas est mater omnium virtutum, et radix," Aquinas wrote (charity is the mother and root of all the virtues), and to be charitable means loving humanity without reservation. We may not judge people as being of equal worth, but we can respond to them equally, regardless of their virtue. Agape love ought to typify all personal relations and replace envy, malice, spite, greed, lust, and hate. Fellowship and brotherhood are higher than personal achievement, especially in relation to the poor, the lowly, the downtrodden.

The supreme prototype of agapeistic love, of course, is God's love for humankind, which is not based on any particular merit but is a constant blessing upon the human race. Divine love does not grace humanity because people deserve it. Rather, it has an unqualified character. Similarly, our caring attitude toward our fellow human beings should be prompted by our relationship to God in agape love: "This is my commandment, that you love one another as I have loved you" (John 1:12), and "Let no man seek his own but each his neighbor's good" (1 Corinthians 10:24). Paradoxically, as we give, we receive; as we lose ourselves, we gain ourselves. When we subordinate our egos in agape love, we become richer within.

The only rule of conduct is not a rule at all, but the spirit of love, which seeks the good of others. Instead of being governed by commandments, the Christian ideal of love should be taken as the sole criterion for action. It does not matter which principle is chosen, provided our choice is motivated by generosity. In some contexts, force will be necessary to defend the innocent; in others, pacifism will be indicated, and both can be correct if prompted by love. In this way Christians can justify the Crusades against the Muslims in the twelfth and thirteenth centuries at the same time that St. Francis of Assisi was preaching to birds. Sometimes honesty will be called for, at other times deceit; and in certain circumstances humility is best, while in others self-assertion—all according to the dictates of love.

Divine Justice

The agape ideal leads to a special conception of justice, which also distinguishes Old and New Testament thinking. The Hebrews believed in people being given their just deserts, whereas the Christian functions in terms of people's need. In Jewish thought the scales of justice must be balanced, so that virtue is rewarded, vice is punished, and people get what they deserve. Justice is retributive. We should return good for good and justice for evil. This is in keeping with the law of talion, according to which people should have done to them whatever they do to others. (In Indian religion it is the force of karma.) This means a proportionate response, punishment commensurate with the offense, balancing the scales of justice. Injustice is the converse: punishment that is not equivalent to the crime. In our criminal justice system that would be a heavy sentence for shoplifting, a light one for grand larceny. The principle is "an eye for an eye and a tooth for a tooth," which does not mean doing to others what they have done, but dispensing an appropriate punishment. A rapist should not be raped but deserves a stiff sentence because that matches the severity of the crime.

In contrast, Christian ethics is concerned with a person's needs regardless of what he or she might deserve. Instead of rewarding or punishing in terms of merit, the New Testament wants to help human beings to improve. People's sins are an index of their need for help, not a way of calibrating their punishment. Christians do not want to make people pay; they want to make them better. They do not want to a point a finger; they want to extend a hand.

Divine justice thus concentrates on needs rather than deserts, redemption of the person rather than compensation for the crime. It looks at the individual's needs and forward to the future, instead of judging the offense and looking at the past. For example, a child who is caught stealing cookies from the cookie jar might deserve a spanking, loss of some privilege, or ostracism (a time-out). But the child might be asking for more affection, for which eating is a substitute, or might be genuinely hungry and need more food. Or the child might be desperate for attention and prefer negative attention to neglect. In this situation, the Christian approach would be to give the child love, nourishment, or more care—whatever is needed—rather than the punishment that the offense deserves.

On a more serious level, murderers might deserve capital punishment, but they might need a prison sentence to bring about their reform and rehabilitation. The Old Testament approach would be to punish the murderer with something equivalent, for example, execution or life imprisonment, whereas the New Testament favors forgiveness for the crime and salvation of the criminal. Although God hates the sin, he loves the sinner. Obviously, the case of the child and the murderer are at opposite ends of the spectrum, but the principle of justice remains the same. To the Christian mind, that means responding to human needs rather than seeking retaliation, much less revenge. Sometimes people need love most when they deserve it least.

The Christian response to violence is a natural outgrowth of divine justice and, ultimately, the agapeistic ideal. In the Sermon on the Mount we are told that if we are attacked, we should not retaliate. "If someone strikes you on the right cheek, turn to him the other also. And if someone wants to sue you and take your tunic, let him have your cloak as well. If someone forces you to go one mile, go with him two miles" (Matthew 5:38–42). We ought not to react to violence, but to act with the kindness the other person lacks. We must return good for evil, not evil for evil, fighting fire with water rather than with fire.

Christ preached a gospel of peace, understanding, and forgiveness rather than force. If injuring others is wrong, it should not be done, even if the other person injures us. We should love our fellow man and not harm him, regardless of the circumstances. "Love your enemies and pray for those who persecute you," Christ tells his disciples, and even when he was being crucified, some of his last words were, "Forgive them for they know not what they do."

A Critical Appraisal

One obvious problem in basing an ethic upon the word of God is that, as we have seen, the reality of that God can be called into question. Many people today are skeptics rather than believers; they demand scientific proof and rational argument, which religion cannot supply.

Sometimes theologians claim that if we believe, we lose nothing, whereas if we do not believe, we risk everything, but then we would have to believe in the Greek and Roman gods on the same grounds, and the gods of the Norsemen and ancient Egyptians. They, too, might exist. But the contemporary mind requires something positive in the way of evidence. Hedging our bets is not enough. Besides, if we believe in God only to save ourselves, we are accepting him out of self-interest and not worshiping God at all.

Similarly, the appeal to blind faith leaves us unmoved today. Belief is not accepting something that we know isn't so; it means going beyond the point at which the evidence leaves off. In the present age a significant number of people think that this foundation of evidence is lacking, and they will not make the leap of faith. To some, faith is what we have in the absence of God.

Of course, Christian ethics does not depend on Christian belief. As discussed earlier, an act does not become right because God wills it, but rather God would will an act because it is right. In other words, ethical value is not derived from God's approval, but God approves of that which is valuable. The question, then, is whether Christian ethics can stand on its own; we would not want to throw out the baby with the bathwater.

The Impracticality of Christian Ethics

When we judge Christian ethics on its own merits, certain problems arise. The principle of agape love—putting other people's needs first—is certainly a high ideal, but the person who operates a business this way, putting his competitor's needs first, is certain to go bankrupt. Similarly, a banker cannot follow the maxim of "Give to him that asketh thee, and from him that would borrow of thee turn not thou away" (Matthew 5:42). In international relations, Christians who act for the good of their enemies would endanger themselves and their nation. A conqueror would like nothing better than such support. Even an attitude of nonresistance would be welcome; therefore Christian pacifism could help evil by default, that is, by not opposing it.

If everyone adopted the ideal of agape love in their interactions, then the Christian approach might work, but in a world where only some operate selflessly and the rest selfishly, altruistic people become casualties and victims in the power struggle. To effect positive change in the world, the approach of universal love is simply naive.

Christian theologians recognize the difficulties involved in applying the agape ideal, and they make various concessions to the business economy and realpolitik. These compromises are more or less successful, but they stray very far from the pure ethics of Christianity. The Protestant theologian Reinhold Niebuhr, for example, concluded that we must abandon the law of love and engage in evil actions if we are to improve the human condition. One person may behave in a loving way toward another person, but "all human groups tend to be more predatory than the individuals which compose them. . . . [T]hey take for themselves whatever their power can command." Therefore, we cannot expect to make progress through example but only by employing the tactics of the groups we oppose. We must get our hands dirty, and "if we repent, Christ will forgive and receive us." Niebuhr may be correct in his assessment, but his formula underscores the impracticality of utilizing Christian ethics in business or political contexts.

This tension is pointed up with regard to war. Although some Christian writers, such as Leo Tolstoy, have taken nonviolence as a basic principle, others have accepted the "church militant," justifying the Inquisition and the Crusades. In fact, there is biblical precedent for both views, for Christ not only advocated turning the other cheek but also whipped the moneylenders out of the temple. Historically, pacifists have been the exception rather than the rule, and it is common for clerics to bless warships, tanks, bombers, and fighter planes—even those armed with nuclear missiles. Our armies are routinely blessed in churches.

The Spirit and the Letter

A second major problem with the agape concept has to do with the conflict that can occur between love and ethical laws—laws such as those cited in the Old as well as the New Testament. Love could point in one direction; ethics in another. Although it appears correct to choose the spirit of love over the letter of the law, can we violate any moral rule in the name of love?

For example, suppose a woman must decide about euthanasia for her husband. He is in the last stages of inoperable cancer, without hope of recovery and beside himself with pain. She believes in the dictum "Thou shalt not kill," especially with regard to innocent people, but out of deep love for him she might want his suffering to end. Which should guide her decision? Principles or compassion?

In a general sense, it seems odd to set aside principles regarding killing, stealing, adultery, and blasphemy, to disregard, in fact, the Ten Commandments and the Sermon on the Mount in favor of love. Agape love is certainly a vital part of Christian ethics, but perhaps it should not override moral rules. Furthermore, in operating this way, we are left without firm ethical guidelines, with too great a burden placed on our consciences to decide which action will express love.

In any case, a tension can exist with Old Testament legalism sinning to the right and the agape of the New Testament sinning to the left.

Dostoevsky's Dilemma
One aspect of this tension was dramatized with considerable power by Fedor Dostoevsky, the great nineteenth-century Russian novelist. Dostoevsky argues that God must incorporate within himself the principle of justice as well as infinite love, which leads to forgiveness. Both are essential to a perfect God, but at the same time they seem incompatible, two sides of an unresolved question.

In the "Pro and Contra" chapter of *The Brothers Karamazov*, Dostoevsky describes an argument between Ivan and Alyosha Karamazov. It takes place in the screened-off corner of a tavern, in an atmosphere that is crowded and hot, thick with smoke, claustrophobic. The two brothers can hear loud shouts and laughter, the click of billiard balls, the clink of glasses.

Ivan had been painted previously as a seething intellectual, a religious skeptic who is still preoccupied with redemption; he sees the absence of God everywhere. Alyosha is a novice at the local monastery, devout and vulnerable, with a sweet, engaging manner. Even though they are separated by disposition and belief, there is great warmth between them.

Ivan turns the conversation to human pain and "the tears with which the earth is soaked from crust to core." He tells stories of the suffering of children, which God does nothing to prevent—a boy torn to pieces by a general's dogs before his mother's eyes, a child locked in an outhouse on a freezing winter night, pleading to God to help him. All of this, Ivan says, is typical of the pain of humanity, while God looks on with benign indifference. He asks Alyosha what should be done to the torturers of the innocent, especially those who cause children to suffer. When Alyosha replies that they should be sent to hell, Ivan remarks, "So there is a little devil sitting inside you too."

The dilemma comes down to this: if God forgives the monsters of this world, then there is no justice; and if he does not, then there is no absolute and infinite love. How can these disparate elements be harmonized?

"I must have justice, or I will destroy myself," Ivan says.

> And not justice in some remote infinite time and space, but here on earth, and that I could see myself. I have believed in it. I want to see it, and if I am dead by then, let me rise again, for if it all happens without me, it will be too unfair. . . . I want to see with my own eyes the hind lie down with the lion and the victim rise up and embrace his murderer. I want to be there when everyone suddenly understands what it has all been for. All the religions of the world are built on this longing, and I am a believer. But then there are the children, and what am I to do about them? That's a question I can't answer. For the hundredth time I repeat, there are numbers of questions, but I've only taken the children, because in their case what I mean is so unanswerably clear. Listen! If all must suffer to pay for the eternal harmony, what have children to do with it, tell me, please? It's beyond all comprehension why they should suffer, and why they should pay for the harmony . . . and so I renounce the higher harmony altogether. It's not worth the tears of that one tortured child who beats itself on the breast with its little fist and prays in its stinking outhouse, with its unexpiated tears to "dear, kind God"! It's not worth it, because those tears are unatoned for. They must be atoned for, or there can be no harmony. But how? How are you going to atone for them? Is it possible? By their being avenged? But what do I care for avenging them? What do I care for a hell for oppressors? What good can hell do, since those children have already been tortured? And what becomes of harmony, if there is hell?

Justice and love are alternatives, yet both are essential for divine harmony, so although Ivan is a believer, it is impossible for him to worship God. He cannot see what it has all been for.

CHAPTER FOUR

Personal Identity and Human Nature: Metaphysics

I Think, Therefore I Am: René Descartes

Just as medieval thought is associated with St. Thomas Aquinas, the pre-Enlightenment that followed is best exemplified by René Descartes (1596–1650). He is often referred to as the founder of modern philosophy, mainly because he relied on individual thought instead of *ex cathedra* pronouncements of authorities, both academic and ecclesiastical. He rejected all traditional philosophy and was the preeminent rationalist, even contradicting common sense and ordinary experience in the pursuit of certain truth.

Some philosophers argue that it is the model of science that makes Descartes' thought modern. Bertrand Russell, for example, writes

> He is the first man of high philosophic capacity whose outlook is profoundly affected by the new physics and astronomy. While it is true that he retains much of scholasticism, he does not accept foundations laid by predecessors, but endeavors to construct a complete philosophic edifice *de novo*. This had not happened since Aristotle, and is a sign of the new self-confidence that resulted from the progress of science. There is a freshness about his work that is not to be found in any eminent philosopher since Plato.

Other commentators note that he placed the individual and subjective thought at the center of philosophy. Still others emphasize his contemporary skepticism about knowledge, his focus on methodology, and the way he set the modern philosophic question, how do we know? In identifying the nature

Figure 4.1. René Descartes, 1596–1650. Engraving by W. Holl after painting by Franz Hals. (Courtesy of the Library of Congress)

of the self, he maintained that thinking defines us, and in doing so, he raised the question of how much our body is part of ourselves.

Descartes was born at La Haye (now called La Haye–Descartes) in Touraine but spent most of his life outside France, especially in Holland, and he died in Stockholm at the age of fifty-four. He was the third child of a prosperous minor nobleman who held the position of judge in the High Court of Brittany. Descartes disappointed his father, even though he was esteemed by the rest of the world. When he published one of his major books, the elder Descartes remarked, "Only one of my children has displeased me. How can I have engendered a son stupid enough to have himself bound in calf?"

Descartes' mother was rather sickly and died shortly after he was born. Descartes himself was weak as a boy, developing a lifelong habit of sleeping late. This practice, he reports, led to deep reflection, especially on mathematics and philosophy. After his father remarried, Descartes was raised by his maternal grandmother and, at the age of eight, was sent to a Jesuit college called La Flèche, which he describes as "one of the best schools of Europe." Here, besides the customary classical studies, he was instructed in mathematics, rhetoric, logic, natural philosophy (science), and theology. His subsequent thought was deeply colored by the religious education he received from the Jesuits.

Descartes then spent some time in Paris but found the life of wine, women, and song not to his taste and so retreated to a contemplative world. He studied law at the University of Poitiers, but although he received his degree, he never opened a practice. Instead, he followed his family's military tradition and joined the Dutch army, then the Bavarian army during the Thirty Years' War, and was even offered the post of lieutenant general. In the military manner, he wore a sword throughout his life and was always fashionably well dressed. Descartes never married, but he did have a daughter, who died at age five—an event he describes as the greatest tragedy of his life.

During a campaign near the Danube in the winter of 1619 he had three remarkable "dreams" while dozing in a room heated by a stove or large oven (*poêle*). These dreams or revelations caused his breakthrough in epistemology, especially his method of systematic doubt, as well as the applications of algebra. Consequently, we now have Cartesian geometry. His mathematical analyses of his reverie also prepared the way for the development of calculus.

Subsequently, Descartes left military service and began a period of philosophic thinking and writing while living in France, Italy, and in particular the Dutch cities of Amsterdam, Deventer, Utrecht, and Leiden. Having sold the land he inherited from his father, he had an income from investments of six thousand to seven thousand francs a year—enough to give him a comfortable living. The twenty-year period he spent in the Netherlands, from 1629 to 1649, was his most creative time. He lived in seclusion, his whereabouts known only to an old school friend, Father Mersenne, who protected him from all intrusions. Unlike most émigrés, he learned Dutch, which proved to be an asset. On one occasion, while traveling in a small boat, he overheard some sailors plotting to rob him. The men assumed he did not know the language, but Descartes quickly drew his sword and the talking ceased.

In his reflections Descartes was preoccupied with the questions, How do we know what is real, and how can we distinguish between the false and the true? He did not want opinion or belief, but certain knowledge, and this became a lifelong obsession. It was as if he were a man whose head was being held underwater, struggling for breath, and this urgency can be felt in everything he wrote about knowledge.

Although content to live in Holland, partly because of its liberal attitudes, Descartes was summoned by Queen Christina of Sweden to tutor her in philosophy and mathematics. She knew his reputation, and he had sent her a treatise on love. Christina dispatched a warship for him, but he must have been reluctant to leave, because he kept the admiral waiting several months.

The queen was a remarkable woman of nineteen, bright, independent, vibrant, and demanding, with a twelve-hour regime of study and sports, especially riding and bear hunting. She spoke five languages, slept three to four hours a night, ate little, and seemed impervious to the cold. She had Descartes lecture at five o'clock each morning, standing on the icy floor of the palace throughout the Scandinavian winter. Descartes, a late riser and used to a more moderate climate, contracted pneumonia and soon died.

Descartes' body traveled almost as much in death as he had in life. His corpse was first buried in Stockholm, then exhumed and returned to France sixteen years later. It was moved to several burial sites in Paris, until it was finally interred in the church of St. Germain-des-Prés. At one point his skull was removed and replaced with that of someone else, which is a good metaphor for the mind/body split that he described. In another bizarre incident a ship carrying his manuscripts from Holland to France sank in the Seine. The pages were salvaged, carefully dried out, and arranged in logical order, otherwise we might not have knowledge of many of his thoughts.

The Cartesian Philosophy
Descartes wrote his first book, *Le Monde* (*The World*), during his seclusion in Holland, but he did not publish it for thirty-one years, because of its heretical content. In it he maintained that the universe was infinite and that the earth revolved around the sun, both of which were contrary to the teachings of the Catholic Church. The more dangerous view was that the universe was heliocentric, not geocentric. His contemporary Galileo had been condemned for just this idea, and Descartes did not want to follow in the path of martyrdom. In fact, the Church offered an apology to Galileo only in 1992—359 years after his appearance before the Inquisition.

Aside from being a prudent man, Descartes seems to have been a sincere Catholic and did not want to depart from church teachings. When he went to Holland, he carried very few books, but two of them were the Bible and the writings of St. Thomas Aquinas. Throughout his life he was torn between a religious scholasticism and a commitment to individual thought, informed by the poise and exactitude of mathematics and science.

Philosophical Essays (1637) was Descartes' first published work, with the celebrated *Discourse on Method* as its fourth section. The *Discourse* also contains his most original philosophic ideas—ideas that were then elaborated in his better known *Meditations on First Philosophy* (1641). Descartes' last book, *Passions of the Soul* (1649), was inspired by his correspondence with Princess Elizabeth of Bohemia. Here he identifies six principal passions: love, hatred, joy, sadness, desire, and wonder; they impel the soul to actions that God considers useful.

In Descartes' time, the late seventeenth century, all intellectual discourse was dominated by the thought of the Schoolmen of the Middle Ages. The pronouncements of Aquinas, Augustine, and Anselm, and the ideas of the ancient Greeks, especially Aristotle, were endlessly analyzed, contrasted, and elaborated. In opposition to this approach, Descartes employed an individual, rational mode of knowing, using the precision of mathematics as his model. "In our search for the direct road to truth," he wrote, "we should busy ourselves with no object about which we cannot attain a certitude equal to that of the demonstrations of arithmetic and geometry." Everything must be tested by the "natural light" of reason, and we should admit only those ideas that are "clearly and distinctly" true. This meant that the warmed-over notions he was fed at school had to be rejected, along with conventional opinions and the evidence of the senses. A radical skepticism was needed, and when the mind was emptied, a method of "systematic doubt" could then be used, leaving a residue of true knowledge. All ideas he had previously accepted had to be called into question, and only those that were indubitable could be believed. Of course, you cannot stop believing in everything, so Descartes accepted temporarily the morality of his society, but he was determined ultimately to discard even that if it could be false.

The "Cogito"

Meditations reads like an intellectual journal, taking readers inside Descartes' mind and inviting them to reason along with him. He begins by stating what seems undeniable: that he is sitting in his chair in front of his fireplace, dressed in a robe, with papers in his hands. No one can doubt this, Descartes says, except a lunatic "whose brain is so troubled and befogged by the black vapors of the bile" that he or she imagines absurd things. But then Descartes has second thoughts: he had sometimes dreamt that he was sitting in his chair in front of his fireplace, dressed in a robe, with papers in his hands, and he can't be sure whether he is now awake or asleep.

Most people are not troubled by such thoughts and believe they can tell the difference between dreams and waking life, but that was not good enough for Descartes. He wanted to doubt everything that could be doubted, and it was at least possible that he was dreaming. This is reminiscent of Lao-Tze, the Chinese sage, who wrote, "The other night I dreamt I was a butterfly flitting from flower to flower, and now I do not know if I was then a man dreaming he was a butterfly, or if I am now a butterfly dreaming he is a man."

However, Descartes then reasons that even if he is dreaming, what he is dreaming about must be real, for we cannot dream about anything that is not of this world. We might combine objects in incongruous or bizarre ways, such as a zebra with wings or a multicolored elephant, but we cannot conjure up purely imaginary things. Even fantasy creatures designed by artists, and mythological chimeras, such as centaurs, dragons, sphinxes, griffons, and unicorns, are only fusions of actual animals.

> Even when painters use the greatest ingenuity in attempting to portray sirens and satyrs in bizarre and extraordinary ways, nevertheless [they] cannot give them wholly new shapes and natures, but only invent some particular mixture composed of parts of various animals.

On the other hand, Descartes reasons, for some time he has believed in God—a God who is almighty and can do anything—at least within the bounds of logic. This includes the ability to invent imaginary objects for us to dream about. In fact, God deceives us all the time for purposes beyond our understanding, so why not in the content of our dreams? Worse still, an evil demon might be in charge of the world, and whereas a benevolent God could deceive us, a powerful and clever devil would delight in doing so.

Therefore, if we are dreaming, we cannot even be sure that our dreams are of something real. What we believe we are experiencing could be an illusion within an illusion, a hall of mirrors, boxes inside of boxes. Even simple proofs of mathematics could be false because reason itself could be some devilish hoax, or the delusions of a madman.

Descartes goes further in his method of systematic doubt and speculates that perhaps the physical objects around him are unreal, along with his own body, and that perhaps he himself does not exist. But here he stops and reasons that if he is thinking, then he must exist, or he could not think. Whatever else he doubts, he cannot question that he doubts; rather, he proves his existence in the very act of doubting it.

This leads to his famous dictum, *Cogito, ergo sum*, "I think, therefore I am." To Descartes, this is a certain truth that defies all skepticism, "self-evident by a simple intuition." Here Descartes has his Archimedean lever with which to move the world.

> While I wanted to think everything false, it must necessarily be that I who thought was something; and remarking that this truth, *I think, therefore I am*, was so solid and so certain that all the most extravagant suppositions of the skeptics were incapable of upsetting it, I judged that I could receive it without scruple as the first principle of the philosophy that I sought.

The "I" in this dictum means "a thing that thinks," that "doubts, understands, conceives, affirms, denies, wills, rejects, and imagines." In short, Descartes sees himself as identical with his mind. To Descartes, each of us is a *res cogitans*, a being whose essence is thought.

Although *cogito, ergo sum* is indubitable, it might also be trivial. If we think, then we exist, but there are times when we do not think. For instance, we sometimes sleep, and even if dreams are considered a form of thinking, we do not dream the whole night. And as the old man said, "Sometimes I sit and think, and sometimes I just sit." The *cogito*, therefore, does not prove that we continue to exist when there are no thoughts in our heads.

Some critics even claim there can be thoughts without a thinker, much like the ideas of Plato, and if that is possible, then Descartes proves only that there are thoughts when there are thoughts. . . . Furthermore, the *cogito* argument shows only the existence of the mind. The body, as well as the physical world, is neglected, for Descartes conceives of the self as basically a mental entity. He, in fact, opens up a schism between mind and body that philosophers have been trying to bridge ever since.

God's Existence
But the world and the human body also seem to be real, so Descartes searched for another clear and distinct idea that would establish physical reality, and he found his proof by a circuitous route, through an argument for the existence of God. Although he had argued previously that God could deceive people for reasons beyond our understanding, he now argues that the Lord would never fool us. A wholly good God is not a trickster and he does not lie. When we are mistaken, we have only ourselves to blame for a misuse of free will. We leap to conclusions without sufficient reasons, or as Descartes puts it, we allow our will to outstrip our understanding. Therefore, if he could prove God's existence, we would be able to trust the evidence of our senses. We must be careful, of course, to filter our sense data through reason, as when we think we see the rising and setting of the sun, but at

least we could accept the external world as real. The existence of God would guarantee that sense experience, combined with deliberate, careful thinking, will bring us to the truth.

At this point, Descartes reverts to a medieval style of thinking, and he presents an argument reminiscent of a proof by St. Anselm. He begins with the statement that the greater can produce the lesser (or something equal to it), but the lesser cannot produce the greater. That is, we cannot get more from less, but we can get less from more. For instance, we can get a rock from a mountain, but not a mountain from a rock.

Assuming this principle is true, if we can find in our minds an idea superior to ourselves, it must have been produced by something greater than we are. God is such an idea, an omnipotent, omniscient, wholly loving being, far exceeding our power, wisdom, and goodness. The only way to account for the notion of God in our heads is to assume the existence of a real God who implanted it. God's existence is therefore a clear and distinct idea that is self-evidently true. In a sense Descartes argues that if he thinks, then he exists, and if he thinks of God, then God exists.

Some philosophers have criticized this notion, saying that the effect is sometimes greater than the cause. A snowball can trigger an avalanche; a spark, a forest fire; and an acorn can become an oak. In all these cases, the effect exceeds the cause. However, this criticism does not seem valid. The avalanche is due to more than the snowball. It is the cumulative effect of the weight of the snow, the angle of the slope, the changing texture of the snowflakes, the temperature differential between layers, and so forth. These factors cause the snowfield to become unstable and separate, and the sum of these causes is equal to the effect, in the way that a straw broke the camel's back. In scientific terms, it can be explained in terms of the conservation of energy. The latent energy contained within the system is destabilized and finally released. In the same way we get a macro nuclear explosion from splitting a micro atom; that causes a chain reaction, but the whole never exceeds the sum of its parts.

Descartes' dictum therefore holds true—but only for the physical world, not for ideas. Through the power of imagination we can conceive of beings greater than ourselves, such as Zeus, Poseidon, Athena, and Hermes—Greek deities who are superior to mortals but cannot be considered real. Or differently put, if Descartes were right, then we should also believe in the gods of mythology. Clearly, then, just having an idea of a being greater than ourselves does not prove there is an actual being behind the idea.

Another criticism carries the name of the Cartesian circle. There appears to be a circularity in claiming that the validity of clear and distinct ideas is guaranteed by God, and that one of the clear and distinct ideas is the existence of God. In logic this fallacy is called "begging the question," that is, assuming the point at issue. It would be like saying, "I believe in God because the Bible tells me so, and I trust the Bible because it is the word of God."

The Mind/Body Split

As mentioned above, one of Descartes' legacies to subsequent thinkers is the mind/body problem. He claimed that we are composed of two different substances, our mind, which is our essence and which understands, senses, imagines, and wills, and our body, which is extended in three dimensions: it has length, width, and breadth, as well as shape, size, and motion. The fundamental part of the self is the mind or soul, which is unextended, indivisible, and continues on after death. The body, on the other hand, is a machine, subject to natural laws, lacking consciousness, and destined to be extinguished. However, the relation between something mental and something physical remained a mystery to Descartes, and that mystery has yet to be solved.

He did think the mind and body interacted to some extent. It is the "pineal gland" that transmits sensations from the nerves, which recall experience to mind, and through the pineal gland the mind, in turn, causes certain motions in the body. Since the ancient Greeks, the pineal gland has been surrounded by myth and superstition; it is the "third eye" in chakra yoga. Biologically, it is an endocrine gland the size of a pea, and because it is situated at the center of the brain, directly behind the eyes, it was the last to be discovered. Perhaps because of its mysterious nature, Descartes posited it as "the Seat of the Soul."

But the pineal gland did not unite the mind and body in any significant way, and Descartes' general view is that two different substances cannot act on one another. But why, then, does it seem that what we think affects what we do? An ingenious explanation was proposed by Arnold Geulincx, a Dutch disciple of Descartes. He suggested a "double-clock" theory, which was echoed by Malebranche and Spinoza: our bodies do not move because of our will, but because of two clocks, one material, the other spiritual, that keep time with each other. These clocks have been set by God in parallel tracks so that our legs move when we need to walk and our mouth utters words when we want to talk. The mind does not feel "sorrow" because the body is thirsty but because the two are on synchronized tracks. All actions can be correlated with mental states, but our actions are not willed by those states; rather, events are timed to correspond to our thoughts.

The Self

The Cartesian explanation for the relation between mind and body is farfetched, and Descartes may have created an even greater split between spirit and matter than Plato did in his doctrine of two worlds.

This raises the question of the nature of the self. In a sense, nothing seems more obvious than our very self, but when we attempt to define it, we become confused. Part of the problem is that we ourselves are analyzing ourselves, which is rather like pointing a flashlight at its own beam of light. The principal problem, however, stems from the self's complexity, which makes it difficult to characterize.

Contrary to Descartes, a commonsense view is to think of the self as a physical entity that exists in the same tangible form as any other object; its existence is verified by sense perception. We recognize ourselves and others as material beings, acting in a concrete world. We are that person in the mirror, the one people recognize on sight, answering to a particular name. In short, we can see that our bodies are something that we *are* rather than something that we *have*.

But perhaps physical appearance does not constitute the self. For example, suppose we knew a girl named Carol who has brown hair, pale skin, and dresses in jeans and T-shirts. But if Carol dyed her hair blond, got a deep tan, and began to dress more formally, she would still be Carol. If we say she had changed, we would not mean she had become another person; she would remain Carol, but with a different appearance. And if Carol is still herself, then physical appearance cannot be what makes her Carol. Similarly, if she had her hair cut, she would not leave part of herself on the salon floor, any more than breaking a tooth means that part of her had broken off.

"Thought experiments" of this kind suggest that the identity of the self may not consist of the body at all. To carry it further, if someone happens to lose a limb in a war, that person's self is not diminished; he remains the same person, but without that limb. Similarly, people who have heart or liver transplants, artificial joints, or reconstructive surgery do not become someone else. And if an athlete becomes handicapped as a result of an accident, or a pianist's fingers are gnarled by arthritis, these people may act differently afterward, not because of the physical trauma, but because of their mental reaction to the trauma. They may become embittered or introspective or despondent, and this is what would make us say they are not the people they were. If there were not any internal changes, then regardless of their physical disabilities, they would be regarded as the same people.

This is reinforced by the fact that we say a person has changed if he or she loses the ability to think, to remember, to recognize people, or to use language. That is, a major mental event, such as severe Alzheimer's disease, could mean a loss of identity in the way that a missing limb could not.

Descartes rejects the materialistic view of the self for similar reasons. He uses the case of wax to illustrate his point, wax being a common material at the time. At one point the wax may be sweet, hard, white, and cold, but the sweet odor could turn sour, and the hardness could become soft, the whiteness grayness, and the surface warm. Still, it remains the same object, which shows that the wax is something other than its external characteristics. The wax, like the self, is its inner nature, known by the understanding.

We can sympathize with this idea because to think of anyone as his or her body alone does not capture the person; it seems superficial, almost extraneous. If people regarded each other just physically, they would become commodities and could be treated as servants, enemies, providers, sex objects.

The self seems more internal, a mental entity lying beneath our appearance and behavior. It is the nonmaterial source of our actions, with the body as the mind's agent. In keeping with this view, the essential self is known through introspection, when we peer inside and uncover our essential core. The body serves only as a shell or housing, the vehicle we drive, the robot we direct; it is our animal form, even though, as Yeats said, we are "chained to a dying animal." The essential person lies within, receiving impressions, storing memories, reflecting, and deliberating. In short, the self can be identified as the mind, which is the way Descartes viewed it.

However, certain problems also beset this interpretation of the self. Our body may not lie at our core, but it does seem important to ourselves; the image in the mirror does appear to reflect us. Conversely, it is hard to imagine being whole, complete, and intact without a body. If our mind could be suspended in a vat, connected by tubes and wires to a life-support system, it would be hard to say that we were still there. Just the presence of mind is not enough to say that the self continues to exist.

Perhaps we assume a mind exists only because we need a subject for every sentence: we say, for instance, "It is raining" or "It is five o'clock." Maybe mind is synonymous with brain rather than soul, an incredibly complex brain with more than one hundred billion neurons. Mind could be reduced to consciousness, and mental health might not be a sound mind but successful functioning.

Besides, the hard-nosed scientist will ask, "Where, exactly, is the mind?" We can locate the brain as a physical organ within the skull, but mind or soul seems like a ghost in the machine. Can it be tested with litmus paper, dissected in the anatomy lab, transplanted to another person? By its very nature mind seems to belong to a mysterious realm beyond the reach of empirical evidence. It cannot be seen, touched, or heard; in fact, no test could detect its presence within the body. If a person reaches for a fork, then a train of physiological events can be described: his or her muscles contracted because of certain nerve impulses that were triggered by neural events occurring in his or her brain. But no evidence can prove that an entity called "mind" was responsible for the movement of his or her arm.

The mind therefore seems unverifiable but at the same time undeniable. Because of this, some philosophers have adopted a dualism that claims both mind and body are real. That is, perhaps both self-awareness and sense evidence can be credited. The self reflects upon itself, and is both subject and object: "I" can contemplate "me."

The issue also plays out in psychology, which can be defined either as the study of the mind or the study of behavior. It impacts religion when believers ask if the soul alone survives death, and whether the body can also be eternal. Christian denominations have varied opinions on the question, especially as applied to the resurrection of Christ. If the spirit alone is resurrected, why should the rock be rolled away from the tomb?

The relation is baffling, even paradoxical, as Oscar Wilde declared:

> Soul and body, body and soul—how mysterious they were! There was animalism in the soul, and the body had its moments of spirituality. The senses could refine, and the intellect could degrade. Who could say where the fleshy impulse ceased, or the physical impulse began? How shallow are the arbitrary definitions of ordinary psychologists! And yet how difficult to decide between the claims of the various schools. Was the soul a shadow seated in the house of sin? Or was the body really in the soul, as Giordano Bruno thought? The separation of spirit from matter was a mystery, and the Union of spirit and matter was a mystery also.

The Self in Space and Time
Another problem in defining the self has to do with its limits in *space*. What should be included as necessary to the self, and what should be excluded as not belonging? What is essential to the person, and what lies outside the circle? How far out does our self extend, and how deeply do we have to descend within ourselves to find our fundamental self?

We wonder, for example, whether personal property might be part of us, the land or home we own, a favorite chair, tools worn from a lifetime of use, a musical instrument we played. Or we might have books or paintings that are meaningful to us, or as Thoreau remarked, clothing that has conformed to our body from repeated wear. If these objects were lost in a flood or fire, we would feel diminished by that much. We might also identify with the people we love, so that their joys are our joys, their tragedies felt as our own. Spectators identify with athletic teams in this way. Perhaps we are a part of everyone we meet, incorporating them within ourselves, and parents live on through their children, an immortality of influence. Or perhaps we can enlarge the self to embrace the whole of humanity within our consciousness; both Eugene Debs and Martin Luther King said, "If any man is in jail, then I am not free." John Donne expressed this thought best in his Meditations:

> No man is an island, entire of itself; every man is a piece of the continent, a part of the main; if a clod be washed away by the sea, Europe is the less, as well as if a promontory were; as well as if a manor of the friends or of thine own; any man's death diminishes me, because I am involved in mankind; and therefore never send to know for whom the bell tolls; it tolls for thee.

Christ said it more simply: "If ye do it unto the least of these, my brethren, ye do it unto me."

A further problem has to do with the persistence of the self through *time*. That which defines a person should remain constant throughout his or her existence. Whether we are referring to mind or body, some element must be the same from birth to death, otherwise it is not the same person. What is the common denominator, the thread of identity that makes a person the same continuous self?

An analogy with a car may clarify the point. If we replace the engine of a car and then the upholstery, the exhaust system, the tires, the body, and so on, until nothing of the original car remains, we could not call it the same car. In the same way, if we have an axe and we change the head and then the handle, it would not be the same axe. Applying this principle to people, if someone changes in all respects, they would not be the same person.

That seems the case with all human beings; nothing of either a mental or a physical nature remains constant throughout a person's lifetime. Our bodies grow, mature, and decay, changing radically in shape and size. Our skin expands and grows slack; our hair thickens, then becomes sparse and changes color; our muscles gain in strength, then atrophy; our senses become more acute, then degenerate in old age. Even our skin cells are replaced every seven years, as well as the RNA in our nerve cells, and although our organs perform the same function throughout our lives, they change in texture and composition. Our DNA stays the same, but that does not separate one identical twin from another, much less clones. What's more, it seems beside the point: our DNA does not make us who we are.

Mutability also characterizes our mind, for every internal element, from thoughts to values to disposition, appears to change. We can go from extreme compassion to bitter cynicism during our lifetime (all cynics are former idealists). Our ideas are different at six years of age and at sixty; our memory and willpower can change from strong to weak; our attitudes can be altered by our experiences, and so forth. And although everyone's experience is unique, that does not tell us what is the unique self that undergoes the experiences. As Heraclitus said, everything is in flux; whirl is king.

What, then, remains constant? Growth and degeneration seem to occur continually between birth and death. In temporal terms, the self is whatever entitles us to declare we are the same person throughout our lives. It is that consistent element underlying all change, the golden thread of identity.

Perhaps we are different selves at different times, and as a corollary, people should not be held responsible for what their previous selves did. What's more, no future self would be bound by a promise made by our present self. In this world, there would be no responsibility and no commitments.

As a final point, some philosophic systems of a mystical nature have denied the reality of the self altogether. Indian philosophies, especially Buddhism, will often make this claim, treating the self as an illusion (*maya*). The enlightened person, it is argued, understands that there are no separate selves and no difference between subject and object. Reality is one, without inner and outer parts, and no distinction exists between our individual soul and the world soul. Indian philosophy further maintains that we can experience the unitary character of reality in privileged moments of heightened awareness. If our spirit is properly prepared, then the Oneness of the universe is revealed to us. Here our sensations are melted and fused, our bones become liquefied, and we are absorbed into the cosmic All.

To conceive of the self in this way—as undifferentiated and, consequently, unreal—is appealing when we long for escape from suffering. Nevertheless, we are aware of our selves with a vividness, immediacy, and power that seem to guarantee authenticity. Western philosophers generally argue that if the "I" is not real, then everything is an illusion, for few things strike us as more certain. As Woody Allen quipped, "We are two with nature."

However, defining this self is challenging for all philosophers, including Descartes, and it persists as a major intellectual problem. It is also a highly personal issue. If we can complete the sentence, "I am nothing if I am not . . . ," then we know who we are.

Beasts, Angels, and Machines: Hobbes and Rousseau

Not only is there a problem defining the self, but we are not sure about human nature. It used to be said that human beings exist somewhere between beasts and angels. Now we must add machines to the list, especially those computers and robots that have been designed with artificial intelligence. To define human nature at this point, we first need to know where we fit in the scheme of things: in the hierarchy of animals, the realm of spirit, the cyberworld, and "the great chain of being."

According to the standard scientific view, human beings are intelligent animals that evolved from primates around ten million years ago. The "out-of-Africa" hypothesis is dominant today, which claims a single origin in the sub-Sahara and subsequent migration to Europe and Asia. Originally tree dwellers, we had front-facing, binocular vision, and through adaptations to ice ages, we developed bipedalism, the ability to walk on our hind legs. This enabled us see predators or game farther away, or as the poet says, it allowed us to see not just the ground, but the stars. Our opposable thumb and finger, along with our superior brain, enabled us to grasp sticks, bones, and stones as both weapons and tools, which was the start of technology. Orangutans, gorillas, and chimpanzees have opposable thumbs on all four hands, and koalas and opossums have opposable toes, but they do not also have a sophisticated brain and fine motor skills. *Homo habilis*, who may have been too close to apes to qualify as a hominid, lived two million years ago and not only used tools but made them. Quite possibly, language, art, and religion were developed at that time, which was the beginnings of culture.

Homo sapiens originated around fifty-five thousand years ago and are our closest relatives as we moved from apelike to humanlike. They took on our physical form and dominated or displaced all other creatures on earth, including the Neanderthals, who preceded them by some 145,000 years. They had a lighter skeleton, a high-vaulted cranium with a near vertical forehead, reduced ridges above the eyes, and a generally modern appearance. Our very earliest ancestor, Ardi, lived 4.4 million years ago, an anthropological Eve.

Aside from physical characteristics, philosophers wonder about the character of humankind from these early beginnings. The question is usually put in terms of the "state of nature": what were human beings like in primitive conditions, before there were social, economic, or political structures? Since we lived in isolated groups in the wild, we wonder about our interior emotions, our ways of thinking, kinship systems, and above all, our moral values. We try to glimpse human nature in pretechnological tribes that have survived into modern times, or by understanding the mentality of infants and children. We rake over geological evidence for fossils that might be revealing, study primates for parallels, and map the human brain to discover how its stem and cerebral cortex function. In the end, we are left with only speculative theories about our fundamental nature.

Thomas Hobbes
Thomas Hobbes (1588–1679) was one of the earliest thinkers to investigate the question of human nature, and his pessimistic conclusions and their political consequences have resonated through philosophy.

Hobbes was born in Malmesbury, England, a south Cotswold town in the county of Wiltshire; as the tale has it, his mother was frightened into labor by the approach of the Spanish Armada. His father was an impoverished vicar of Charlton and Westport, who "disesteemed learning . . . as not knowing the sweetness of it." The vicar fled to London after being involved in a brawl outside his own church, and Thomas was raised by a wealthy uncle. He managed to thrive, but his brother Edmund "drowned his wit in ale."

Because he seemed unusually bright, his uncle sent him to Magdalen Hall, Oxford, at age fifteen, and after graduating, he was employed by William Cavendish, Earl of Devonshire. Hobbes remained connected to the Cavendish family throughout his career, as secretary, tutor, and general advisor, and he took the sons on Grand Tours of France, Italy, and Germany. Here he interacted with the outstanding minds of his times, such as Pierre Gassendi, Descartes, and Galileo, and back in London, Francis Bacon and Ben Johnson, the playwright and poet.

Hobbes lived most of his life in England, except for eleven years spent in France because of civil unrest in his home country. This was the time of a civil war between Parliamentarians (called Roundheads) and Royalists (Cavaliers). It led to the execution of Charles I, the exile of Charles II, and eventually the establishment of a protectorate under Oliver Cromwell. When the monarchy was restored, it could rule only with the consent of parliament.

During this historical period Hobbes was a highly controversial figure, antagonizing almost every faction. The parliamentarians thought he supported the rights of the sovereign, but because he rejected the divine right of kings, the royalists also distrusted him. He did write that subjects can unseat the monarch if he no longer protects them. At the same time he was alienated from the Church of England because of atheistic passages in his published works, and in France his "godless" views antagonized the Catholics. He was often accused of anticlericalism for maintaining the priority of the state over the church. Toward the end of his life, when parliament considered criminalizing atheism, he was prohibited by law from publishing anything, and two of his books were burned at Oxford four years after his death.

Thanks to John Aubrey, a contemporary of Hobbes, we know a great many personal details about him. Aubrey reports that Hobbes had a "fresh, ruddy complexion," an ample forehead, yellowish red whiskers, "goose-skin," and hazel-colored eyes that showed "a bright live-coal" within them. In old age he was "very bald" and his "greatest trouble was to keep off the flies from pitching on the baldness."

He is described as "a proper man, brisk, and in very good habit," "in love with geometry" and "much addicted to music"; he played the bass viol and sang to exercise his lungs. He also played tennis up to the age of seventy-five. Hobbes wore a black velvet coat lined with fur on his habitual long walks, which were a time for reflection. "He walked much and contemplated, and he had in the head of his cane a pen and ink-horn, carried always a notebook in his pocket, and as soon as a thought darted, he presently entered it into his book." After a breakfast of bread and butter at seven o'clock, he would stroll and meditate, have dinner at eleven o'clock, smoke, nap for half an hour, and then write his reflections in the afternoon. Like Descartes he believed "leisure is the mother of philosophy."

Hobbes wrote a number of works, mainly on politics and philosophy, ranging from his first book, *Short Tract on First Principles*, to *De Cive* (*On the Citizen*), *Human Nature*, *Objections*, *Of Liberty and Necessity*, and his major work, *Leviathan*. A leviathan is a large marine animal, such as a whale, and Hobbes meant this book as his magnum opus. In *Objections* he disputed Descartes' belief in mind as primary, asserting that there is only matter in motion, and in *Of Liberty and Necessity* he rejected the idea of free will. His mechanistic philosophy did not allow him to accept free choice. He thought that we do not decide our preferences but choose from our preferences, which are determined. Hobbes also translated Homer and Thucydides, the latter as a warning against democracy, and he wrote his autobiography, in Latin verse, when he was eighty-four years old. His final words were, "I am about to take my last voyage, a great leap in the dark."

Political Philosophy
Politics was Hobbes's central concern, specifically why the many allowed themselves to be ruled by the few, and what would be the best form of government. To answer these questions, he first had to know what constituted human nature, and his conclusions are at the opposite extreme from sentimentality.

Hobbes regarded people as closer to beasts than angels, although he also compared them to machines. When we look within ourselves to discover our fundamental thoughts and passions, we find self-interest as the primary motivating force. "Homo homini lupus," Hobbes writes, "man is wolf to man" (which may be unfair to wolves, which are social and cooperative). By nature, human beings are prone to be aggressive, selfish, and mean, and are interested only in advancing their own preservation and well-being. The desire to "shun death" is very strong; we fight for life, power, position, and material goods; and we possess a general distrust of one another. Because all people are equal, at least in their ability to threaten each other's lives, this leads to constant struggle and violence. In a *state of nature*, prior to civil government, turmoil and insecurity are the rule. As Hobbes famously writes, it is a

> dissolute condition of masterless men, without subjection to Lawes, and a coercive Power to tye their hands from rapine and revenge.... [There would be] no place for industry, because the fruit thereof is uncertain; and consequently no culture of the earth; no navigation, nor use of the commodities that may be imported by Sea; no commodious Building; no Instruments of moving and removing such things as require much force; no Knowledge of the face of the Earth; no account of Time; no Arts; no Letters; and which is worst of all, continuall feare, and danger of violent death. And the life of man, *solitary, poore, nasty, brutish, and short* [my italics].

The state of nature, then, is one of warfare, *omnium contra omnes*, all against all, because of our basic animal aggression. Human existence is mean and violent, with everyone struggling for domination; people interpret "right" as whatever is necessary for their self-preservation. Individuals, living in isolation, personally decide what is moral and what is pious, what goods they deserve and the respect they themselves should be accorded. But general notions "of right and wrong, justice and injustice have no place" in the natural world.

To escape this misery, people voluntarily submit to an absolute sovereign, surrendering some of their liberty in exchange for security and peace. We relinquish our desire for "all things" and enter into a *social contract* with a monarch, whom we agree to obey if he will only protect us from each other. Civilization is therefore based on fear, not love, on mutual advantage and not on the fact that we are social animals.

Since there is no consensus on right and wrong, a shared authority decides moral matters, and law is nothing but the commands of the "sovereign." The sovereign does not have a God-given right to rule but maintains a "covenant" with the people. For their part, citizens join in an implied promise of obedience to the sovereign who has saved them from a state of nature, which expressed only their baseness. The alternative is chaos, "slaughter, solitude, and the want of all things." Even despotism is preferable to anarchy.

At a time of civil war over the rights of the monarchy, which Hobbes experienced, we can understand why a doctrine of obedience to the sovereign put Hobbes in the center of the storm.

Criticisms

Philosophers, of course, have challenged the notion that a promise made under coercion—the fear of a natural state of violence—is freely made. More technically, people in an amoral state cannot make promises, since amorality means not having duties or obligations. In addition, the idea of an implied promise is questionable. If we are born in a country, we do not tacitly promise to support the government simply by living there. Critics of a state are not in breach of the social contract; there can be a loyal opposition. If we give testimony in court, we expressly promise not to lie, but in ordinary conversation there is no implied promise to tell the truth, the whole truth, and nothing but the truth.

Another question concerns the absolute authority of the sovereign. If people have the right to depose the sovereign for failing to defend them properly, then there are natural, perhaps inalienable, rights that are higher than the sovereign. This implies the existence of objective values even in a state of nature, and that neither the people nor a sovereign decides right and wrong. It also means faith in human judgment, which should not be surrendered to a king.

For our purposes a more fundamental question is whether Hobbes is right about the selfishness of human nature, a view called psychological egoism. Although Hobbes was apparently a nonbeliever, his idea of innate evil is reminiscent of original sin, the inherent depravity of man. Anachronistically, it also carries reverberations of Freud's "id," a seething cauldron of selfish desires.

In our more jaded moments we tend to agree with Hobbes: everyone appears to act selfishly, and generosity may only be apparent—a mask for the self-satisfaction that comes from being kind. Those who give to charity are not motivated by concern for the poor but want to view themselves as superior to the people they have helped. In explaining why he gave money to a beggar, Hobbes wrote, "I was in pain to consider the miserable condition of the old man; and now my alms, giving him some relief, doth also ease me."

What's more, doctors are not humanitarians but receive great personal and financial rewards; they practice medicine because of the power, prestige, and wealth it provides. In modern terms, they are type A personalities who relish their achievement and could not live with themselves if they failed. In the same way, parents who sacrifice for their children will receive reflected glory at their success, as well as feeling proud of themselves for their sacrifice. Religious people, who practice agape love, hope for God's protection in this life and heavenly rewards in the next. As for martyrs, they would rather live a brief, glorious life than have a banal, average existence; their martyrdom is essentially pride and vanity.

This cynical view is tempting at times, but in the last analysis, it presents a distorted picture of human nature. Although we might feel good about ourselves after performing a generous act, it is unlikely that we acted generously in order to feel good about ourselves. We may experience a sense of pride as a *result* of being kind, but that is rarely the *motive* for the kindness. The driver who swerves into a tree to avoid hitting a child is trying to save the child's life, not thinking of the praise he might receive. Doctors Without Borders medical teams are rightly celebrated for the dangers they face in combat zones, and it is far-fetched to think that celebrity is their purpose in alleviating suffering and saving lives.

Some of the time, at least, we do seem to act in unselfish ways. We place our family's welfare above our own, support Medicaid for the poor, contribute money to victims of disasters. In fact, we could be hardwired to empathize and to practice compassion. Some recent evidence suggests that we have an inborn ethical faculty comparable to our natural capacity to acquire language, a universal moral grammar that judges actions as permissible, obligatory, or prohibited.

Critics have also pointed out that people violate their self-interest by self-destructive behavior, such as drinking to excess, taking drugs or chain-smoking, and eating to the point of obesity, attacking themselves with a knife and fork. Some seek blood revenge, even though it might mean a prison sentence. We know the consequences but act in perverse ways, which implies that we do not always act for our own good; we bite off our nose to spite our face. Some individuals carry around a weight of pathological guilt, so that any pain is thought of as just deserts, atoning for that much. In referring to the English, G. B. Shaw remarked, "They always think they're being moral when in fact they are only uncomfortable."

In short, we act in self-destructive ways some of the time, which means we are not always rationally self-serving. And we also seem capable of putting other people's good above our own, not for our ultimate self-interest but as genuine self-sacrifice. Hobbes's view of human nature, therefore, seems more jaded than realistic. Even primates exhibit altruistic behavior. Nevertheless, as one analyst wrote, "Where [Hobbes] is wrong, he is wrong from oversimplification, not because the basis of his thought is unreal or fantastic. For this reason, he is still worth refuting."

Jean-Jacques Rousseau

A very different picture of human nature is painted by Jean-Jacques Rousseau. His dates, 1712 to 1778, place him squarely in the era of the Enlightenment, although he helped initiate the age of Romanticism that followed. Even though Rousseau was born in Geneva, he is considered a French philosopher because that city had not yet become part of Switzerland. French was also his native tongue and shaped his oblique mode of thinking.

Rousseau's mother died in childbirth, and he was raised by his father, a watchmaker. He reports that he had a happy childhood, even though he was never allowed to play with children his own age (sic!). Without any formal schooling, his only education came from reading Plutarch's *Lives* and some Calvinist sermons (Geneva was the home of Calvin). Like Hobbes, Rousseau's father had to flee his native city because of a row in which he brandished his sword, and Rousseau was taken in by his mother's relations—apparently a humiliating and degrading experience.

At age thirteen he was employed by a notary, who complained of his incompetence, then apprenticed to an engraver for three years. Rousseau left this trade because of poor treatment and struck out on his own, ending up in the employment of Baronne Louise de Warens in Savoy.

In Madame de Warren he found a benefactress, a colorful Swiss woman who had robbed her husband of his money and run off with the gardener's son. She had converted to Catholicism and was dedicated to converting young Protestants to her new faith—including Rousseau. She was twelve years his senior, and their relationship was multileveled. Rousseau treated her as a mentor, a mother, and a romantic figure, becoming her secretary, steward, companion, and eventually her lover. Because of Madame de Warens's taste and intellect, she guided his education, particularly in music, and within four years he had established himself as a music teacher and general tutor. Subsequently, although he never attended school, Rousseau became a leading French intellectual who influenced the wider world.

At about age thirty, when Madame de Warens's affections shifted to a wig maker, Rousseau went to Paris and fell in with some radical philosophes. The group was led by Denis Diderot, editor of the *Encyclopédie*, which was intended as a compendium of all human knowledge (from the standpoint of the Enlightenment); when completed it numbered twenty-eight volumes. Nothing so massive or ambitious had ever been attempted, and the contributors included famous people of the time, such as D'Alembert, Montesquieu, Turgot, and Condorcet, as well as Rousseau, who wrote articles on music. However, because of its opposition to the establishment, including religion and royal power, the encyclopedia was periodically suppressed by the authorities. Eventually, Rousseau quarreled with the editors and left the group. He turned to music more than writing, composing operas, such as *Le devin du village* (*The Cunning Man*), that were good enough to be praised by the king and court.

Although he could have had a respectable career as a composer, Rousseau felt uncomfortable in that role, perhaps because it was fashionable. Furthermore, he experienced an "illumination" that was decisive for his career. While walking to Vincennes to visit Diderot, who had been imprisoned for his sacrilegious writings, he saw an advertisement for an essay competition by the Academy of Dijon, the subject matter of which was whether the arts and sciences had improved or corrupted humankind.

> All at once I felt myself dazzled by a thousand sparkling lights, crowds of vivid ideas thronged in my head with a force and confusion that threw me into unspeakable agitation; I felt my head whirling in a giddiness like that of intoxication.

In a "terrible flash" Rousseau understood that in a state of nature, human beings are good but that the forces of civilization have ruined us. His essay expressing this idea, *Discours sur les sciences et les arts* (1750), won the competition, establishing Rousseau's fame and setting the dominant theme of his subsequent writings.

At this time he began a relationship with Thérèse Lavasseur, a maid and seamstress in his hostelry, who is reputed to have been both illiterate and unattractive. Rousseau's association with her may not be surprising given his belief in natural goodness; he said that he admired her "pure and innocent" heart. It is unclear whether they were ever married, but they had five children and remained together until he died. In one of the most surprising episodes of his life, Rousseau gave all his children to an orphanage. As might be expected, this generated a great deal of criticism, especially from Voltaire and Enlightenment thinkers, since Rousseau had professed admiration for the simplicity of children and contempt for institutions. Edmund Burke, the Irish statesman and political theorist, wrote that Rousseau expressed

> benevolence to the whole species, and want of feeling for every individual . . . [He] melts with tenderness for those only who touch him by the remotest relation, and then, without one natural pang, casts away, lustful amours, and sends

his children to the hospital of foundlings. The bear loves, licks, and forms her young; but bears are not philosophers.

Rousseau seems to have loved humankind until he saw one of them walking toward him. The rationalization for his actions was that, because he was poor, his children would have a better life in an institution than he could offer; they would also be less exposed to society's deviousness. In later life, however, he expressed regret at abandoning them, realizing his own hypocrisy. He felt he had not lived up to his ideals, which, of course, does not invalidate them.

In 1754 Rousseau published another *Discours*, this one on the origin of inequality among people; and in 1762 his masterwork, *The Social Contract*. It begins with the famous sentence, "Man is born free, and everywhere he is in chains." Embedded in this book is the slogan of the French Revolution and the motto of modern France: *Liberté, égalité, fraternité* (Liberty, equality, brotherhood). Rousseau's novel *La nouvelle Héloïse* (1761) was the most popular of his books, and *Émile* (1762) contains his theory of education. His autobiography, *Confessions* (1781), has the same classic status as that of St. Augustine's, after whom it was named, and as Cardinal Newman's *Apologia pro Vita Sua*.

All of Rousseau's books were controversial, causing political turmoil throughout his life. His notion of an "elective aristocracy" was heretical in itself. For this reason he moved from place to place in Europe, living in Montmorency for four years (a seminal time), then Luxembourg, Venice, Môtiers in Neuchâtel, and Ashbourne, England. He even returned to Geneva for a brief period, where he recovered his citizenship and reconverted to Protestantism.

Rousseau quarreled with almost everyone, including the benign David Hume, and seemed hypersensitive, tormented, and suspicious to the point of paranoia. He had wide mood swings and frequently accused others of plotting against him, which alienated even close friends. These psychological peculiarities may have been due to his unsympathetic upbringing (early rejection is difficult to overcome), as well as the real persecution he experienced during his stormy career. Although Rousseau was never imprisoned, some of his books were censored and banned. *The Social Contract* was burned, his house was stoned, and he was periodically banished from France and cantons of Switzerland.

In his final years he found a certain tranquility, as witnessed by his last major work, *Reveries of the Solitary Walker*, which has a lyrical quality of acceptance and closure. Nevertheless, Rousseau supposedly died insane; some of his friends even believe he committed suicide. His remains were placed in the Pantheon, directly across from Voltaire, in a tomb that resembles a rustic temple.

Human Nature
An abiding faith in the goodness of human nature is the cornerstone of Rousseau's philosophy. To Hobbes, human beings are brutal when they live among animals, while Rousseau believes that we are innocent, happy, and free in that state of nature. He exonerates the natural state and condemns human society for our depravity. Society provokes passions that lead to vices. Once we left the golden age of the past, where nature belonged to everyone, and we began owning property and houses, the first steps were taken toward conflict. Private goods lead to inequality, as each person measures himself against his neighbor, and love, too, carries with it destructive jealousy. When we shared the earth, we did not envy or hate one another; in fact, we have an innate tendency toward pity and compassion. Civilization engenders *amour-propre*, self-love.

Unfortunately, Rousseau says, we cannot go home again and become noble savages, and with the fatal curse of property, government must be instituted with laws to safeguard everyone's possessions. The rich do better than the poor because society legalizes their ownership of larger tracts of land, but everyone is benefited to some extent by the enforced peace. A civil animosity persists, however, because social man is never satisfied, not having what he wants, not wanting what he has. Separated from nature, we have lost our innocence and contentment; we live amid converging lines of self-interest.

To provide a remedy, Rousseau argues, people must enter into a social contract, not a false contract, such as Hobbes proposed, that subjugates people to an absolute ruler, but a genuine contract that enhances their liberty. In a social context, people cannot do as they like, because they must interact with others who also want free choices. Instead, people must follow the *volonté générale*, or general will, pledging to support the public, common interest. Citizens must surrender their natural rights, based on might, skill, or intelligence, in exchange for civil rights that maximize their freedom within the group. These will be legitimate rights, enforced by the community for the welfare of all.

But as he moves from idyllic nature to necessary government, Rousseau's ideas become incrementally more menacing. For example, he is uncompromising about the treatment of the rebel, criminal, or nonconformist who breaks the law. Here he sounds like a stern, almost vengeful judge. The individual who is pursuing his personal welfare must be compelled to obey the "general will" within him; he must be made to realize his personal interests, which ultimately coincide with those of the group. In a chilling phrase, Rousseau speaks of "forcing a man to be free," including liberating him from his private passions.

Furthermore, in passages that seem almost fascist, Rousseau argues that a *lawgiver* must draft a rigid constitution and a strict system of statutes for the masses to follow. Despite the fact that he championed the natural goodness of people, he did not trust the average person to identify the good, so a great mind, like that of Solon or Calvin, is needed to enact true laws. In this he resembles Plato. And to persuade the unintelligent populace to conform to these laws, the lawgiver can claim they come from God.

Although Rousseau believed in a supernatural being, as revealed in forests, lakes, and mountains, and he spoke of "the divine voice in the soul of man," he did not think of him as a legislator. However, here he wants to use God to intimidate people into obedience. Machiavelli, whom Rousseau admired, also advocated the public worship of God, and for cynical reasons: religion kept the people from revolting.

Rousseau's thinking seems to have been erratic and inconsistent. Some of it has a Romantic quality to it—it is anti-Enlightenment, rather than a product of the Age of Reason—and that is the humane part. It can be seen in his battle with the music critic Jean-Philippe Rameau over which opera was superior: the new Italian or the traditional French. Rameau, a composer and leading musicologist, championed harmonious music, in which the French excelled, whereas Rousseau argued for the Italian model, which made melody primary. That is, Italian opera emphasized the melodic line and therefore a more individual and creative expression, whereas adherence to rules of harmony, the French condition for art, meant order and structure, imposing rationality on the chaos of nature.

Rousseau won the day, "liberating music" and helping to change the direction of European art. During the late eighteenth to the mid-nineteenth century emotion—the senses over the mind, the spontaneous over the planned—dominated in music, painting, and literature. Composers, painters, and writers wanted freedom from classical restraint and tried to express their personal spirit. Like Rousseau they wanted a return to nature, or a close approximation—but without authoritarian features.

Rousseau traveled an enormous distance, beginning with trust in human goodness and ending with distrust of people's ability to know what is good for them; from viewing society as the corrupting influence to empowering a lawgiver to control people in society; from a naturalistic democracy to a near totalitarian regime.

But in all fairness, the questions he raises are enormously difficult to answer: What should be done if people want what they should not have, if they do not recognize where their freedom lies? In a democracy, should government enforce the values of equality and justice, even if they are opposed by the will of the majority? Does freedom consist in obedience to principles, in identifying with the welfare of the community, or is that surrendering too much personal liberty?

To some critics Rousseau presents a maze of contradictions that could support a democratic republic, a socialist collective, individualistic anarchy, or a fascist nation. Others see coherence in his scheme, which addressed some of the knottiest questions in political philosophy. Wherever the truth lies, his influence has been varied and enormous, stretching from G. W. F. Hegel and Immanuel Kant to back-to-nature movements. It reaches from German and English Romanticism to modern theories of education. Goethe, Tolstoy, Marx, and Freud all acknowledge their debt to him.

Overall, Rousseau is known for championing the innate goodness of humankind, rejecting Hobbes's cynicism and declaring human nature benevolent. In a sense, he never departed from the Christian story of Eden, a paradise of grace and simplicity before the fall made us complex and sinful.

New Directions
Other characterizations of human nature exist, of course; we may not be exclusively beasts or angels. We could be a mix, or our nature may be fluid at birth, changing with experience: children sometimes think of their mother as both the good witch and the bad witch on different days. Perhaps the definition of *humanness* changes according to the interaction between biology and culture. Breakthroughs in biomedical engineering, for example, could result in post-humans or trans-humans, such as we see in mechanical implants and in cyborgs.

Cyborgs, short for "cybernetic organisms," are a combination of the human and the mechanical. In collaboration with engineers, researchers in medicine have introduced a variety of artificial parts into our bodies, mainly to improve our health or physical functioning. The resultant cyborg is part natural and part synthetic, both organic and inorganic. Bones are combined with steel, flesh and blood with wires and circuits, so that the person is partially transformed into a machine.

We already accept the notion of cyborgs when we insert a pacemaker or use hearing aids, teeth implants, or contact lenses; when we substitute artificial joints in fingers, elbows, or knees, and attach prosthetic devices, such as artificial arms or legs. Pacemakers and drug dispensers are now incorporated into our bodies, just as paralyzed patients can have direct interface with machines through electrodes in their brains.

As we exchange more and more of our body parts for synthetic materials, will the human being be displaced? Are we simply machines, clever enough to invent machines brighter than ourselves, or are we spiritual beings created in the image of God? Perhaps we are input/output mechanisms programmed by heredity and environment, or incorporeal minds on the verge of transcending the limitations of our bodies. If we are programmed like computers, maybe we never make free choices, or on the other hand, perhaps we have to attribute consciousness to machines that can think.

Above all we wonder, as Descartes did, whether our mind is basic, so that when robots begin to perform higher brain functions, we will lose our distinct human nature. IBM's Deep Blue has already beaten Gasparov at chess.

CHAPTER FIVE

How Things Seem and What They Are: Epistemology

The question of what is real naturally leads us to the question of how we know what is real. That is, what means should we use to determine the truth of things? Can we depend on the evidence of our eyes and ears, our senses of smell, taste, and touch? Should we use our rational mind and its logic, or rely perhaps on what our heart tells us? Are things true for one person but not for another, so that people invent rather than discover what is so? Can we, in fact, ever achieve reliable knowledge, or must we be satisfied with theories, conjectures, assumptions, opinions, and beliefs?

Epistemology is the branch of philosophy that deals with these issues and tries to establish the most reliable way of knowing. When anyone makes a statement, how do we know it is true? How are truth-claims established? What warrant validates them?

Skeptics claim we cannot know anything, which seems self-contradictory since that, at least, is something we know, while most epistemologists will only claim that we cannot know anything certain about the world. "There are more things in heaven and earth, Horatio, than are dreamt of in your philosophy," Shakespeare writes. But how do we know there are things we cannot know?

Within epistemology the most common theory is *empiricism*—the view that sense perception, mainly our ability to see and hear, is the best instrument for grasping reality. In fact, we say "I see" in place of "I understand." A hard-nosed empiricist will claim that only the senses can be trusted, and that whatever we accept as true is justified by sense evidence. We know the

Figure 5.1. *Portrait of David Hume,* by Allan Ramsay, 1766 (Scottish National Portrait Gallery, Edinburgh).

apple is red by seeing it, that it is smooth by touching it, and that it has a sweet flavor by tasting it. The apple also has an aroma, and when we bite into it, there is a satisfying crunching sound. This is the model for knowing whatever we do know, not just apples, but tigers and kangaroos, locomotives, birch trees, and oysters. Plato claimed that we come into life already containing knowledge, but the empiricist maintains we don't know anything beforehand; we acquire knowledge by sense experience during our lifetime.

Most people accept this latter view, and it is usually tied to materialism—the belief that the physical world, revealed by the senses, is the only world.

However, as we saw in discussing Zeno of Elea, our senses can deceive us. We claim to see the sun rise and set, and to gaze at the stars, when, in fact, these are illusions. The earth may appear to be stationary, terra firma, but it is rotating on its axis, orbiting the sun, wheeling round the cosmos with the Milky Way galaxy, and moving outward with the expansion of the universe, like dots on a balloon that is being inflated. All these facts are contrary to our direct sense experience but are real nevertheless, and the more science discovers, the less it resembles the world of the senses.

Sense perception is therefore fallible, and what's more, it might be too narrow for the breadth and richness of life. For example, the religious person claims that God is a reality, even though we can never perceive him, any more than we can see our conscience, our will, or our mind. In the same way, we call the sunset beautiful, even though we never see beauty, but only variegated colors, and we judge cruelty as wrong, even though its wrongness is nothing tangible. Time may be real, but it is an invisible shell in which things happen, and if we believe in love, we are reaching far beyond our senses.

Rationalism is a rival position, offering an alternative theory of knowledge. According to this view, we should use our reason, rather than sense perception, to determine reality. As Descartes said, everything must be tested in the light of rationality, which can correct the mistakes of the senses. For example, we realize that the lake we see in the desert is probably a mirage caused by shimmering heat, a projection of our need for water. Deserts do not normally contain lakes. And if a magician pulls a rabbit out of an empty hat, we realize there must be a trick to it. The hat might have a false bottom, or maybe the rabbit was in the magician's sleeve, but rabbits cannot materialize out of thin air.

When people in New Mexico claim to see a flying saucer, they are probably misinterpreting lights in the sky, a type of mass hysteria. The Swiss psychoanalyst C. G. Jung has a provocative theory about such sightings. He suggests that the human race needs a higher intelligence to come down to earth and help us solve our problems. In a scientific age, that salvation would not take a spiritual form but that of a spaceship in the perfect shape of an oval, with superintelligent aliens inside. Wishful thinking can reach the wrong conclusions from raw sense data, such as flying saucers.

Mathematicians employ reason, not sense perception, to devise systems of thought using numbers. For example, if a square has one side of four inches, then the volume is four inches times four inches times four inches, or sixty-four cubic inches. This theorem can be logically proven; it is conceived rather than perceived. Science, too, uses reason to form hypotheses and proofs. Galileo, for example, devised an experiment about gravity. He dropped balls of different weights from the Leaning Tower of Pisa, and when they all landed at the same time, that proved velocity is independent of mass. This was contrary to common sense. And drifting in a boat one day, while the bank seemed to move and the boat to remain stationary, he reasoned that the sun and the earth have the same relation: that is, the earth revolves around the sun, not the sun around the earth. Today astronomers claim that the stars and galaxies appear to be moving away from us, when actually it is the universe that is expanding. Of course, we wonder what the universe is expanding into, or whether it is creating more of itself.

Being rational is often considered the prime mark of humanness, but rationality has certain weaknesses as an epistemic theory. The principal defect is that we never know whether a structure of thought, however rational, accurately diagrams reality. In other words, although ideas may fit together coherently, they may not represent the actual world.

Suppose we argue that the earth is resting on the back of a tortoise, which is allegedly part of a Hindu creation myth. As the tortoise walks, the earth rotates, clouds form from his breath, and hurricanes are created when he coughs, and earthquakes when he stumbles. Even if we make everything fit, at the end of the day the earth is not on the back of a turtle; it is only a "just so" story. When this idea was quoted by a member of the audience during a lecture by William James, he asked what the tortoise rested on. The person announced that it rested on another tortoise, declaring, "It's tortoises all the way down."

We are also familiar with detective novels where the evidence points to a certain person as the killer. He or she had the opportunity and the motive, was heard uttering a threat, has a history of violence, and so forth. Everything makes sense, but it turns out that someone else committed the crime. As Bertrand Russell remarked, if we are empiricists, we will be partly right, but if we are rationalists, we can be entirely wrong.

Intuitionism is a third channel to reality, although it is not on a par with empiricism or rationalism. According to this theory, we gain knowledge through an "immediate apprehension" or "sudden awareness" of reality. We feel we understand something that did not come from our senses or from our mind but nonetheless is genuine and undeniable. We simply have a gut feeling, or gain an insight in a rush of emotion, and even though we may not convince other people or even articulate the knowledge to ourselves, we feel that we have grasped a truth that can transform our lives.

Intuition lies outside empiricism, which is regarded as a clumsy instrument, and beyond reason, which is that "old definition cutter with his logical scissors." It concerns spiritual, aesthetic, or moral matters—that angels are real, that a rose is truly beautiful, and that we should care for one another.

The problem, of course, lies in verification. If an insight cannot be communicated, much less verified by any external test, how do we know it is genuine? The private understanding we think we've gained could be purely imaginary. In other words, if our intuition is beyond all confirmation by the senses or the mind, then we have no protection against self-deception. Even if our lives are transformed as a result of a "revelation," that would not be proof of its authenticity; believing we have received some intuitive insight could have the same effect. In medicine, it is the placebo effect.

In all the ways of knowing discussed, an overall problem is that we need to assume a reliable means of knowing in order to determine the most reliable means of knowing. That is, in deciding whether empiricism, rationalism, or intuitionism is best, we first have to decide which way of knowing is best, otherwise we have no basis for a decision. Can we get beneath this fundamental tautology? If, for example, we say sense perception is most trustworthy because we perceive that truth, we are going around in circles. Can the world truly be known, then?

Thinking Makes It So: Bishop Berkeley

George Berkeley (1685–1753) is classified as an empiricist, but an empiricist of a unique sort, because he did not believe the physical world is real. He was an Anglo-Irish philosopher, born in a cottage near Dysert Castle, Thomastown, Ireland, the eldest son of an English customs official. Throughout his life, though, he considered himself emphatically Irish. Berkeley (pronounced Bark-lee) was raised at the castle as part of the nobility, and he received a proper eighteenth-century upbringing. Interestingly enough, several major composers were also born the year of his birth: Johann Sebastian Bach, George Friedrich Handel, and Domenico Scarlatti.

At age eleven Berkeley was enrolled in the school at Kilkenny, the Eton of Ireland, and at fifteen he entered Trinity College, Dublin, where he studied classics, mathematics, and philosophy, including Descartes. The authorities could not decide whether he was the greatest genius or the greatest dunce in the college's history, which is reminiscent of St. Thomas's label as the dumb ox. In any case, he succeeded in receiving a B.A. and an M.A. degree, and was subsequently appointed fellow of the college. In 1710, at age twenty-five, he was ordained a priest of the Church of England.

Three years later he traveled to London and was presented at the court of Queen Anne, and he subsequently joined a glittering circle of intellectuals. This included the satirist Jonathan Swift, the poet Alexander Pope, and the essayists Joseph Addison and Richard Steele. He attended gatherings where the major ideas of the day were discussed, and he contributed several articles to the *Guardian* newspaper.

It was during this time that he met a woman named Hester Van Homrigh at a dinner party (Swift's Vanessa). They met only once, but she was so impressed by the conversation that she left him half her property; she might also have been trying to spite Swift when she found out he was secretly married.

Holding various positions common at the time, Berkeley traveled onto the Continent, first as chaplain to Lord Peterborough, then as tutor to the son of the Bishop of Clogher. In Italy he witnessed the eruption of Mt. Vesuvius, and in France he met the metaphysician Nicholas Malebranche, which was equally volcanic; their quarrel on Malebranche's deathbed probably hastened his death.

Shortly after returning home, he was given a D.D. degree by Trinity and appointed senior lecturer and university preacher. At this time he married Anne Forster—an educated, talented woman, the daughter of the chief justice of Ireland. They had six children, and one of his four sons followed him into the church, becoming canon of Canterbury.

Berkeley then made the most adventurous move of his life. He conceived a plan to establish a college in Bermuda, a college that was intended "to reform the manners of the English colonists" and preach the gospel to "American savages." Berkeley had become disillusioned with Europe as a decaying and decadent civilization; it did not suit his virtuous ways. He even diagnosed the poverty in Ireland as due to "an unhealthy combination of English greed and Irish sloth." Bermuda, on the other hand, had children of nature who were innocent and uncorrupted. The British colonies, therefore, were humanity's only hope. In fact, he predicted greatness for North America: "Westward the course of empire takes its way. . . . Time's noblest offspring is the last."

For his venture the British crown promised him twenty thousand pounds, and he bravely set sail for the New World, first landing in Newport, Rhode Island. But once he got there, both he and the British government realized the impracticality of the scheme: Bermuda was six hundred miles from the mainland, with little food or water. After three years the funds were rescinded, and Berkeley was forced to retreat to England.

Before leaving the New World, he divided his library of Shakespeare, Milton, Pope, Ben Johnson, and so forth between Yale and Harvard, and deeded property to Yale, specifying that the income should be used for scholarships. The recipients were to be chosen by a competitive exam in Latin and Greek. It was the first merit scholarship in this country, and it is still given to three students annually. Another legacy is that the University of California, Berkeley, was named after him, as was the city of Berkeley, but little else remains of his misadventure, except for his house at Newport, which is still preserved.

It is worth mentioning that Berkeley bought a farm named Whitehall while in Rhode Island and "several Negro slaves," according to a bill of sale in the British Museum. Apparently Berkeley supported slavery, along with baptism, for "it would be advantageous to their [slave masters] to have slaves who should obey . . . not with eye-service as men-pleasers but in the singleness of heart as pleasing God . . . their slaves would only become better slaves by being Christian." Berkeley can be criticized for not transcending the mores of his time; wearing similar blinders, Pope referred to him as possessing "every virtue under heaven."

In 1734 Berkeley returned to Ireland and was appointed Bishop of Cloyne in Dublin. By all accounts he carried out his responsibilities in a highly conscientious manner. As well as being a cultural center, his home was a medical dispensary in times of sickness and epidemics. He also established a school "for the working class" to teach spinning and the manufacture of linen. His parishioners, both Protestant and Catholic, regarded him as a genial, devout, and generous man. In his books he defended the Anglican Church and upheld the superiority of supernatural explanations over the natural explanations of science. Above all, his aim was to refute atheism and materialism, especially that of Hobbes.

Except for serving in the Irish House of Lords in 1737, Berkeley led a quiet life for twenty years—a life that ended in Oxford in 1753, while he was visiting his son George. He was listening to his wife read from the Bible and apparently died abruptly of a stroke. In accordance with his will, his body was "kept five days above ground . . . even till it grow offensive by the cadaverous smell." Presumably this was to ensure there was no mistake. Some caskets even had bells that people could ring if they had been buried alive. His body was later interred in Christ Church Cathedral, Oxford.

Philosophy

Berkeley formed his philosophy at Trinity College before he turned thirty, and he presented it in two main works: A *Treatise Concerning the Principles of Human Knowledge* (1710) and *Three Dialogues Between Hylas and Philonous* (1713). The latter was meant as a popular version. In addition, he wrote

Essay Toward a New Theory of Vision (1709), which dealt with the relation between sight and touch, and in Newport he completed *Alciphron* (1732), a dialogue against skepticism and liberal thinking. He also attacked the logical foundation of calculus as developed by Newton and criticized Newton's conception of absolute space and time. Berkeley's oddest book, *Siris* (1744), is an exposition on the virtues of tar water to cure almost every bodily ill. "Hail vulgar juice of never-fading pine!" he writes. "Cheap as thou art, thy virtues are divine."

Since Berkeley was an Anglican priest he could not very well endorse materialism over spiritualism. At the same time he trusted the evidence of his senses, so the trick was to combine empiricism as an epistemological theory with spiritualism as a metaphysical one. He did this by treating sense perception as part of the mind rather than the body, which meant that he was an empirical idealist.

Empiricism, of course, relies on the validity of sense evidence, and the famous British empiricists included John Locke and David Hume, as well as Berkeley. Idealism is a more ambiguous term. In our ordinary language an idealist is someone who pursues noble (and unrealistic) principles, a visionary who tries to achieve utopia, but philosophically an idealist maintains that thought or ideas are what we know and they make up the whole of reality. Plato adopted an "objective Idealism," asserting that forms, universals, or ideas are the basic reality, but Berkeley maintained a "subjective Idealism," whereby reality depends upon a perceiving mind.

Berkeley's philosophy is most clearly expressed in *Three Dialogues Between Hylas and Philonous*, where Hylas represents common sense, supported by science, and the character Philonous represents Berkeley's idealism. Philonous, in fact, means love of mind. The dialogue begins with the two friends talking in the quadrangle of a college—presumably Trinity College, Dublin. Hylas states that he has heard Philonous does not believe in external things, that he thinks objects have no reality. Philonous corrects him by saying that he does believe in an external world but not a physical one. Everything we know is based on our senses, and sense perception is part of our experience, not part of material objects. We never know things in themselves, but only the perceptions of our mind.

This sounds vague, even evasive, but Philonous illustrates his point in terms of various senses, beginning with touch. If we sit too close to a fire, it will burn us, but the pain we feel is not in the fire but in ourselves. Similarly, if we put our hand in lukewarm water after having it in cold water, the water will feel hot, and if we have had our hand in hot water, the lukewarm water will then feel cold. A warm day to an Eskimo will be cold to an Egyptian, but the day itself is neither warm nor cold; it only feels a certain way to the person. We can say "I am hot" but not "It is hot." In the same way, we sometimes refer to a warm coat, but the coat is not warm. It merely keeps us warm; the heat is in us.

We might add that silk feels smooth to a person but rough to a flea, a pin drop is soft to us but loud to a gnat, and a load of straw might be heavy for a donkey but light for an elephant. The sensations we feel, therefore, are not in things but in the mental perception of them. In other words, we never experience any physical causes of sensations, only sensations "existing in our minds."

The same holds true for taste and smell. Food may be zesty to one person, sharp to another, and too salty or too bland to someone else, depending on the person's palate. This is because food does not have a *flavor* but only a *taste*, and taste depends upon the individual. Likewise, smells may be pleasant or unpleasant, agreeable or disagreeable to a person, but things themselves do not have a smell, any more than they have a sweet or sour flavor. They are not musty, dank, earthy, or foul. Horse barns smell awful to some, but are perfume to others. In fact, we never smell things at all, not even a rose, but only the scent of a rose, and flowers are nothing but their hue, texture, form, and aroma.

Color is also a matter of mental perception. The sea is not green or blue, pearl gray, or wine dark. In fact, it does not have any color apart from a perceiver. Autumn leaves have shades of color only when they are seen, and perceptions vary. Colors look different under a microscope. If there were a red sweater inside a closed drawer, no one could say it was still red. The sweater is red only when the drawer is opened and we can see it. It's not that the color is still there, invisible to the eye, but that if it is not visible, we cannot say it is there. In other words, the red color is not on the sweater but a function of perception.

As for sound, that also depends on being perceived. We do not hear a gong, but only the sound of a gong; not a storm, but the thunder. That is, we are never aware of physical objects per se, but only perceptions, and that is what we know of an object. This, of course, introduces the well-known philosophic chestnut, If a tree falls in the forest, and no one is there to hear it, is there a sound? Berkeley's answer is that since sound means that which is heard, if no one hears it, there is no sound.

But suppose we set up a recording device that detected sound when we weren't present. Berkeley would answer that that would only be an extension of perception, not the absence of it, rather like a camera that captures the color of leaves when people aren't in the woods.

But wouldn't there be sound waves regardless of whether anyone was there? Hylas asks whether sound isn't "motion in the air"? Philonous's reply is that then we are changing the definition of *sound*. Sound waves may be seen and vibrations felt, but they cannot be heard. Sound is that which strikes the ear and cannot exist without an ear to strike, just as color does not mean light waves of a certain intensity but something that is seen. Again, knowing is a matter of mental perception.

Some critics would add that since color is a function of light, if there is no light, there is no color. It is questionable whether this holds true for a pigment theory of color, with red, yellow, and blue as the primary colors. If we mix the colors of a prism, we get white; if we mix the colors in a painter's palette, we get black. But Berkeley's challenge still remains. These considerations led Berkeley to assert his famous dictum: *Esse est percipi,* "To be is to be perceived."

Hylas feels something is wrong somewhere, and he returns to the attack by making a distinction between primary and secondary qualities. The primary qualities include characteristics such as figure (shape), whether solid or liquid, moving or stationary, extended like our bodies or immaterial like numbers. Secondary qualities consist of taste, smell, sound, touch, and color. Hylas admits that these secondary qualities depend on perception, but he insists that the primary qualities inhere in the objects themselves. For example, an iron ball is round, dense, still, and extended in space, whether or not anyone perceives it.

However, Philonous counters that objects look large close up and small far away (the moon, for example), and that movement is fast to one person, slow to another (a year to a child). A river seen from a mountaintop looks like a silver ribbon, not liquid but solid, and not moving but motionless. We can measure distance with a yardstick or in light years, and the instrument makes the difference. "The [perceiving] mind is therefore the deepest reality"; there is only mind and its perceptions.

Hylas then tries another tack. If all knowledge is individual, then why do people consistently perceive something as a tree and not as an oyster, and why do two people both perceive an object as a tree? Since perceptions are consistent and uniform, it's reasonable to assume there is a common cause for the perceptions. That is, there must be an external, physical world, independent of any perceiver.

Philonous (Berkeley) answers that he did not say that reality depends on *human* perception but only on perception, and the only way to account for the continuity and agreement of perceptions is to posit a God who is constantly aware of the world. Whether we are awake or asleep, God maintains the world in being by his mental perception of it. He is omnipresent and omniscient, and whatever is real exists through his eternal consciousness.

This position gave rise to the limerick by the cleric Ronald Knox over a century later:

> There was a young man who said, "God Must think it exceedingly odd
> If he finds that this tree Continues to be When there's no one about in the Quad."
> Reply:
> Dear Sir:
> Your astonishment's odd: *I* am always about in the Quad. And that's why the tree Will continue to be,
> Since observed by Yours faithfully,
> God.

In this way Berkeley's philosophy defends idealism. He eliminates a material world independent of thought and treats reality as an idea in the mind of God.

A Critical Evaluation

Berkeley's theories are troubling because they run counter to our conventional understanding. We think of the world as existing physically outside of us and all perceptions of it. In his *Life of Johnson*, Boswell reports that Samuel Johnson "struck his foot with mighty force against a large stone" and said, "I refute [Berkeley] thus." This seems a fair reaction to the idea that the physical world is unreal, and that perceptions are not of any material objects. Oddly enough, Berkeley regarded his theory as self-evident, an antidote to skepticism. In *The Principles of Human Knowledge* he wrote,

> Some truths there are so near and obvious to the mind that a man need only open his eyes to see them. Such I take this important one to be, to wit, that all the choir of heaven and the furniture of earth, in a word all those bodies which compose the mighty frame of the world, have not any subsistence without a mind, that their being is to be perceived. . . . The all-seeing eye of God makes possible the continued apparent existence of things.

Modern philosophers, however, have not treated his theories as obvious at all. To take Berkeley's example of temperature, under normal conditions people can judge it correctly and recognize scalding water and icy water when they feel it. Although there could be differences of opinion about in-between cases, that does not mean temperature is in the mind. The fact of twilight does not make it impossible to differentiate between night and day.

And although it is people who experience the pain of a burn, the cause of the pain lies in the fire that burns them.

In the same way, people experience pleasure at tasting a strawberry, but it is the sweet flavor in the strawberry that causes the pleasure. A flavor is not the same as the sensation of flavor, or as the philosopher G. E. Moore commented, yellow is separate from the experience of yellow.

In addition, if everything depends on perception, then how can God exist when he is not perceived? The answer sometimes given is that God perceives himself, and does so continually. However, he must first exist in order to perceive; he cannot perceive himself into existence.

In the end, Berkeley's defense of spiritualism against an atheistic materialism was ingenious, but it had no lasting effect. He is something of a philosophic curiosity, a starting point for the study of epistemology, but he did not persuade many people to his point of view. The classic epitaph is, "His arguments produce no convictions, though they cannot be refuted."

In the final analysis, the reality of matter seems undeniable. Dr. Johnson's stone appears substantial enough, and because natural law is constant, the falling tree makes a sound even when no one is present. Trees remain existent, physical things, even without a God in the forest to watch them.

At times, however, we can sympathize with Berkeley's point of view. Sometimes the world does seem to be our idea, or perhaps a dream in the mind of God (maybe a nightmare). External things can appear insubstantial; and our thoughts alone, vivid and real. When we return to a place after being away, we are surprised that things happened while we were not there watching. We can wonder about the existence of anyone or anything outside ourselves and feel locked inside the world our perceptions have created. Each of us views things through lenses of different curvatures, shapes, and colors, and the broken window could be a crack in our eyeglasses.

Luckily, these are only passing thoughts, and we soon accept the reality of the physical world. To separate fantasy from reality seems part of the maturing process.

Seeing Is Believing: David Hume

The Scottish philosopher David Hume (1711–1776) appears to be a more straightforward empiricist than Berkeley, but paradoxically, his reliance on the senses eventually led him to deny common sense. Beginning with the evidence of sense experience, he ultimately became a skeptic with regard to personal identity and causation, as well as theism, miracles, and the foundation of religion.

David Hume was born in Edinburgh on April 26, 1711, the youngest son of Joseph Home, an attorney and minor lord (laird), and Katherine Lady Falconer, daughter of the president of the College of Justice. He assumed the name Hume so that the English could pronounce it in the proper Scottish way. The family was not wealthy but was fairly influential, especially in legal circles. They lived in the village of Chirnside, nine miles from Berwick-upon-Tweed, just over the Scottish border, on an estate named Ninewells, so named because of the springs at the front. Hume considered it the "fair domain" of the family, and it remained his home for the first forty-one years of his life.

At age two, however, disaster struck the household. In his autobiography, he describes what happened:

> My father, who passed for a man of parts, died when I was an infant, leaving me, with an elder brother and a sister, under the care of our mother, a woman of singular merit, who though young and handsome, devoted herself entirely to the rearing and educating of her children.

His mother educated David at home and, being a pious woman, instilled strong religious feelings in him. He attended the Church of Scotland and took to heart the moral teachings of *The Whole Duty of Man,* a Calvinist devotional. He would catalog the sins he wanted to correct, and according to a manuscript book he kept, he was preoccupied with arguments about the existence of God. However, early in his life he abandoned religion and belief in divine providence and could later write, "Ignorance is the mother of Devotion."

David's mother recognized his intellect and academic talent, noting that he was "uncommonly wake-minded," and along with his brother, she sent him to the University of Edinburgh before he was twelve—several years earlier than was customary. There he studied history, mathematics, philosophy, and the science of his day, and read the classical Latin and Greek texts. However, as he reports, he decided not to become a lawyer, as his family expected, but to pursue literature, which was broadly defined to include philosophy.

> I passed through the ordinary course of education with success, and was seized very early with a passion for literature, which has been the ruling passion of my life, and the great source of my enjoyments. My studious disposition, my sobriety, and my industry, gave my family a notion that the law was a proper profession for me; but I found an insurmountable aversion to every thing but the pursuits of philosophy and general learning; . . . Cicero and Virgil were the authors which I was secretly devouring.

Leaving the university at age fourteen or fifteen, Hume then suffered a psychotic break accompanied by hypochondria and psychosomatic illness, probably due to intense thought and reading. But he recovered without any aftereffects; in fact, throughout his life he was regarded as unusually high-spirited, optimistic, and gregarious. He exemplified his own view of human nature as being essentially benevolent and sociable.

Following this incident, though, Hume thought that he needed a more active, worldly, and prosperous existence. So he took a position as clerk to a sugar importer in Bristol, thinking a life of business might benefit him as well as his family. But after "a very feeble trial" of a few months, he found it "totally unsuitable" and decided to travel to France to pursue philosophy.

He first visited Paris, then spent some time in Rheims before settling in La Fléche, a pastoral town in Anjou, in the Loire Valley. Here he remained for three years, constructing a "new science of thought." Descartes had studied at the Jesuit college at La Fléche, and Hume found the atmosphere conducive to writing and to the development of a new life purpose. To quote again from his autobiography, *My Own Life*, written four months before his death, Hume says that in France

> I laid that plan of life which I have steadily and successfully pursued. I resolved to make a very rigid frugality to supply my deficiency of fortune, to maintain unimpaired my independency, and to regard every object as contemptible except the improvements of my talents in literature.

Hume returned to Great Britain with the manuscript of *A Treatise of Human Nature* under his arm, a work subtitled *An Attempt to Introduce the Experimental Method of Reasoning into Moral Subjects*. In effect, he took an empirical approach to knowledge, using a naturalistic view of everything: the self, cause and effect, and God. All that we know depends on "experience and observation," he stated. In the name of empiricism, Hume even rejected the popular concept of the human mind as a microcosm of the divine mind; knowledge, he thought, should be based on science, not metaphor.

During 1739 and 1740 Hume supervised the publication of his *Treatise*, fully expecting that it would ensure his reputation in philosophy. He hoped for "vehement attacks, which he would meet with brilliant retorts." However, as he describes it, the work "fell dead-born from the press, without reaching such distinction as even to excite a murmur among the zealots." Critics described the book as "abstract and unintelligible," and in later years Hume himself repudiated it as a youthful aberration. Today, however, the *Treatise* is regarded as one of the principal works of philosophy—written when Hume was barely twenty-six years old.

After suffering this rejection, Hume retreated to Ninewells to lick his wounds, but being "naturally of a cheerful and sanguine temper," he "soon recovered from the blow." After deliberating about the nature of public taste, he decided that the manner of the book was at fault, not the matter. So he prepared a simplified, less skeptical version in two volumes: *Enquiry Concerning Human Understanding* (1748) and *Enquiry Concerning the Principles of Morals* (1751). Both books proved successful, and Hume put his signature to them; the *Treatise*, by contrast, had first been published anonymously. Like the previous work, the books attempted to explain the principles of human knowledge but in a less complex way.

In addition to writing philosophy, Hume was also an economist and a historian; he described himself simply as "a man of letters." His economic views can be found in *Political Discourses* (1752), but he won widespread acclaim (and financial independence) for his six-volume *History of England* (1754–1762); this was the standard history in Great Britain for fifty years. He recounted England's past from the Saxon kingdoms to the Glorious Revolution, which overthrew King James II and put William of Orange on the throne. In his view, an impartial history was needed, "neither Whig nor Tory," that would present political decisions as a consequence of historical contexts and changing conditions.

Hume wrote a variety of other books, including *The Natural History of Religion* and *Dialogues Concerning Natural Religion*, the latter frequently cited in discussions on the philosophy of religion. His *Essays, Moral and Political* covered more popular topics, such as national character, aesthetic taste, political systems, and philosophical character types. Some of his works were successful, some notorious, and some were both. Because of his antireligious views and his championing of Newtonian science, Hume remained a controversial figure to the very end.

Along with writing and studying, Hume participated in the wider world, holding several government positions, from secretary to aide-de-camp. He participated in diplomatic missions to Austria, Italy, and France, and as secretary to General St. Clair, he saw military action in Brittany. At one stage he tutored the Marquise of Annandale, who was officially declared a "lunatic." He also held the post of librarian to the Edinburgh Library of Advocates, but this caused controversy because of his "indecent books." In addition, Hume served as under secretary of state for Scotland and secretary to the British Mission in Paris under Lord Hertford.

Apparently, he was well received in the Paris salons and conversed regularly with Diderot and D'Alembert. When he returned to England, he brought Jean Jacques Rousseau with him, but Rousseau, who was probably suffering from delusions of persecution, accused Hume of plotting against him, and their relationship ended in a public row.

On two occasions Hume tried to obtain a university position, once as professor of moral philosophy at Edinburgh and once as professor of logic at Glasgow, but powerful figures in the church opposed him, including Thomas Reid of Aberdeen. At the University of Glasgow, a charge of heresy was brought against him, but even though he was acquitted, the appointment was given to someone with more orthodox views. Hume certainly had enemies throughout his life, but his enemies seemed to be the right people (unless you have enemies, you have no character).

Although Hume never married, he seemed very responsive to women. When he built his house in Edinburgh in 1769, he entertained a wide coterie of male and female friends, including "the young and careless." At one point he wrote, "As I took particular pleasure in the company of modest women, I had no reason to be displeased with the reception I met with from them." Nancy Orde was a prominent member of the group, a woman described as attractive, intelligent, and vivacious. In Hume's will he designated ten guineas (10£, 10s) "to buy a Ring, as a Memorial of my Friendship and Attachment to so amiable and accomplished a Person." It was Nancy Orde who playfully wrote on his house "St. David's Street," and the name has persisted up to the present. He was, in fact, canonized as a saint by the populace because of his geniality and kindness, despite his antireligious views.

Hume's self-obituary, or "funeral oration," as he termed it, seems a fair summation of his personality: "I was a man of mild dispositions, of command of temper, of an open, social and cheerful humor, capable of attachment, but little susceptible of enmity, and of great moderation in all my passions." His disappointments, he writes, never soured his sunny outlook on life.

Hume's last years were spent revising and editing his earlier works, enjoying social gatherings, and keeping in contact with many of Europe's intellectuals. He publicly supported American independence, so it was appropriate that his last dinner party was held on July 4, 1776. We know that he influenced his good friend Adam Smith in the ideas contained in *The Wealth of Nations*, and both Charles Darwin and T. H. Huxley paid tribute to him. He caused the "scales to fall" from Jeremy Bentham's eyes and awakened Immanuel Kant from his "dogmatic slumbers."

At the time of Hume's death a crowd gathered outside his home to see whether fear would cause him to renounce his atheism (there are no atheists in foxholes). But as Adam Smith reported in one of his letters, Hume maintained "a steady cheerfulness" to the last, despite intense suffering from cancer of the intestines. In fact, he invented "several jocular excuses" he might make to Charon, the mythological Greek figure who ferries souls across the river Styx to the land of death:

> "Good Charon, I have been correcting my work for a new edition. Allow me a little time, that I may see how the public receives the alterations." But Charon would answer, "When you have seen the effect of these, you will be for making other alterations. There will be no end of such excuses; so, honest friend, please step into the boat." But I might still urge, "Have a little patience, good Charon. I have been endeavoring to open the eyes of the public. If I live a few years longer, I may have the satisfaction of seeing the downfall of some of the prevailing systems of superstition." But Charon would then lose all temper and decency. . . . "[T]hat will not happen these many hundred years. Do you fancy I will grant you a lease for so long a term? Get into the boat this instant, you lazy loitering rogue."

Hume's Philosophy

Hume was the last of the three great British empiricists, and he built on the ideas of his predecessors, George Berkeley and John Locke. He thought seeing is believing, or more precisely, that we know only what we perceive and do not possess any knowledge prior to experience. "Adam, though his rational faculties be supposed, at the very first, entirely perfect, could not have inferred from the fluidity and transparency of water that it would suffocate him, or from the light and warmth of fire that it would consume him." But the logic of this epistemology led him to radical conclusions, especially about the self and about cause and effect.

We discussed the nature of the self in connection with Descartes' philosophy, but Hume disagreed with the Cartesian notion that we are "a thing that thinks." In fact, he did not believe there is a substance that is our persistent self. To Hume, we are only a series of sense impressions, "nothing but a bundle or collection of different perceptions, which succeed each other with an inconceivable rapidity, and are in perpetual flux and movement." To think otherwise, that some invisible self lies beneath our perceptions, is to accept something that is not given to sense perception.

In any case, Hume maintains that everything we know comes from the senses, and that ideas differ from sense impressions by being less lively or vivid. "An experienced feeling or emotion is more pronounced than any idea of it." When we recall the original sensation, we may think we are reliving it, but in fact we can "never reach the force and vivacity of the original sentiment."

Now, we might believe we are free in the ideas we can conjure up—imagining monsters with fantastic shapes, picturing the most distant planets—but in actuality we can only "compound, transpose, augment, or diminish" the material furnished to us by sense experience. A golden mountain or a virtuous horse is simply a recombination of simpler impressions of gold, a mountain, virtue, and a horse. Also, if we lack a sense, such as seeing or hearing, we cannot form an idea related to it. Someone who is blind cannot conceive of blue, and we can never explain B-flat to a deaf person; colors and sounds must be experienced in order to be understood, and that holds true of all other ideas.

We may also think that our ideas follow one another in random order, but Hume claimed there are "principles of association" that account for the way ideas succeed one another in our heads. Sometimes ideas are connected by *resemblance*, as when a picture reminds us of the person himself; *contiguity* operates when we see an anchor chain and think of the anchor attached to it; and *cause and effect* is used when we see a glass of wine and imagine the enjoyment of sipping it. This shows how the mind works.

The last notion of causation is especially important to Hume, not just with regard to ideas in our minds, but in explaining sequences in history. (It is sometimes said that even God cannot change the past, but historians can.) Here causal knowledge is the most instructive, because we can then learn to avoid or encourage different effects. We learn not to walk on thin ice, that a match can burn down a house, and that war produces a "blood-red blossom."

Causation

In analyzing cause and effect, Hume developed his most controversial theory. In section IV of the *Enquiry* he first makes a distinction between "relations of ideas" and "matters of fact." An example of a "relation of ideas" statement would be "All circles are round," "Murals are on walls," and "Three times five equals half of thirty." These propositions simply show the relation between parts of the sentence; they "unpack" the subject term in the predicate so we can see what it implies. Although we cannot deny the truth of these statements without contradicting the meaning of the terms, we are only talking about words or ideas, not the external world. That is, "All circles are round" is a necessary truth, but only in the way we define the term "circle."

"Matters of fact" are the more important types of statements, because they make claims about reality. For example, "The sun will rise tomorrow," "Horses like to eat clover," and "Diamonds are harder than glass." These sentences refer to actual things, although they could be false. "That the sun will not rise tomorrow," Hume writes, "is no less intelligible a proposition, and implies no more contradiction, than the affirmation that it will rise."

Hume then argues that the truth of "matters of fact" depends on cause and effect. In proving a claim, we always point to some fact as the cause of our believing it. That someone is standing in a dark room is proven by hearing his voice; that a man is out of the country is proven by the fact that we received a letter from him. Everything therefore depends upon the validity of causation.

However, when we think about it, we never see a cause, and since knowledge depends upon sense impressions, cause is not a meaningful idea! We may believe we see one event causing another, but strictly speaking, that is not true.

For example, we think we see the balloon burst because it was pricked by the pin, the glass shatter because it hit the ground, and the light go on because we threw the switch, but all we really saw was a sequence of events. The skin of the balloon was pierced by the pin, followed by the balloon bursting; the glass struck the ground, then shattered; and after the switch was thrown, the light went on. We did not actually see cause and effect but assumed the temporal sequence was a causal connection.

Hume does not believe there is a mysterious "causal power" in one event that compels another event to happen. Rather, what we mean by cause is "constant conjunction"—that one event is consistently followed by another. This builds up a psychological expectation, a habit of thought, so that we come to expect the second event when the first occurs. However, there is no inevitability to the sequence, no necessary connection. "After the constant conjunction of two objects, heat and flame, for instance, weight and solidity, we are determined by custom alone to expect the one from the appearance of the other."

This view of cause and effect, as regular succession, is certainly contrary to ordinary experience. If a child cries when it scrapes itself, that seems a natural response to pain, and if we lose our appetite after eating, we assume the meal was responsible. As Tom Stoppard remarked, St. Sebastian did not die of fright. To Hume, however, "If we believe that fire warms, or water refreshes, 'tis only because it costs us too much pain to think otherwise."

Regardless of its truth, Hume's view of causation does not change science or our everyday plans. Nature is regular and falls into a predictable pattern; only the explanation is different for whatever happens. We cannot be sure of the future, because events are not necessarily connected, but we can have sufficient confidence that nature is predictable. When we hit a nail with a hammer, we can behave as if that action drove the nail into the wood.

Religion and Miracles

Hume is usually considered an atheist, and that seems accurate, but he had to conceal his ideas because criticizing religion was both an obstacle to fame and downright dangerous. At the close of the seventeenth century a student named Thomas Aikenhead was hanged on the road between Edinburgh and Leith for railing against the Holy Trinity. In the court's words he had to "atone with blood, the affronts of heaven's offended throne." That execution for blasphemy was the last in Britain's history, but it cast a long shadow into the eighteenth century.

So as not to offend a bishop, Hume deleted the section on miracles from his *Treatise*. What's more, his essays "Of Suicide" and "Of the Immortality of the Soul," along with his *Dialogues Concerning Natural Religion*, had to be published posthumously. Writing in dialogue style is itself a form of protection, for one can always deny that the characters' speeches express the author's opinions.

Some critics have suggested that Hume might not have been an atheist but an agnostic, or even a deist, because of passages such as this:

> The whole frame of nature bespeaks an intelligent author, and no rational enquirer can, after serious reflection, suspend his belief a moment with regard to the primary principles of genuine Theism and Religion.

But the following excerpts seem more representative:

> Examine the religious principles which have, in fact, prevailed in the world. You will scarcely be persuaded, that they are anything but sick men's dreams. Or perhaps you will regard them more as the playsome whimsies of monkeys in human shape than . . . a being who dignifies himself with the name rational.
>
> The life of man is of no greater importance to the universe than that of an oyster.

Hume also rejected the validity of miracles, which he regarded as the basis of religion. Since "the Christian religion not only was at first attended with miracles, but even at this day cannot be believed by any reasonable person without one," the weakness of this pillar threatens the entire edifice of belief.

Hume identifies three main criticisms: (1) None of the witnesses to miracles are credible. "There is not to be found in all history, any miracles attested by a sufficient number of men, of such unquestioned good sense, education, and learning, as to secure us against all delusion." (2) Although we accept as most probable whatever is most usual, "when any thing is affirmed utterly absurd and miraculous . . . the passion of surprise and wonder . . . being an agreeable emotion, gives a sensible tendency towards the belief of those events." (3) And finally, "all supernatural and miraculous relations

". . . are observed chiefly to abound among ignorant and barbarous nations." People believe the incredible as much as they doubt the indubitable.

Above all, Hume rejects miracles because he agrees with John Locke's notion that the mind at birth is a tabula rasa, or blank slate. We derive our knowledge through the ordinary experiences that are written on that slate. A miracle, on the other hand, "is a violation of the laws of nature, and as a firm and unalterable experience has established these laws, the proof against a miracle, from the very nature of the fact, is as entire as any argument from experience can possibly be imagined." In other words, unlike genuine knowledge, which has a foundation in repeated experience, miracles have the weakest claim to be believed precisely because they are unique events.

Hume therefore rejected religion for a variety of reasons, including its basis in the miraculous, regarding it as not only false but treacherous. "Generally speaking, the errors in religion are dangerous," he wrote, "those in philosophy only ridiculous." In *Dialogues Concerning Natural Religion*, he also rejected the argument from design, which was one of the mainstays of belief.

Conclusion

To Hume, then, there is no self, no cause, and no God—all because they violate the empirical view of knowledge. Critics have seized on this as a seminal weakness, arguing that with a more inclusive epistemology, he would have rejected a lot less.

More specifically, if Hume had relied more on reason, he might have been more sympathetic to the reality of the self. He could have wondered why, if the self is nothing but a series of sensations, it can be aware of itself as a series. Using the senses alone, we cannot solve this problem, but it might be accurate to hypothesize a self that is aware of itself. With regard to causation, if we scream after burning our hand, it certainly seems as though we screamed because we burned our hand, and when a blister forms, that appears to be the effect of the burn. Although we do not see the one cause the other, it is a reasonable assumption. The fact that the burn would not occur without the fire might be due to the regularity of nature, but more probably the fire is a condition for the burn. Besides, if the frequent conjunction of A and B causes us to assume they are causally connected, then that itself is a type of cause, in which case there are causes.

As for miracles and religion, Hume claims that nature is consistent and miracles cannot be authentic, because they constitute breaks in that constancy. But why is that impossible, especially since "Nature is consistent" is a "matter of fact" statement that could be false? For all we know, events could occur tomorrow that are without precedent.

These are called "black swan" events because at one time it was assumed that all swans were white, but after the discovery of black swans in Australia, that was seen as a contingent statement—a matter-of-fact claim that happened to be false. It only seemed true because the observers were in Great Britain. The trick is to turn black swans into white ones, that is, not to be surprised by new findings.

Some of these objections were raised during Hume's lifetime, but he remained a skeptic throughout. He was, however, a benign, benevolent, and beloved skeptic. His nature and his philosophy seemed at variance, even to himself, so that after completing one "proof" against common sense, he could write,

> Most fortunately it happens, that since reason is incapable of dispelling these clouds, nature herself suffices to that purpose, and cures me of this philosophical melancholy and delirium, either by relaxing this bent of mind, or by some avocation, and lively impression of my senses, which obliterates all these chimeras. . . . Here then I find myself absolutely and necessarily determined to live, and talk, and act like other people in the common affairs of life.

Although he was serious about his theories, Hume regarded philosophy as a "point of pleasure" and "an agreeable way of passing the time."

CHAPTER SIX

The Purpose of Living: Ethics

Doing the Right Thing: Immanuel Kant

Ethics is the field of philosophy that deals with right and wrong, with judgments of good and bad, and worthwhile goals in living. It concerns the value of conduct and our purpose in being; what is praiseworthy and blameworthy, just and unjust; and the nature of fairness, integrity, shame, and virtue. People reflect upon their lives throughout the living of them and try to determine whether they are living well or badly. Ethics comes into play when we deliberate about the rightness of our behavior and the quality of our existence altogether.

Immanuel Kant (1724–1804) is one of the leading theorists in the field of ethics, as well as in epistemology. In fact, Plato, Aristotle, and Kant are arguably the most significant figures in philosophic history, although Kant is not as well known outside the academy. .

Born in Königsberg, Prussia (now Kaliningrad, Russia), Kant was raised in a blue-collar family of harness and saddle makers. He changed his name from Emanuel to Immanuel as the latter is more faithful to the Bible. His father, Johann Georg, had migrated from Lithuania; his mother, Anna Regina Porter, came from Nurenberg but was of Scottish descent. Immanuel was the fourth of nine children, only five of whom survived into adulthood, and the large family lived modestly in a working-class district of the city. Pietism was their religion, a sect that endorsed personal faith over formal orthodoxy, strict devotion, humility, and the infallibility of scripture. Anna apparently

Figure 6.1. Immanuel Kant, black-and-white reproduction of eighteenth-century portrait.

was a devoted mother, dedicating her life to God and family: *Kinder, Küche, Kirche* (children, kitchen, church). Kant wrote of his parents:

> [They] were perfectly honest, morally decent, and orderly. They did not leave me a fortune (but neither did they leave me any debts). Moreover, they gave me an education that could not have been better when considered from a moral point of view. Every time I think of this I am touched by feelings of the highest gratitude.

When Immanuel was eight, the family pastor, Franz Albert Schultz, noticed his promise and sent him to a well-known school for classics, the Collegium Fredericianus. The training was highly disciplined and rigorous, consisting of Latin, Greek, Hebrew, French, theology and, to a lesser extent, science and mathematics. Immanuel remained at the school for eight years, studying six days a week from 7:00 a.m. until 4:00 p.m., until at age sixteen he was admitted to the University of Königsberg.

Here he indulged his interest in philosophy, mathematics, and science, especially Newton's physics. But like many of his fellow students, he also enjoyed cards and pool, and often came home late at night half inebriated. One instructor, Martin Knutsen, took an interest in him, guiding him past the shoals of Berkeleyan idealism and the rationalism of G. W. Leibniz (whose notion of preestablished harmony he considered "the pillow for the lazy mind").

Kant's studies were interrupted by the death of his father, which was followed soon after by his mother's death, perhaps from the strain of repeated childbirth, and this precipitated a financial crisis. He had to leave the university, and in order to survive he worked as a private tutor in the towns surrounding Königsberg. He lived frugally in a one-room apartment with a bed, a table, and a chair. The walls were bare except for a silhouette of Rousseau, whose "rights of man" he admired.

For the next seven years Kant continued to struggle, returning to the university when he could to complete his degrees. His financial troubles seemed over when, at age thirty-one, he received an appointment as *Privatdozent* (university lecturer) at Königsberg, teaching science and mathematics. But the position was non-salaried, and for the next fifteen years he lived on student fees and odd tutoring. At this point, he experienced something of a mid-life crisis, feeling that he should have had a clear direction by this time. Finally, in 1770 at age forty-six, with increasing recognition for his lectures and writings, he was made professor of logic and metaphysics and could live comfortably.

Kant was a late bloomer. His most important books were published in the last third of his life. His masterwork, *Critique of Pure Reason* (1781), was the result of ten years' labor and proved to be one of the most influential books in modern philosophy. Following this success, he published *Groundwork of the Metaphysic of Morals* (1785), *Critique of Practical Reason* (1788), and *Critique of Judgment* (1790). These works made his reputation, and for the next twenty-seven years he attracted a substantial following across Europe; Kantianism, in fact, dominated philosophy for one hundred years.

In his later years Kant became a finicky bachelor, as well as a hypochondriac. He was noticeably undersized and frail, with a slightly deformed shoulder, and as he aged, he became unusually anxious about his health. He regulated his diet carefully, was afraid of getting wet, and always breathed through his nose, "on the theory that nothing invited disease so much as an open mouth." Although he enjoyed reading geography, he never traveled more than forty miles from his home, even to see the Baltic, which was one hour away.

One incident may be telling about his disposition: Kant was in the habit of gazing at a church steeple when he was working at home, but some trees grew up in a neighbor's garden, obscuring the view. Kant became agitated, unable to think or write until the neighbor, out of esteem for him, agreed to trim the trees.

Essentially, Kant was a methodical, stiff, solitary, formal individual who led an uneventful life, much more logical than emotional. He had a tin ear for music, was indifferent to painting, and had only one artwork in his house. His daily routine never varied. According to his servant, he rose immediately at 5:00 a.m., worked all morning, dined promptly at 12:00, took a daily walk at precisely the same hour each day, and was in bed every night before ten o'clock. He lectured two hours per day, six days a week, for twenty-five years without missing a day. As one biographer described it, his life passed like the most regular of verbs. "Rising, coffee-drinking, writing, lecturing, dining, walking—each had its set time. And when Immanuel Kant in his grey coat, cane in hand, appeared at the door of his house, and strolled toward the small avenue of linden trees, which is still called 'The Philosopher's Walk,' the neighbors knew it was exactly half past three by the clock."

At the same time, Kant held dinner parties regularly, in part because conversation and laughter were good for one's constitution. His lectures at the university were extremely popular, both because of the quality of his thought and his witty comments on other philosophers. Students who wanted to attend his classes had to arrive one hour early to ensure a place. Kant's lectures were also notorious because of his rational, unorthodox views on religion, including his refutation of St. Anselm's ontological argument. He said, "I do not add to the value of 100 imaginary dollars by taking a real one out of my pocket." At one point in 1792, King Frederick William II prohibited him from teaching or writing on religious subjects—a ban that Kant obeyed, at least until the king's death five years later.

In his final years Kant's mind went into decline and he became rather confused, perhaps due to Alzheimer's disease, and since he was aware that it was happening, it was a sad end. When he died, he was entombed in a mausoleum adjoining the city cathedral. His statue, which used to stand in front of the University of Königsberg, has been placed on the grounds nearby.

Epistemology
Kant's epistemological ideas brought about a "Copernican revolution," but like most original ideas, they seem simple and obvious in hindsight. He had inherited a split between rationalism and empiricism, and he bridged that divide through an analysis of the way the mind functions.

The rationalists had referred to "a priori" ideas, which are known before we experience the physical world—ideas such as Descartes' *cogito, ergo sum*. The empiricist regarded the mind as an empty vessel that we fill "a posteriori" through sense experience; they rejected the notion of innate ideas or Platonic forms. Kant combined the two approaches. He accounted for knowledge by postulating that the mind contains categories of thought that we bring to bear upon sense experience.

More specifically, our mental apparatus organizes our experience in terms of categories of thought, especially time, space, and causation. Because our mind is so constructed, we can identify events *temporally* as before or after, yesterday, today, or tomorrow; we can place objects *spatially* as above or below, beside, between, and among; and we can judge events *causally*, recognizing that the eight ball dropped into the side pocket because it was struck by the cue ball. (In this last premise, Kant answered Hume's skepticism about causation.)

The structure of the mind therefore determines how objects and events are understood, ordering the data that appear to our senses. As Kant phrased it, concepts without percepts are empty; percepts without concepts are blind. We would not gain any knowledge if we just had the mental categories; neither would we know anything if there were just a random inundation of impressions. Both the categories and the sense data are needed to obtain intelligible ideas.

The downside of all this, of course, is that we are "hardwired" in a particular way and see the world through fixed lenses. That is, we cannot know the world as it is, the *Ding an sich*, but only as the categories of our mind structure it. Reality is therefore more made than given, and we can never get outside ourselves to see whether we have captured nature itself. This is "the scandal of reality," that there is no proof of the outside world. We can never know what lies beyond experience, what Kant calls the "noumenal world," but only the "phenomenal" world arranged by our minds. The categories of thought provide the conditions under which objects are perceived and understood, but they cannot be proven in themselves.

This is one of the great paradoxes of knowledge. If we approach the world with prior concepts, we are selective in our perception and therefore distort the evidence, but unless we have some structure to lay over experience, it cannot be organized into anything comprehensible. We have a choice between contaminated findings or no findings at all.

Despite the impossibility of knowing ultimate things, Kant thinks we ought to hold certain beliefs for our personal well-being. Even though they are unprovable, we should believe in God, freedom, and immortality in order to give meaning to life. "Practical reason" requires that we think there is a source directing human life, a God that lies behind our moral instincts and free choices. Since we can never fully know God, we must rely on faith, not reason, to affirm his existence. Sometimes Kant refers to a "logical understanding" that provides us with knowledge of the divine, of freedom of the will, and of the immortality of the soul.

"I have found it necessary to deny knowledge in order to make room for faith," Kant observed. For a leader of the late Enlightenment, or *Anfklärung*, this seems an unusual conclusion. Such a position has more in common with the pragmatist who believes things because they are useful, not as a result of rational evidence. But Kant's position becomes understandable if reason is disqualified and faith is a necessity for meaningful living. We can, of course, question both premises. Reason may not be that limited, and atheists seem able to lead meaningful lives. Even Mother Teresa confessed to doubts about her faith but led an exemplary existence, perhaps as a secular saint.

Our Moral Obligations

Kant is known for his epistemology but also for his theory of ethics, and the latter has had a more general impact on society. In his ethical system the value of actions is judged according to two main elements: the intention of the agent, that is, the motive of the person performing the action, and the moral nature of the act itself. The latter, doing the right thing, is more important, and within school philosophy it is termed formalism or deontologism.

First, the correct intention, motive, or purpose is an indispensable condition for moral conduct. At the beginning of the *Foundations of the Metaphysics of Morals*, Kant declares, "Nothing in the world . . . can possibly be conceived which could be called good without qualification except a good will." In other words, conduct should not be evaluated in terms of the consequences that flow from it, but in terms of the will that lies behind it. People who do things with a pure heart are praiseworthy, regardless of whether their actions achieve anything worthwhile: "like a jewel, [the will] would still shine by its own light, as a thing which has its value in itself." Bad luck, unfavorable circumstances, historical accidents, and so forth may prevent the accomplishment of what a person intends to do, but the significant factor is whether the person meant well, whether his or her heart was in the right place. If so, then praise is appropriate, and if not, then no praise is due, regardless of whether the results are benefical. As William Blake wrote, "A truth that's told with bad intent, beats all the lies you can invent."

For the will to be good, however, Kant describes the second factor: that it must operate not from inclination but out of recognition of rightness. For example, if we are moved to help a blind person across the street out of an impulse of pity, that would not constitute a moral action; but if we offer our help because we realize we have a duty to help those in need, then the action would be moral.

Kant distrusted the emotions, regarding them as too unreliable to determine correct behavior. The emotions could impel us to act with sympathy and generosity, but they could also provoke cruelty and destructiveness. Just because we feel a certain emotion, that is no reason to act upon it, but if we recognize a moral duty, then we have a reliable basis for conduct. One should always behave on principle, not by inclination. Contrary to Kant, of course, we could ask whether we would rather have a neighbor who is good on principle or because of a generous nature.

The next question Kant addresses is how we know where our duty lies. His answer is that if our action can be subsumed under some universal moral principle, then we know we are in the presence of correct behavior. That is, if our action is an instance of a broad rule of conduct, then we can feel confident that it is right. For example, suppose we are hungry and are conflicted over whether to steal food to fill our stomachs or to respect the right to property, including food. In order to test the morality of this action, we must ask ourselves whether it can be placed under a universal rule. Can we recommend that anyone who is hungry should steal food? Obviously not, and since stealing cannot be considered a general moral obligation, it cannot be considered right.

The core of Kant's ethical system is contained in what he calls the *categorical imperative*. He renders it in various ways, but broadly speaking, it can be expressed as follows: We should always act in such a way that the principle for our actions could become a universal moral law. That is, in order for an action to qualify as right, we must be able to affirm that all people at all times and all places should do the same. "So act that your principle of action might safely be made a law for the whole world," or negatively put, "I should never act in such a way that I could not also will that my maxim should be a universal law." If we make an exception for ourselves, declaring that the act is wrong in general but nonetheless we can do it, that is a certain indication that our action is immoral.

Kant gives various examples of the categorical imperative to help clarify its meaning. Suppose we are considering borrowing money—money that we do not intend to pay back but promise to repay in order to get the loan. Should we, Kant asks, make an insincere promise so that we can obtain the money? Would it make a difference if it were needed for a worthwhile purpose, say, a child's operation? To decide this question, we must apply the categorical imperative. Could we will that everyone should act according to that principle, that whoever wants to borrow money is justified in making a false promise to repay it? Obviously not, Kant says, for if everyone did so, no one would ever lend money. The conduct cannot be universalized and therefore cannot be right.

Another example is that of truth telling. We may be tempted in various circumstances to tell a lie, perhaps to extricate ourselves from an awkward situation or to spare someone's feelings, but to Kant the ultimate test of the rightness of our behavior is whether it can be universalized. Can we will that lying be practiced by everyone, everywhere, at all times? No, because if everyone lied, saying the opposite of what they believed to be true, no one would ever be deceived. Lying cannot be universalized and therefore is wrong.

It is important to understand that Kant is not restating the golden rule, that we should all do as we would be done by, or the silver rule, that we should not do unto others as we would not have them do unto us. Kant's point is that if an action becomes *impossible* if everyone were to carry it out, then it cannot be right.

Kant formulated the categorical imperative in another way, sometimes called the *practical imperative*, which seems quite different from the concept of universalizability, although Kant regarded it as the same. He stated that we should "treat humanity, whether in thine own person or in that of any other, always as an end and never as a means only." Here he emphasizes respect for persons (specifically, rational beings) and affirms that people should not just use one another as means. Now, to some extent, people must treat each other as a means, whether as doctors, plumbers, mothers, or letter carriers, but human relationships ought to be more than that. We should, Kant believes, regard people as worthy of respect in and of themselves. People should be treated as the end of our actions, not as a way of achieving some other purpose. Only then are human beings given the dignity they deserve.

The practical imperative provides a second reason for condemning deceit and dishonesty: we are treating someone as a means only. This is why we feel insulted when we discover that someone has lied to us. We have been regarded as an obstacle, rather than a person. Interestingly enough, Kant condemns suicide on the same grounds. We are treating ourselves as a means of solving a problem and ignoring the ultimate worth of human beings, which includes ourselves.

Treating humanity as an end is an important element in Kant's ethics, but his main theory turns on the notion of universal principles. An act is not right because it has good results. Our conduct must fall under principles that can be advocated for all human beings, categorically and unconditionally.

A Critical Appraisal
Kant's ethical system is very high-minded, even noble in tone, but it is also strict and uncompromising. If a principle has exceptions, it is inadmissible to Kant, and that seems unduly harsh. For example, there are times when telling the truth would hurt someone deeply; lying might then be best. But that does not imply that truth telling is not a virtue. It only means that in general we should be truthful, but sometimes there are overriding considerations. Not hurting someone's feelings can be more important than telling the truth, which is why we can excuse "white lies."

An exception actually reinforces a principle, rather than invalidating it, for the implication is that, with some exceptions, the principle holds true. Put differently, Kant fails to differentiate between an exception and a qualification. It might be self-serving to think we are an exception to a rule, but we could qualify rules without making an exception for ourselves. We could, for instance, respect private property and oppose stealing but make allowances for spies whose job it is to steal enemy secrets. Granted, it is wrong to argue, "No one may break a promise except me"; nevertheless we might want to qualify promise-keeping by saying, "No one may break a promise unless a person's life would be endangered by keeping it." In this case, the qualified rule might be universalized without exceptions, which would satisfy the standard of the categorical imperative.

Kant's attitude toward ethics was extremely severe, especially toward sexual morality. He condemned homosexuality and masturbation, although not going as far as St. Thomas, who said these practices are worse than rape because they do not produce children. But his rigidity can be seen in the following excerpts:

> A child that comes into the world apart from marriage is born outside the law . . . so that the commonwealth can ignore its existence (since it was not right that it should have come to exist this way), and can therefore also ignore its annihilation.
>
> It is far better to die honored and respected than to prolong one's life . . . by a disgraceful act. . . . If, for instance, a woman cannot preserve her life any longer except by surrendering her person to the will of another, she is bound to give up her life rather than dishonor humanity in her own person.

Such declarations, about children born out of wedlock and death before dishonor, have a callousness about them that amounts to malice. In fact, the Kantian system as a whole can be inhumane, adhering to principles and ignoring the harm that can follow as a consequence. Keeping a promise to return a weapon to someone who is criminally insane could produce havoc. Kant always put principles ahead of people, distrusting even feelings of compassion, which ought to modify our obligations.

On a more technical level, Kant has been criticized for not realizing that two universalized principles can conflict, and for failing to provide a means of resolving the conflict. Suppose, for instance, we maintain as part of our absolute principles that human life should be preserved *and* that we should always tell the truth. Then one day a man runs up to us with a smoking gun in his hand and asks, "Which way did my wife go?" Here we can either tell the truth and contribute to a murder or save a life by telling a lie. Under Kant's moral system, in which genuine moral rules cannot be broken, we are faced with an impossible dilemma. Is saving a life more important than honesty? It seems so, but then people go to the wall for the truth, valuing their integrity above life itself.

To take another example, a doctor is bound by the Hippocratic oath to preserve life *and* to alleviate suffering, but suppose a terminally ill patient asks to have his life ended rather than experience more pain. Which value should be given priority? The quality of a person's life can be more significant than its quantity, but the doctor has an obligation to do no harm.

This leads to another major criticism of Kant's ethic. Not only can universal principles conflict, but it is difficult, if not impossible, to find a principle that can be applied without exception. That is, only universal rules are right in Kant's system, but we wonder whether there are any universal rules. Each one covers a certain number of cases, perhaps a majority, but none can be said to apply in all circumstances. We should not kill, except in self-defense; we should keep promises, except those made on a deathbed; we should be truthful, except where we shouldn't. By insisting that only principles without exceptions are moral, Kant created an ethical system that does not contain any genuine principles. Nothing qualifies. The analogy is of the donkey loaded with salt that crossed a stream and had only empty sacks on the other side.

Part of the problem is that some principles might be moral even though they cannot be universalized. For example, self-sacrifice does seem admirable in certain circumstances, but it cannot be practiced by all people in all places at all times. For if everyone were self-sacrificing, there would be no one left to accept the sacrifice. On Kantian grounds, then, we would have to say it is not a virtue. However, it seems more reasonable to say that self-sacrifice should be practiced some of the time, that there are occasions in which we should put other people first. In other words, a principle need not be universal in order to be moral.

Kant's absolutism also trips him up with regard to the practical imperative. Sometimes we must treat others entirely as a means. For example, we might justify sacrificing a squad of soldiers, rather than risking an entire company to rescue them. Sometimes the greater good takes precedence over individual well-being; the squad is expendable. Even in ordinary life we must sometimes decide between the conflicting interests of two individuals, making one subservient to the other. Having said that, though, we should treat people with respect insofar as we can. As Kant says, we should not use people as instruments or objects but as the end for which actions are done.

Conclusion

Despite the flaws, Kant's philosophy is intriguing, perhaps because of a combination of purity, sincerity, and rational simplicity. The world we perceive is, in fact, edited by the structure of our minds, and it seems reasonable that if an action is intrinsically right, it should be done.

Kant famously wrote, "Two things awe me most, the starry sky above and the moral law within." His life's work was to understand both, insofar as his scholarly approach allowed. Like many philosophers, he advocated the absence of passion for the sake of clarity. His rationalism was softened by Rousseau and religion, and he was a liberal with some antidemocratic tendencies, which did not stop him from sympathizing with the French Revolution and even the Reign of Terror. He believed "there can be nothing more dreadful than that the actions of a man should be subject to the will of another." War, he thought, was contrary to reason, and only an international government can ensure peace.

He also thought the only right use of the intellect was in the service of moral good, and that there must be a God to bring about justice. Virtuous people should be rewarded, and only a divine providence could make that happen. He tried to include himself among the virtuous and earnestly sought to answer the philosophic questions, "What can I know? What ought I to do? What can I hope?"

The Greatest Happiness Principle: John Stuart Mill

The atmosphere surrounding Kant's ethics is of a radically different character than that of John Stuart Mill, and the two are often juxtaposed. As we have seen, Kant believed in doing what is right because it is right, following the logic of principles. Mill, by contrast, chose actions because of their beneficial outcomes, that is, according to whether they produced beneficial or harmful results for society. This approach is labeled consequentialism or teleologism. The difference is due in part to the temper of the two men and to the philosophic traditions of their two nations.

John Stuart Mill, who is considered the most important English philosopher of the nineteenth century, was born in 1806 in Pentonville, a suburb of London, and was buried in France in 1873. He received an extraordinary education from his father, James Mill, a Scot who attended the University of Edinburgh. When he moved to London, James joined a group called the Philosophical Radicals, dedicated to promoting the ideals of a philosopher named Jeremy Bentham (1748–1832), and he groomed his son to be a disciple. The group was opposed to "natural rights," which Bentham called "nonsense on stilts," and endorsed a doctrine of maximizing happiness.

James Mill published a book entitled *History of India* and, on the strength of that, obtained a position with the East India Company. Along with the British crown, the company governed the Indian colonies, and James Mill rose through the ranks to become chief examiner, the highest executive officer.

John Stuart, the eldest of nine children, never attended a school or university but was educated exclusively by his father in a remarkably demanding regimen of studies. He read Aesop's *Fables* in Greek by age three and mastered Latin by age eight, along with algebra and Euclidian geometry; he also tutored his siblings three hours a day. By age fourteen he had digested most of the classical authors, including Xenophon, Herodotus, and the philosophic historian Diogenes Laertius. The following year he was fluent in French, as a result of travel on the Continent with the Bentham family, and he had read Adam Smith's economics, as well as the works of Plato and Aristotle.

Such an education is impressive but also appalling, and in later years Mill attributed his "mental crisis" at age twenty to this rigorous intellectual training; he rightly believed it had stunted his emotional growth. Reading some of the Romantic poets, such as Wordsworth, Coleridge, and Goethe, restored his equilibrium—that plus the realization that, aside from walks with his father, some music, and reading *Robinson Crusoe*, he had hardly had a childhood. His father was so far removed from the world of feeling that he considered poetry "the expression of barbarous people before they can speculate." Mill's travels in France also made him aware of a sweeter life and a sense that happiness requires more than a commitment to social progress.

Like his father, Mill began working for the East India Company and remained there for thirty-five years, becoming chief examiner at India House in turn. At the same time, he began to write a series of books, beginning with *A System of Logic* (1843), followed by *Principles of Political Economy* (1848), the latter expressing a liberal economic theory. His best-known work, *On Liberty* (1859), stands as the classic defense of individual freedom within society, and *Utilitarianism* (1863) contains the definitive statement of the utilitarian ethic, modified to include the quality of happiness. *The Subjection of Women* (1869) contributed significantly to the suffragist movement, even though Mill made a generalization about all women based on a study of his wife! His *Autobiography* (1873) offers insights into his personal history, as well as the psychological sources of his philosophic ideas.

At age twenty-five Mill met Harriet Taylor, who proved to be the most significant person in his life, both personally and professionally. She was married to a druggist, who allowed Mill and Harriet an intimate relationship for twenty years. They all went on vacation together, and when Harriet invited Mill to dinner, Mr. Taylor went to his club. She was a very attractive woman, something of an invalid, described by the essayist Thomas Carlyle as "pale and passionate and sad looking, a living romance heroine." Under her influence, Mill expanded his vision to include the insights of poets as well as scientific method, Romanticism as well as Enlightenment thinking. Harriet seems to have mellowed his outlook, even though he always appears dry, pinched, and earnest in his portraits.

Throughout their relationship Mill claimed it was platonic. Nevertheless it scandalized Victorian England and, in particular, outraged the elder Mill. A few years after her husband's death in 1851, Mill and Harriet finally married, alienating the rest of Mill's family but apparently enjoying an idyllic relationship. Mill regarded her intellectual abilities as superior to his own, even attributing to her joint authorship of his major works. However, after only six years of marriage Harriet died unexpectedly. Mill was nearly inconsolable, and he instructed that he be buried with her in Avignon. Their life together seems to have been a genuine love story.

Mill was elected to the House of Commons in 1865, warning his constituency that he would not support their special interests but only what he thought to be right; he was not reelected. His political views might have been too liberal and lofty for Parliament altogether. At his maiden speech the prime minister, Benjamin Disraeli, remarked, "Ah, the finishing governess." To his credit, Mill opposed slavery and supported women's rights against the sentiment of his times, although he opposed suffrage for the illiterate. He argued that people must be properly educated, otherwise we have "false democracy" and "the selfishness and brutality of the mob." He was called "the most open-minded man in England."

Although Mill's life was unexciting, it was also filled with controversy because of his personal affairs and his radical views. He wrote provocative articles in the *London Review* and the *Westminster Review*, and his books on economics, religion, history, and politics, provoked a great deal of intellectual debate. He was especially challenged for championing personal freedom and for his consequentialist theory, neither of which is now considered disgraceful.

Politics

In his political philosophy Mill is known for his support of individual liberty against government encroachment in our private lives. In *On Liberty* he wrote,

> The only purpose for which power can be rightfully exercised over any member of a civilized community against his will, is to prevent harm to others. His own good, either physical or moral, is not sufficient warrant. He cannot rightfully be compelled to do or forbear because it would be better for him to do so, because it will make him happier, because in the opinion of others, to do so would be wise or even right. These are good reasons for remonstrating with him, or reasoning with him, or persuading him, or entreating him, but not compelling him, or visiting him with any evil in case he do otherwise. To

do that, the conduct from which it is desired to deter him, must be calculated to produce evil to someone else.

This means that the law should not interfere with people for their own good but only to prevent harm to others. Society may think a person's actions are wrong or even destructive to that individual, but the state has no right to restrict conduct on those grounds. It has no authority to protect people from themselves but only from other people.

In a modern context, then, Mill would oppose laws against marijuana or even hard drugs; he would not force people to wear seat belts or crash helmets. Driving "under the influence," on the other hand, should be punishable by law because other people's lives are put at risk. Mill might even object to laws against euthanasia, prostitution, polygamy, and homosexuality on the basis that these are "crimes" without victims. Provided there is no compulsion, consenting adults in private should be able to do as they please. The opposite position has been held by thinkers such as Lord Patrick Devlin:

> If men and women try to create a society in which there is no fundamental agreement about good and evil they will fail . . . [for] society is not something that can be kept together physically; it is held by the invisible but fragile bonds of common beliefs and values. . . . A common morality is part of the bondage of a good society, and that bondage is part of the price of society which mankind must pay.

In other words, even actions done in private can fall under the rule of law, because we need that cement to hold society together. Even if other people are not at risk, whatever the group judges unethical should be made illegal, otherwise we lose our social cohesion. For example, if society judges pornography to be immoral, vulgarizing men's view of women, then it should be banned, even if it cannot be linked to sex crimes. The government must exercise a "legal paternalism," using the power of law to keep the fabric of society from unraveling.

The two sides are thereby drawn, and Mill clearly wants to limit the state's interference in the lives of its citizens. He is afraid of the actions of the minority being criminalized and of the values of the ruling party becoming the law of the land—all in the name of social unity. According to his view, we should not prohibit whatever we consider wrong, but only those actions that threaten other people. In this way we protect our individual liberty.

In American society we are of two minds about the matter. We allow the sale of cigarettes, even though they are harmful, because we want consumer choice, and we allow people to own guns, even though they cause bloodshed, because that is a citizen's right. At the same time, we ban drugs because they are destructive to the individual, and we prohibit prostitution, even though it involves consenting adults in private, because we disapprove of it. Can there be a crime without a victim?

Utilitarianism

In keeping with the education he received from his father, Mill became a follower of Jeremy Bentham, the leading figure in the social and ethical movement called utilitarianism. According to the "Principle of Utility," which is its foundation, "actions are right in proportion as they tend to promote happiness; wrong as they tend to promote the reverse of happiness," or "the principle of utility is that principle which approves or disapproves of every action whatsoever, according to the tendency which it appears to have to augment or diminish the happiness of the party whose interest is in question." Whether we are deliberating about individual acts or public policy, the primary question is whether it will provide "the greatest amount of happiness for the greatest number of people."

Utilitarianism, therefore, is a consequentialist ethic, judging actions by their outcome, as distinct from a Kantian, formalistic approach, which considers the ethical nature of the act itself as paramount. In utilitarianism we do not know what to do ahead of time, but we can judge what we should have done in retrospect.

To strengthen predictability, Bentham devised a *hedonic calculus,* or a *calculus of pleasures,* which was a scheme for scientifically measuring the amount of pleasure and pain that any action would yield. To Bentham's mind, ethics had been too imprecise in the past, but the time was ripe to introduce scientific rigor and exactitude into ethical thinking. Each of the factors that are involved in obtaining pleasure and pain could be identified, and actions could be rated according to the enjoyment that each provided. Furthermore, pleasure could be broken down into certain elements, called *hedons*—units of pleasure or pain capable of being added and subtracted, and these units could be fed into a calculus. In this way the happiness quotient of any act could be precisely measured.

Bentham isolated seven factors, or "marks," and rated actions in terms of each, assigning numerical values according to the degree of pleasure or pain produced. For example, *intensity,* the first mark, assesses the strength of a pleasure. *Duration* refers to whether the pleasure is extended or brief; a pleasurable experience of long duration is obviously preferable to one of short duration. By their very nature, intensity and duration are opposed to each other (there cannot be a long, intense pleasure), but both seem to be important factors to take into account. What's more, many activities aim at the prolongation of pleasure rather than vivid sensations.

Certainty or *uncertainty* is another mark, the meaning of which is self-evident. An experience we are certain to enjoy would be given a higher rating than one where enjoyment is merely possible. Since the certainty of a pleasure could be a function of its nearness, Bentham introduced a fourth mark, *propinquity* or *remoteness*. This means that the experiences we can enjoy immediately are superior to those we hope to have at some future point. If we defer pleasures, hoping to obtain them at another time, we run the risk of never experiencing them at all.

Bentham's other factors include *fecundity*, the tendency of a pleasure to be followed by sensations of the same kind; *purity*, which he defined as the chance a pleasure or pain has of *not* being followed by sensations of the opposite kind; and finally *extent*, meaning the number of persons to whom the pleasure or pain extends. As a utilitarian, Bentham believed that a pleasurable action that affects more people is better than one affecting fewer people.

Having determined the relevant factors, the hedonic calculus would work this way: When judging the value of an action, a person would draw up a list of the number of hedons that each of the marks would yield, perhaps on a scale of one to five. The hedons would then be added together. The same process would be carried out with regard to pains. Then the negatives would be subtracted from the positives to see whether the act was pleasurable overall.

The attempt to put ethics on a scientific footing is certainly commendable, and as a utilitarian, Bentham wanted to determine the amount of happiness that would be provided by any given action. If we are to bring the greatest amount of happiness to the greatest number of people, we would have to know the extent to which various actions provide happiness. However, is happiness the kind of thing that can be precisely measured? Can a person say exactly how happy or sad he or she is, how ecstatic or depressed, on a scale of one to five? Perhaps Bentham is trying to quantify something that is not quantifiable.

Mill's Version of Utilitarianism
Mill departed from Bentham on this point, introducing a more thoughtful version of the utilitarian doctrine. He pointed out that Bentham took into account only the *quantity* of pleasure that an action would yield and not the *quality* of enjoyment that is experienced. Bentham would compare activities, such as hearing a classical concert and wallowing in mud, only

with regard to the amount of pleasure that each produced; if the latter was more pleasurable, it would be preferable. But surely, Mill thought, pleasures should be differentiated in terms of higher and lower kinds, and not judged solely in terms of amount. Qualitative distinctions between pleasures seem at least as significant as quantitative ones—and are probably more important altogether. He argued that poetry is far better than pushpin (pick-up-sticks).

Because of Bentham's failure to consider the type of pleasure involved, Thomas Carlyle, the Scottish essayist, referred to his ethics as "pig philosophy": the pleasures of a pig and those of a person were considered of equal value as long as they were of the same degree. To Carlyle and Mill, we should be concerned with better and worse pleasure, not just more or less.

When we see sheep or cows grazing in a field, we might experience some envy. We might think, Wouldn't it be marvelous to lead the life of a farm animal, with food readily available and nothing to do but graze, sleep, stare, and reproduce the species? But even though the simple existence of an animal might be appealing for a moment, we really would not want to trade places. If we had the option, we would choose the deeper, more complex life of a human being, even if it were less enjoyable. We believe human life to be qualitatively superior in the kind of happiness it brings, and we are not impressed by the fact that a sheep or a cow might enjoy itself more at a lower level.

This is Mill's point regarding quality. Utilitarianism has to take into account the higher pleasures if it is to become dignified enough to be the goal for human beings. In his book *Utilitarianism* Mill declares that some kinds of pleasure are more worthwhile than others. "It would be absurd that while, in estimating all other things, quality is considered as well as quantity, the estimation of pleasures should be supposed to depend on quantity alone."

But how are we to determine which of two pleasures is qualitatively superior? What makes one pleasure higher and another lower? Mill's answer is that the better pleasure is the one chosen by the majority of people. He wrote, "Of two pleasures, if there be one to which all or almost all who have experience of both give a decided preference, irrespective of any feeling of moral obligation to prefer it, that is the more desirable pleasure."

The choices of "experienced" people, then, can be safely taken as the index of higher quality. "No intelligent being would consent to be a fool; no instructed person would be an ignoramus, no person of feeling and conscience would be selfish and base, even though they should be persuaded that the fool, the dunce, or the rascal is better satisfied with his lot than they are with theirs." Mill goes on to say, "It is better to he a human being dissatisfied than a pig satisfied; better to be a Socrates dissatisfied than a fool satisfied."

In short, superior pleasures are the ones knowledgeable people choose because they engage our higher faculties.

A Critique
Certainly utilitarianism needed the addition of qualitative factors, since the goal of happiness could produce a crude philosophy. But it is extremely difficult to find a criterion for high versus low, for refined or vulgar pleasures.

For one thing, it is simply a mistake to believe that people who have experienced two pleasures will necessarily choose the higher one—however broadly we define "higher." The millions of people who watch soap operas are by and large acquainted with good plays, but they prefer to watch these programs instead. And in choosing soap operas, they do not claim they are a higher pleasure; they simply want the lower one. The same holds true with regard to professional wrestling as contrasted with a dance concert, monster truck rallies compared to art shows, comic books and Shakespeare. Even within the same field, the higher type of pleasure is usually less popular than the lower. Better literature sells fewer copies than pulp fiction, serious drama attracts fewer people than musical comedies, and artistic films do not have the box-office success of commercial ones. In short, popular taste can be bad taste, which means that, contrary to Mill's contention, the choice of the majority cannot be taken as an indication of higher quality.

However, to talk about good and bad taste today makes us uneasy. In a democracy, where everyone is considered equal and each person is entitled to his or her own opinion, it seems snobbish to talk about uplifting or degrading forms of enjoyment. We sympathize with Mill, but we wonder whether any criterion is possible, or whether it is simply elitist to differentiate between superior and inferior pleasures.

From a cultural standpoint, are all pleasures equal, or can we identify higher and lower forms of pleasure? Is Bentham right in arguing that we cannot enjoy ourselves in the wrong way but only not enough?

Another charge against Mill is that his emphasis on higher modes of experience places him outside of utilitarianism altogether. That is, when he stated that it is better to be a dissatisfied person than a satisfied pig, or a Socrates dissatisfied rather than a fool satisfied, he was saying that a qualitatively higher life is more valuable than a pleasurable one. A consistent utilitarian would never approve of *dissatisfaction*, but Mill preferred this over animalistic or foolish pleasures. In this way, he chose a qualitatively rich existence rather than the goal of enjoyment itself.

The general point is that when Mill (or anyone else) attempts to refine a pleasure theory by introducing qualitative distinctions, he places himself outside the system altogether. That is, the criterion used to differentiate between higher and lower pleasures becomes the basic ethical standard. Mill ultimately took as his goal the life of a cultured human being, and although that may be right, it leaves utilitarianism far behind.

Utilitarianism Broadly Considered

This leads to the criticisms of utilitarianism itself. The main problem with the theory is a moral one. The goal of "the greatest happiness for the greatest number" is the foundation of the theory; actions are right insofar as they promote the social good. But the flaw is that whatever secures that good is allowable, even immoral actions. For utilitarians, the ends justify the means, just as in Kant's ethic the means justify the ends. The utilitarians would accept awful means, provided the end is good enough, just as Kant ignores awful consequences if the principle is worthwhile.

The problem may be illustrated by the following story, written by the Danish writer J. H. Wessel. A blacksmith killed a man in a fight and was in jail awaiting execution, but an eloquent spokesman for the citizens reasoned with the judge:

> "Your wisdom, we know you are thinking of the welfare of this town, but this welfare depends on getting our blacksmith back. His death won't wake up the dead man, and we'll never find such a good blacksmith ever again."
>
> The judge said, "But a life has been taken and must be paid for by a life. . . ."
>
> "We have in town an old and scrawny baker who'll go to the devil soon, and since we have two bakers, how about taking the oldest one? Then you still get a life for a life."
>
> "Well," said the judge, "that is not a bad idea. I'll do what I can." And he leafed through his law books but found nothing that said you can't execute a baker instead of a blacksmith, so he pronounced this sentence:
>
> "We know that blacksmith Jens has no excuse for what he has done, sending Anders Petersen off to eternity, but since we have but one blacksmith in this town I would be crazy if I wanted him dead, but we do have two bakers of bread . . . so the oldest one must pay for the murder."
>
> The old baker wept pitifully when they took him away.

In our contemporary society we want to operate with fairness and justice, not just in terms of favorable outcomes. It might, for instance, increase the happiness of the majority to hang the minority, but that would hardly be fair. We should not steal from the rich, even if we are giving the proceeds to the poor, and U.S. policy does not approve of assassinating foreign leaders, even if the people would be better off. Using a cost-benefit analysis, Ford built the

Pinto with a gas tank positioned too close to the rear of the car; that caused the vehicle to explode on impact. But Ford knew the cost of settling claims would be less that retooling the assembly line, and the value of human life was ignored. Actions should be judged right or wrong in themselves, independent of the consequences. Utilitarianism, therefore, does not provide us with a proper standard of behavior and could well approve of conduct that is morally wrong.

Another criticism is that not all pleasures are worthwhile, whether for the individual or society at large. The sadist who enjoys inflicting pain can be condemned for deriving pleasure that way, just as we criticize schadenfreude, finding joy in someone else's misery. Drunkenness, philandering, drug addiction, or enjoying blood sports seems the wrong way of being entertained. Bullfighting was banned in this country, not because it caused pain to the bull, but because it brought pleasure to the spectators; there are some things we ought not to enjoy.

Finally, utilitarianism has been plagued from its inception by an inherent problem known as the hedonistic paradox. The paradox, quite simply, is that pleasure or happiness is not something that can be obtained directly but comes about as a byproduct of the pursuit of some other goal. People who serve others, for example, may find that they are happy in their dedication, but people who deliberately try to be happy usually discover that happiness eludes them. Happiness or pleasure seems to come about indirectly, and any conscious effort to attain it becomes self-defeating. It is a side effect of our effort and is destroyed when it becomes our goal, like putting on a light to see the darkness. Therefore, the search for happiness tends to be an unhappy one. Utilitarians are faced with the further paradox that by advocating the pursuit of happiness, they are decreasing the likelihood of people achieving it.

Mill made this concession in his *Autobiography*. "Those only are happy who have their minds fixed on some object other than their own happiness. . . . Ask yourself whether you are happy, and you cease to be so. . . . Treat not happiness, but some end external to it, as the purpose of your life . . . and if otherwise fortunately circumstanced you will inhale happiness with the air you breathe."

This observation appears to be true, but it also gives the game away. Here Mill is recommending some other purpose in life besides the pursuit of happiness. Perhaps we never do seek pleasure, but only value, and pleasure is an accompaniment to the pursuit of value in our lives.

Still, in the last analysis there is a natural appeal to happiness as our life purpose. This was expressed by Joseph Butler (1692–1752) in his comment that "when we sit down in a cool hour we cannot justify any pursuit 'til we are convinced that it will be for our happiness, or at least not contrary to it."

Investing Life with Meaning: Jean-Paul Sartre

In the twentieth century ethics underwent a sea change. Instead of issuing pronouncements that certain goals, such as duty or happiness, are fundamental, philosophers began to wonder whether there were any ideals to be found. They questioned whether existence has any inherent value, whether God provides direction, and whether right and wrong are written in eternal, invisible letters in the sky.

A movement called existentialism arose, pivoting round these questions, with its origins in the ideas of Socrates (470–399 BCE) and Pascal (1623–1662), and the nineteenth-century thought of Friedrich Nietzsche (1844–1900) and Sören Kierkegaard (1813–1855). But it flourished in the uncertainties of the modern era through the literary writings of Albert Camus (1913–1960), Andre Gide (1869–1951), and Jean Genet (1910–1986), and the works of philosophers such as Martin Heidegger (1889–1976), Karl Jaspers (1883–1969), Gabriel Marcel (1889–1973), Simone de Beauvoir (1908–1986), and the dean of existentialism, Jean-Paul Sartre (1905–1989).

Sartre was born in Paris and lived his life there, the quintessential Parisian. His father, Jean-Baptiste Sartre, was a naval officer and died in Indochina when Jean-Paul was fifteen months old; his mother, Anne-Marie Schweitzer, was first cousin to the medical missionary Albert Schweitzer. In his autobiography, *The Words*, Sartre describes his childhood as "unnatural," with no companions his age, "encountering the universe through books." After being home tutored, he graduated from the prestigious École normale supérieure in 1929, the classmate of Simone de Beauvoir, who became his lifetime companion. Their relationship was volatile and intense, built around the motto "Free but faithful."

Initially, Sartre taught at the lycée in Le Havre and was a research student in Freiburg and Berlin, but the academic life did not suit him. He was drafted into the French army during World War II, was imprisoned by the Germans in 1940, and was released or escaped in 1941. Back in Paris, Sartre joined the Resistance, fighting the Nazi occupation, and he wrote articles for magazines such as *Combat* and *Les Lettres Françaises*. He frequented the cafés of the Left Bank, holding spirited discussions with intellectuals and writing voluminously. He found the atmosphere of the café conducive to reflection, a combination of activity and anonymity; at home, he said, he was tempted to stretch out on his bed. Also, there were women, and nothing was more annoying than a woman trying not to be annoying, that a woman's solicitude could penetrate through three locked doors and make a man stop working altogether.

Sartre was extraordinarily versatile, writing fiction, essays, film scripts, criticism, and philosophical works. He first found success with the novel *Nausea* (1938), which was followed by the celebrated short story "The Wall" (1939), and the plays *The Flies* (1943) and *No Exit* (1944); his best dramatic work is often considered to be *Dirty Hands* (1948). Sartre's main contribution to philosophy is *Being and Nothingness* (1948), a book that provides the theoretical underpinnings of existential thought. He is known to the public for his manifesto "Existentialism is a Humanism" (1956); it began as an address to a Paris crowd, and after publication it made his name synonymous with existentialism.

Sartre was not an armchair philosopher but a public figure, conspicuously supporting social causes and manning the barricades during political protests. His politics were left-wing, but he opposed the Soviet invasion of Budapest and never joined the Communist Party. In fact, he became disillusioned with the Russian experiment and condemned the totalitarian oppression, just as he criticized the United States at the International War Crimes Tribunal for invading Vietnam.

Sartre lost the use of one eye as a boy and in his last years was nearly blind, but he continued writing, using a tape recorder. When he died, thousands followed the funeral cortege, for he had become the best-known philosopher in France.

Philosophic Movement

Existentialism can be difficult to define, partly because it rejects all definitions, including its own. Sartre said, "I am not an existentialist," just as Marx said, "I am not a Marxist" (and historians claim the Holy Roman Empire was neither holy nor Roman nor an empire). Nevertheless, existentialism can be characterized by certain common features.

First, the existentialists do not want to begin philosophizing from abstractions, to derive the role of human beings from a higher scheme of things. Rather, they start at the level of the concrete, individual person, here and now. What does it mean to be in existence as a human being at this particular time and place? We are thrown into the world, and once we become conscious of existing, we must ask ourselves what the terms of our existence are, the circumstances in which we find ourselves. This is the proper starting point for understanding human beings, not Freudian theory, which begins with the id or the Oedipus complex, or Platonic theory, which regards the idea of a person as more real than any actual person. To the existentialist, the world is not a shadow or copy of any form. Rather, the reverse is true: ideas are reflections of physical reality. We must begin with our experience of life as it presents itself to our consciousness and not as detached, uninvolved observers. "Existence is not something which can be thought from a distance," Sartre wrote. "[It] overwhelms you brusquely . . . it weighs heavily on your heart like a fat, loathsome beast."

Once we become aware of ourselves as existent beings, we realize that we experience certain psychological states that have philosophic significance. They give us insight into the human condition. These states include anxiety, anguish (angst), dread, forlornness, boredom, alienation, estrangement, despair, and melancholy. Each arises from our awareness of being in the world, and although they seem a curse, they may be a blessing in disguise. For they can be catalysts, enlivening us to the possibilities of living, arousing us to a more intense experience.

The phenomenon of anxiety can illustrate this point. Both Kierkegaard and Heidegger contrast anxiety with the more easily definable emotion of fear. When we are frightened, we can always specify the source of our fear. We may be afraid of a gun pointed at us or a contagious disease or a qualifying exam. "In fear we are always in the presence of this or that determinate being which threatens us in this or that determinate manner," Kierkegaard wrote. Once we are able to name the threat, we gain a certain control over it. With anxiety, however, nothing can be specified as the cause. There does not seem to be any particular reason why we are anxious, yet we feel profoundly uneasy, as though a shadow were lying over us, some impending doom. Heidegger says that if we are asked what we are anxious about, we usually reply that it is nothing.

But this answer is revealing. Our anxiety is over nothing, that is, the nothingness that awaits us at death. With anxiety we confront our terror at being snuffed out, realizing that the world offers no protection against the void. It is the state, as Tillich described it, of a being aware of not being, feeling abandoned and helpless to avert our ultimate extinction. We become conscious of the emptiness that preceded our birth and that will succeed our death. In short, we become acutely aware of our limited lives surrounded by endless time and space.

In facing nothingness, we come to terms with our temporary existence, but instead of denying death and living in "bad faith," people can choose to exist in an authentic way. Although we may lie to others for their good, we should never lie to ourselves and deny that our lives are transitory, for then we are deprived of the chance to fully exist.

Most human beings live as if they were going to live forever, but the confrontation with nonexistence can jolt people out of their stupor; they can then utilize the time available to them to become something before they are nothing. Anxiety, nothingness, and existence are, therefore, intimately connected, for as Camus wrote, "There is no sun without shadow, and it is essential to know the night."

Another important point to the existentialists is that feeling and the emotions are superior to reason. Therefore they do not attempt to demonstrate the truth of their ideas in syllogisms ("the poor definition cutter with logical scissors"), but try to provoke a personal response by their poetic style. This is why so much of existentialism is cast in literary form and why existentialists feel contempt for pedantry. In place of (mere) objectivity, the existentialist wants to stimulate our affective understanding.

If we are ruled by reason, we also relinquish our freedom, for then we can do only what reason dictates, not as we please. We become intimidated by the need for consistency and must justify our ideas before some imaginary logical tribunal sitting inside of us. The existentialist believes we have to liberate ourselves from the straitjacket of thought if we are to live fully. We should be free to behave rationally or irrationally, just as we like. To contradict ourselves is a great relief, "so refreshing," as Camus wrote in his play *Caligula*. And as Dostoyevsky commented in *Notes from the Underground:* "What sort of free will is left when we come to tables and arithmetic, when it will all be a case of two times two makes four? Two times two makes four even without my will. As if free will meant that." That is, if we defer to logic, we become machines and are no longer people; we lose our distinctive freedom.

Existence Precedes Essence
Perhaps the most important tenet of existentialism is that, for human beings, *existence precedes essence*, and this idea was best articulated by Jean-Paul Sartre. He explains the concept by contrasting the mode of being of objects with that of human beings. Objects already possess their essential nature when they come into being; their essence, or the set of qualities that identify them, is fully formed the moment they exist, and they will not develop any further. To use Sartre's example, a paper knife is imagined in someone's mind before it is brought into existence. Its shape, color, texture, and material are all decided beforehand. Humans, on the other hand, first exist, then fill out their essence by their decisions and actions. People do not possess an essence prior to their existence, but only become what they are by the choices they make after they come into being. Different decisions create different people. For the existentialist, "I choose, therefore I am."

In making these assertions, the existentialist assumes that human beings have the power to decide their lives, that we are creatures with free will. We can become whatever we choose, and so we are burdened with a "terrifying freedom" to choose the kind of person we want to become. They therefore oppose all forms of fatalism and determinism, refusing to believe we are string marionettes or cause-effect mechanisms. Existentialists also reject theories of a fixed human nature, for to regard people as possessing a basic "humanness" when they come into being would make them into objects; our essence would then precede our existence. In fact, people are nothing other than the consequence of their free choices, the ensemble of their actions.

"Man is the future of man," Sartre writes, and history does not teach us anything, since humanity is constantly reinventing itself in every age. Whatever generalization we make is contradicted by the "choice of themselves" of the next generation. We can describe human beings during a particular era, but only as the sum of individual actions at that time. Sartre even based his atheism on these grounds, arguing that if God created human beings, then they would resemble paper knives, with their essence already imagined in the mind of God. In Christianity, in fact, man is believed to be born with original sin. It is only without the notion of God that existence precedes essence and human beings can have full freedom. Then we choose our own identity and act to create ourselves.

Furthermore, to Sartre's mind, there is no reason for either humans or objects to exist. All forms of matter burgeon and blossom, multiply and proliferate to no purpose. Everything in existence is *de trop*, that is, pointless, unnecessary, excessive, superfluous. Matter has become self-conscious in humans only to realize the pointlessness of matter, which is the great cosmic joke.

But at least we are aware of the absurdity of our existence, and even though life itself makes no sense, we are able to invest life with purpose. "Before you come alive," Sartre wrote, "life is nothing; it's up to you to give it a meaning, and value is nothing else but the meaning you choose."

Our efforts to lead a meaningful life naturally produce conflict, for each person is striving to do the same, so Sartre devotes considerable space to describing how we stymie, block, and frustrate one another. In fact, in his play *No Exit* a character declares that hell is other people. Sartre feels we must learn to share our freedom with our fellow human beings. We are all in the same boat, trying to project meaning onto life, and we should not make our situation any worse than it is. We also have an obligation, Sartre maintains, to assume responsibility for what we do, because it has been freely chosen and constitutes ourselves. Our actions are not based on any ultimate values, for they do not exist, but we are still accountable to others for our decisions: we have "total responsibility in total solitude."

In fact, our responsibility is even greater than we imagine, because in choosing to become a particular type of person, we are also choosing for others. We are presenting a model for all humankind. "If I want to marry, to have children; even if this marriage depends solely on my own circumstances or passion or wish, I am involving all humanity in monogamy and not merely myself. Therefore, I am responsible for myself and for everyone else. I am creating a certain image of man of my own choosing. . . . [We] fashion an image [that is] valid for everybody and for our whole age."

To exist as a human being, then, meant to Sartre acting in good faith with a clear awareness of our existential condition. Our capacity for freely chosen acts must be engaged for the maximization of our being, and in acting, we should not interfere with other people's freedom or evade full responsibility for what we do. Without illusions, with a lucid recognition of our solitary state, we must decide on the meaning of our lives, thereby achieving an authentic existence.

Some Problems with the Existential Ethic

To begin with, critics often worry when reason is rejected and personal feelings are substituted. Having strong emotions about something is a dangerous standard for truth. As Bertrand Russell remarked, "[S]ubjective certainty is inversely proportional to objective certainty." In addition, the preoccupation with conditions such as anxiety, dread, forlornness, and alienation might border on the pathological. The existentialists claim they are revealing the psychological states that are endemic to the human condition, but perhaps they are merely reflecting their own, rather morbid personalities, jaded by two world wars.

The existentialists also carry the concept of freedom too far in claiming that people are wholly responsible for their lives. Common sense tells us that, to some extent, circumstances do affect what we become. Some people have diminished responsibility because they were raised in an awful environment or have disabilities that limit them. It also seems extreme to think that everything we do affects other people and therefore we are responsible for what they do.

The most important criticism of existentialism, however, centers on the idea that values are created, not discovered, and that an action becomes valuable by virtue of our choosing it. "All human activities are equivalent," Sartre wrote. "Thus it amounts to the same thing whether one gets drunk alone or is a leader of nations." But aren't some ways of living better than others, and can't we make bad choices? Aren't there richer and poorer types of lives?

More importantly, tyrants, dictators, despots, and mass murderers may have freely chosen their lives, but that hardly makes them worthwhile. Wrong actions cannot be made right by virtue of choosing them. In fact, the existentialists contradict themselves by recommending a life full of awareness and freedom; presumably, that is valuable.

Despite these criticisms, existentialism does challenge us to confront the basic terms of our lives and to decide how to exist. It enlivens us to the necessity for decisions and commitments, to the responsibility we bear for the person we become, and to our very ephemeral condition. In all of these ways it has a beneficial effect on our existence because it forces us to account for ourselves and to lead more intense and meaningful lives.

We will end with a passage from *The Myth of Sisyphus* by Albert Camus, a contemporary of Sartre, who expressed some of the insights of existentialism in a moving way.

> The gods had condemned Sisyphus to ceaselessly rolling a rock to the top of a mountain, whence the stone would fall back of its own weight. They had thought with some reason that there is no more dreadful punishment than futile and hopeless labor. . . .
>
> You have already grasped that Sisyphus is the absurd hero. He is as much through his passions as through his torture. His scorn of the gods, his hatred of death, and his passion for life won him that unspeakable penalty in which the whole being is exerted toward accomplishing nothing. . . . Myths are made for the imagination to breathe life into them. As for this myth, one sees merely the whole effort of a body straining to raise the huge stone, to roll it and push it up a slope a hundred times over. . . . At the very end of his long effort measured by skyless space and time without depth, the purpose is achieved. Then Sisyphus watches the stone rush down in a few moments toward that lower world whence he will have to push it up again toward the summit. He goes back down to the plain.
>
> It is during that return, that pause, that Sisyphus interests me. A face that toils so close to stone is already stone itself! I see that man going back down with a heavy yet measured step toward a torment of which he will never know the end. That hour like a breathing space which returns as surely as his suffering, that is the hour of consciousness. At each of those moments when he leaves the heights and gradually sinks toward the lairs of the gods, he is superior to his fate. He is stronger than his rock. . . .
>
> I leave Sisyphus at the foot of the mountain! One always finds one's burden again. But Sisyphus teaches the higher fidelity that negates the gods and raises

rocks. . . . [He] concludes that all is well. This universe henceforth without a master seems to him neither sterile nor futile. Each atom of that stone, each mineral flake of that night-filled mountain, in itself forms a world. The struggle itself toward the heights is enough to fill a man's heart. One must imagine Sisyphus happy.

CHAPTER SEVEN

Contemporary Trends

Figure 7.1. Mary Wollstonecraft, photograph of a stipple engraving by James Heath, ca. 1797, after a painting by John Opie. (Courtesy of the Library of Congress)

Fiddling with Words While the World Burns: Linguistic Philosophy

The twentieth-century movement of existentialism arose on the Continent and seems expressive of a European sensibility. Some commentators remarked that it was morbid, a blend of Nordic melancholy and Parisian pornography, that the French would not let sewers flow underground but had to rechannel them along the Champs-Élysées. In any case, it did not suit the Anglo American mind, which is more pragmatic, rational, and optimistic, a no-nonsense, can-do attitude. Existentialism seemed too speculative and romantic, good poetry but bad philosophy.

Rather than making pronouncements on how life should be lived, philosophers in Britain and America focused on more modest problems, those that could be solved, resolved, or dissolved through traditional tools of analysis. They focused on "meta-problems," problems that had to be addressed through the language in which philosophic issues were contained. Once the language was clarified, the issue could often be seen as not a real one at all, but a matter of semantics, of ambiguous words, vagueness, connotation, misleading grammar, and so forth.

For example, during the Middle Ages some theologians argued that atheism was impossible. One either believed something or one believed nothing, but in either case one was a believer. However, the linguistic philosopher dissected this argument as a verbal confusion. When a person believed nothing, the nothing was not the object of belief but the absence of belief; the person did not believe anything. The grammatical form gave the impression that nothing was a thing (as Parmenides pointed out).

Another instance where analysis deconstructed an argument is in the writings of John Stuart Mill. In making a case for happiness as the goal in life, Mill argued that if something is seen, it is visible; if it's heard, it's audible. Likewise, whatever is desired must be desirable. Happiness is desired by all humanity, which proves it is a desirable purpose in living.

However, if we analyze the language, we discover a flaw in the reasoning. "Visible" and "audible" mean what *is* seen and heard, whereas "desirable" refers to what is *worth* desiring. In that sense, people can want things that are not worth wanting—an addict craving drugs, an overweight person lusting after that candy bar. The syntactical similarity of "visible," "audible," and "desirable" makes it appear as though they behave the same way logically, when in fact they do not.

Likewise, if we think that because we have a word, it must represent something real, we commit a linguistic error. "Between," "since," and "then" do not refer to any objects, and "centaur" and "unicorn," "troll" and "elf," "fairy" and "dragon" are all labels for mythical creatures. (Nonbelievers wonder if "miracle," "revelation," "angel," and even "God" fall into the same category—words without a referent.)

Similarly, we must not think of the mind as a receptacle just because putting an idea in someone's head has the same grammatical form as putting marbles in a box (Gilbert Ryle's example). If we do, we are being misled by language into making a conceptual mistake, confusing figurative and literal meanings.

The twentieth-century philosophers who use this approach are not concerned with how we know, what is the best form of government, or whether there are standards of good art. They insist that we answer questions about language first, and once these questions are addressed, then we can see the issue more clearly. In many cases, the problem will vanish altogether, withering under the spell, and saving us a lot of trouble; that is, we may not have to erect a new structure on the cleared ground. Or as one linguistic philosopher put it, "Hercules was asked to clean out the Aegean stables; he wasn't asked to fill it up again."

Logical Positivism

This approach to philosophy first took the form of logical positivism, a movement popularized by an Englishman, A. J. Ayer. He imported the idea from Austria, where it was first proposed by the "Vienna Circle"—philosophers such as Rudolf Carnap, Otto Neurath, and Moritz Schlick.

In his seminal book *Language, Truth, and Logic* Ayer asks under what conditions a statement is meaningful. Some sentences make sense; others do not, even though they appear to do so. This was illustrated by C. L. Dodgson (Lewis Carroll), an Oxford logician and the author of *Alice in Wonderland*. In "The Jabberwocky" he writes

> 'Twas brillig, and the slithy toves
> Did gyre and gimble in the wabe;
> All mimsy were the borogroves,
> And the mome raths outgrabe

Although some of these words make sense (as shown in *The Annotated Alice*), most are nonsense words that sound convincing because of the grammatical structure. In the same way, some sentences appear to be meaningful, when in fact they are not. To separate the authentic from the bogus, we must use the "verification principle":

> A sentence is factually significant if, and only if, we know how to verify the proposition it purports to express—that is, if we know what observations would lead us to accept the proposition as true or reject it as false.

In other words, if a statement can be tested by our senses, then it is significant; otherwise it is a meaningless assertion masquerading as a meaningful one.

For example, G. W. F. Hegel, the nineteenth-century German idealist, wrote, "The Absolute enters into but is itself incapable of evolution and progress." This appears to make sense, but what is the Absolute, and what evidence would be relevant to its truth or falsity? Since nothing could count, the sentence is nonsensical, neither right nor wrong, but meaningless. The historian Oswald Spengler said the color of philosophy is brown, but how can this be proven? It is the same as "'Twas brillig, and the slithy toves"; it makes no sense to begin with, so to ask if it is correct is an inappropriate question.

Wielding this principle as a cleaver, Ayer dismissed all moral principles, such as "Take care of your ageing mother"; aesthetic expressions, such as "The music of Bartok is purple"; legal propositions, such as "People are innocent until proven guilty"; and religious claims that "God's in his heaven, all's right with the world." What proof would count for or against such assertions? Ayer asks. The poet Shelley wrote, "Life, like a dome of many colored glass, stains the white radiance of eternity," but this can't be verified using the color chart or the refraction of light. In fact, no sense evidence is applicable; therefore we are in the presence of nonsense.

But critics soon realized that propositions can make sense without being either true or false. One philosopher named Peter Strawson pointed out that the phrase "The king of France is bald" is meaningful, even though there is no present king of France, much less a bald one. More importantly, too much was being excluded. That is, a great deal that was worth saying was declared nonsense: the discourse of ethics, aesthetics, politics, and religion, for example, as well as history and literature. Furthermore, the "verification principle" itself does not satisfy the verification principle: it fails the test and has to be declared meaningless. The positivist was like a person who loses his or her keys on a dark road, then walks to a streetlight to look for them.

Because of such realizations, logical positivism was short-lived, although A. J. Ayer went on to professorships at the University of London and at Oxford. Like his compatriot, Bertrand Russell, he became a humanist and debated the Jesuit scholar Frederick Copleston, declaring that the proposition "God exists" is false, even though it is meaningless (sic!). He also speculated that "death may not be the end of me" . . . "though I continue to hope that it will be."

One anecdote about him is instructive. At age seventy-seven he attended a party in New York at which Mike Tyson was harassing a model. When Ayer intervened, Tyson said, "Do you know who I am? I'm the heavyweight champion of the world." Ayer replied, "And I am the former Wykeham Professor of Logic. We are both preeminent in our field. I suggest we talk about this as rational men." They then sat down to discuss the nature of harassment; presumably, it was a meaningful discussion.

Linguistic Analysis
When cracks began to appear in logical positivism, an alternative theory appeared called linguistic analysis, associated with the names Bertrand Russell (1872–1970), G. E. Moore (1873–1958), Ludwig Wittgenstein (1889–1951), Gilbert Ryle (1900–1976), J. L. Austin (1911–1960), Peter Strawson (1919–2000), R. M. Hare (1919–2002), and numerous others at "Oxbridge." They agreed with the positivists that most disagreements were not substantive but a misuse of language, and that philosophers should spend their time analyzing these verbal mistakes. As Wittgenstein put it, people must stop tracing round the picture frame; we should show the fly the way out of the fly bottle.

But rather than categorizing sentences as good sense or nonsense, the linguistic analysts had a more open-minded attitude. Sentences could be meaningful on various levels and need not be supported by empirical evidence alone. Problems in philosophy arose by confusing one type of language with another; conversely, they could be eliminated by separating the varieties of discourse and their distinctive modes of proof. Most, if not all, philosophic problems are pseudo-problems, rooted in the misuse of language. As Ludwig Wittgenstein remarked, "Philosophy is a battle against the bewitchment of our intelligence by means of language."

For example, when we refer to a good steak, a good deed, a good painting, a good time, a good job, a good profit, a good sleep, and good manners we use the term "good" in different senses. If we think that good candy is good for us, we mistakenly ignore the ambiguity. Or as C. S. Lewis remarked, if a man shoots his mother at one hundred yards, we would call him a good shot but not a good man.

Many linguistic distinctions can be made to avoid mistakes in thinking, for example:

- There is an "is" of equivalence ("Four is twice two"), an "is" of attribution ("A jaguar is fast"), and an existential "is" (God is). The ontological argument, which claims a perfect God must contain goodness, power, wisdom, and existence, confuses attribution and existence. We do not attribute existence to God if we say God is; we posit the existence of God with his attributes.

- We cannot buy a chunk of the equator; we cannot measure the size of happiness; our conscience does not have color, size, or texture; sunlight can't be swept away with a broom; and pi can't be cut into slices.
- All civil and criminal laws are enacted by legislators, but that does not mean the law of averages or the law of gravity must have a lawgiver. They are merely descriptions, not prescriptions, and do not require a cosmic legislator.
- If someone visits a college and is shown the library and student center, the classrooms, residences, faculty and students, and then asks, "But where is the college?" they have misunderstood the meaning of the term, placing it in the wrong category.
- The egoist, who thinks everyone is selfish, argues that people always do what they want to do, but that does not mean they never want to help others; that could be what they want to do.
- Does God answer all prayers? Theologians answer "of course" but say sometimes the answer is "no." However, this trades upon an ambiguity in the term "answer," which usually means giving people what they ask for.
- In *Alice in Wonderland* subtle questions are raised by the word play. For instance, the March Hare invites Alice to take some more tea. "I've had nothing yet," Alice replied in an offended tone, "so I can't take more." "You mean you can't take *less*," said the Hatter: "It's very easy to take *more* than nothing." To tease apart the tangle, we realize that "more" usually means something additional, although, of course, some tea is more than none.

Linguistic distinctions must also be made in more serious contexts, otherwise we end up making important conceptual errors. This is the task that linguistic analysis sets for itself: clarificatory analysis.

Some linguistic philosophers thought ordinary language was helpful, that a great deal of wisdom was contained in common speech. Philosophers can be too rarefied in their thinking, acting like hothouse flowers, when they should be grounded in everyday expression. For example, some philosophers have taken the skeptical view that our body is not real, but G. E. Moore responded, "Here is one hand, and here is another." Such realism is not naive, Moore asserted; people should not be talked out of their common sense.

J. L. Austin believed, in fact, that ordinary language contains all practical and useful distinctions.

Other analysts who identified with the "linguistic turn" in philosophy thought the philosopher's job was to clarify ordinary language and the errors rooted in it. Gilbert Ryle, for example, believed that people confuse one sort of sentence with another, religious with scientific, historical with poetic. This is a "category mistake," causing muddles and mischief.

Whether common speech is trustworthy or untrustworthy, each type of sentence must be separated into its proper logical category, and each must specify the type of proof appropriate to it. Empirical propositions may not be the only ones that are meaningful, but other sorts of statements must show in what way they, too, are meaningful, that is, the type of warrant behind their claims. They must demonstrate what would count for them and what would count against them, albeit in their own terms, otherwise they can be dismissed as nonsense.

To illustrate this, let's take a story contained in the book *New Essays in Philosophical Theology*. Two explorers tramping through a jungle come upon what might be a clearing. The first explorer says, "Some gardener must tend this plot." The second explorer says, "There isn't any gardener," thinking the land has always been a wilderness. So they pitch their tents and set watch, but no gardener ever appears. The second explorer says, "You see, there isn't any gardener," but the first explorer says, "There is a gardener but he is invisible."

So they set up a wire fence, which would reveal the presence of an invisible gardener, but the wire never moves. They electrify the fence, but no one ever shrieks. They patrol with bloodhounds, but the dogs never howl. At this point the second explorer declares, "Clearly, there isn't any gardener." But the first explorer persists. "There is a gardener, but he is invisible, intangible, and eternally elusive."

Exasperated, the second explorer then asks, "But how does an invisible, intangible, eternally elusive gardener differ from no gardener at all?"

The obvious analogy is to belief in God. If people say God exists, they must specify factors that would constitute proof and other factors that would count as disproof, at least, theoretically. These factors do not have to be empirical or scientific, but something must be relevant to confirm or deny the claim, otherwise it is meaningless. If nothing conceivable would apply to verify or falsify a statement, then it makes no sense.

Obviously various types of discourse will employ different kinds of proof, whether we say "The autumn foliage in New England is beautiful," "Alexander died young," or "Do not steal other people's property." After we categorize these utterances, each must account for itself. There are many mansions, but every construction must be well built.

Critics charge that this orientation to philosophy certainly has value but only modest value; it might even be judged frivolous in the light of real global problems. We are fiddling with words while the world burns. It is sanitized, fastidious philosophy, reminiscent of the priest in Ignazio Silone's *Bread and Wine* who remarked, "Good taste has always kept me from action."

Linguistic philosophers respond that they are qualified to do analytic work but have no special revelations that would qualify them to pontificate on worldly matters. They are more gardeners than botanists. However, philosophy has traditionally reflected on important questions, and some philosophers, such as Rousseau, Mill, and Sartre, have actively tried to have a significant effect. Karl Marx said that philosophers have tried to understand the world but the point is to change it. Linguistic philosophers, by contrast, focus on how thought and language interact, which is a relatively minor matter. For this reason, the linguistic approach is usually accepted as a preliminary activity, prior to doing "real" philosophy. Certainly the existentialists regarded it as trivial when faced with the urgent question of how best to live.

Some critics have even charged that language philosophers have focused exclusively on English as their model and have not engaged in linguistic comparisons across cultures. This seems arrogant, and it did not help when one analyst remarked, "If English was good enough for our Lord, it should be good enough for us."

Nevertheless, being precise about our language can yield benefits. An "accident" is bad luck, whereas a "mistake" is our fault; we cannot make an accident or have a mistake, and we can't excuse a mistake by calling it an accident. Commending is not the same as recommending, which means we can judge an action right but advise against doing it. For example, a mass murderer might deserve to be tortured to death, but as civilized people we should not inflict cruel and unusual punishment. Making such distinctions, therefore, can affect our decisions, but they do not move the earth.

The Voices of Women: Feminist Perspectives

Women have been noticeably absent from our survey of philosophy, mainly because few women philosophers have achieved prominence. This, in turn, is due to the fact that women have been discouraged from pursuing philosophy; abstract, logical, profound thought was considered the province of men. As one feminist put it, men regard women philosophers the way they do an elephant dancing: it's not that they do it well; it's only surprising they can do it at all.

Because of this suppression, philosophers have, by and large, been men, and as creatures of their male-centered cultures, many have ascribed a subordinate role to women. Here is Aristotle:

> It is fitting that a woman of a well-ordered life should consider that her husband's wishes are as laws appointed for her by divine will, along with the marriage state and the fortune she shares. If she endures them with patience and gentleness, she will rule her home with ease. . . . If through sickness or fault of judgment, his good fortune fails, then must she show her quality, encouraging him ever with words of cheer and yielding him obedience in all fitting ways—only let her do nothing base or unworthy. Let her refrain from all complaint, nor charge him with wrong, but rather attribute everything of this kind to sickness or ignorance or accidental errors. Therefore she will serve him more assiduously than if she had been a slave bought and taken home.

Plato took a sunnier view of women, arguing in *The Republic* that they are capable of the same responsibilities as men. Women's reproductive capacity should not preclude them from the military or from participation in government, any more than a female watchdog is exempt from work as a guardian. Likewise, John Stuart Mill in *The Subjection of Women* held that one sex should not be subordinated to another; there should be "a principle of perfect equality [with] no power or privilege on one side."

But whether they had dark or sunny opinions, philosophers have almost always been men—with conspicuous exceptions. Aspasia and Hypatia of Alexandra were exceptions in the sixth century BCE; so were the eighteenth-century thinkers Mary Astell, Catharine Macaulay, and Anne Louise Germaine de Staël, and nineteenth-century suffragists, such as Susan B. Anthony and Elizabeth Cady Stanton. During the nineteenth and twentieth centuries more women philosophers emerged from obscurity: Mary Wollstonecraft, Rosa Luxemburg, Hannah Arendt, Simone de Beauvoir, Susanne Langer, Simone Weil, Ayn Rand, G. E. M. Anscombe, Iris Murdoch, Philippa Foot, Martha Nussbaum, and so forth. Revisionist history has brought to light a number of women who were overlooked, not because of the quality of their thought, but because of their gender. It is time for "herstory" as well as history, "sheroes" along with heroes.

Mary Wollstonecraft (1759–1797) broke new ground for women, and she is often taken as the prototype of the female philosopher and feminist. Contrary to British society, she held that women were equal to men in rationality and only appeared inferior because they lacked education. She echoed Elizabeth Cady Stanton that women should regard themselves not as adjectives but as nouns. During her brief, tempestuous years she wrote novels, essays, a travel narrative, treatises, a children's book, and a history of the French Revolution. Her best-known work, A *Vindication of the Rights of Women*, argues for women's equality and rails against eighteenth-century notions of femininity.

In *Thoughts on the Education of Daughters* she advocates coeducation and instruction for girls "after the same model" as for boys. Girls should be educated as equals and treated as neither ornaments to society nor property traded in marriage. This book also contains autobiographical elements, with a chapter entitled "Unfortunate Situation of Females, Fashionably Educated, and Left Without a Fortune." These were Wollstonecraft's own circumstances, forcing her to work as a governess until she bravely launched herself as an author. In this she was supported by Samuel Johnson, the dictionary maker, as well as by good friends, such as Jane Arden and Fanny Blood. It was Fanny's death that prompted the novel *Mary: A Fiction*, an apparent alter ego.

Part of Wollstonecraft's appeal is her colorful, liberated, unconventional, and sometimes scandalous life. She had two passionate love affairs, one with a married man named Henri Fuseli, about whom she waxed lyrical: "the grandeur of his soul, that quickness of comprehension, and lovely sympathy." He broke it off when she proposed moving in with the couple. Even though it was to be a platonic relationship, he was nearly as appalled as his wife. The other affair was in France, with Gilbert Imlay, which produced an illegitimate daughter. Despite Wollstonecraft's renunciation of sex in *The Rights of Women*, it was apparently a torrid relationship, conducted in the midst of the French Revolution, when Louis XVI was guillotined and the Terror was at its height. When Imlay left her, she returned to England and tried to commit suicide (for the second time in her life) by throwing herself into the Thames. She walked about in torrential rain until her clothes were heavy, then jumped into the river; a passerby managed to rescue her.

She then married William Godwin, a seminal figure in the anarchist movement (who, ironically, had advocated the abolition of marriage), and gave birth to a daughter, Mary. This daughter became the future Mary Shelley, wife of the poet and author of *Frankenstein*. But there were complications with the birth, and Wollstonecraft died a few days later at the age of thirty-eight. In his *Memoirs* Godwin celebrated his wife, but the details of her life that he disclosed, her love affairs, illegitimate child, and suicide attempts, shocked the English and almost destroyed her literary reputation.

Although Wollstonecraft is regarded as a proto-feminist, she never fully embraced the equality of the sexes. She wrote, "Let it not be concluded that I wish to invert the order of things . . . men seem to be designed by Providence to attain a greater degree of virtue." Apparently she thought we are equal only before God. And though she attacked the aristocracy, she never completely transcended her bourgeois upbringing, recommending an education that would enable girls to join the middle class, "the most natural state." In contrast to most of today's feminists, she believed that women should be valued because they raise the nation's children.

Nevertheless, Wollstonecraft decried the treatment of women, who were not companions to their husbands, but wives, and were regarded as silly, sentimental, weak, and superficial, as "spaniels" and "toys." She thought that so many women were trapped in loveless marriages. Rousseau was one of her idols with his naturalism until he wrote in *Émile* that women should be educated for the pleasure of men. Above all else, she championed rationality, asserting that women should not fall "prey to their senses" or be enslaved by their form. "Taught from infancy that beauty is woman's scepter, the mind shapes itself to the body, and roaming round its gilt cage, only seeks to adorn its prison." Above all, women deserve the same rights as men, for although there are differences between the sexes, they have nothing to do with politics.

Feminist Thought
Wollstonecraft is an early feminist, and women who join the ranks of philosophers usually bring with them a feminist consciousness. Let's first look at the feminist position in terms of epistemology, theory of knowledge.

Feminists claim that gender affects our understanding in significant ways, and that philosophy thus far has been skewed toward the male perspective. Viewing matters through a female prism can affect the subject of our inquiry, the questions we ask, and the method we use to obtain knowledge; it can also determine what constitutes good evidence and which findings are valuable. The cognitive styles of women have often been dismissed, rendering their claims invalid and invisible, but a woman's criteria of proof is simply different, not worse; women's standpoint has equal authority.

A pivotal idea among feminists is that all knowledge is "situated," that is, relative to the perspective of the viewer. Everything we understand reflects the relation between the knower and the known; it is contextual and personal, not universal and objective. A chicken is surprised when its head is chopped off, but the chicken farmer is not. In the same way, men and women will regard the same object in different ways, depending on the attitudes, interests, and emotions of their gender. For example, a woman might see a house as home and family, whereas to a man it might represent a mortgage; and a woman might view a waterfall as beautiful, and a man as a source of hydroelectric power.

Feminists usually treat knowledge gained through personal experience as more reliable than any inferences gained secondhand, and these experiences are also interpreted according to one's background, assumptions, and worldview (*Weltanschauung*). Race, class, and gender, as well as status, age, occupation, ethnicity, sexual orientation, and so forth, determine our outlook, and none are objectively justified. Each of us is a living coalition that determines how we view reality. As Picasso remarked, perception must be relative, or there could not be a thousand paintings of a tree, or as the French say, if we all had the same taste, there would be only one sauce for the meat.

Gender in particular is highlighted by feminists as significant in our viewpoint on the world, and to them gender means a culturally assigned role for men or women, rather than the natural tendencies of our sex. From boyhood on males are encouraged to be physical, loud, cool, assertive, and athletic, to assume competitive jobs in business, sports, or the military. Females are socialized into being modest, neat, gentle, soft, and deferential, to aspire to nurturing tasks, such as teaching, housekeeping, or motherhood. Boys play rough-and-tumble games of dominance, while girls are encouraged to interact as caregivers. Boys are offered guns; girls flowers. Gender is therefore a social construct, while sexual identity is a biological matter of XX or XY chromosomes, of genitals, hormones, or reproductive organs. To feminists, there are no fixed traits of gender; instead, maleness and femaleness are fluid images based on our culture's ideals. Even the division of people into only two genders is a polarizing idea, an either/or, socially imposed.

The knowledge we acquire is connected to our gender situation. Even in academic research the gender of the investigator is relevant, because a woman in molecular biology might be interested in gene therapy for childhood diseases, not just the structure of RNA; a woman in psychology might trust the insights of her subjects rather than empirical data; and a female philosopher might not want to argue a theory in an adversarial way, but to teach through narratives, enabling people to empathize with a position. In terms of gender stereotypes, men are deductive, analytical, quantitative, and theoretical, whereas women are qualitative, holistic, contextual, and personal. G. K. Chesterton wrote, "A woman uses her intelligence to find reasons to support her intuitions"; men are more logical, while women are more often right. A woman's perspective, then, could radically change our knowledge, adding experiences that are differently perceived.

The notion of "situatedness" or "standpoint theory" is largely based on a European movement popular in the twentieth century called deconstruction or postmodernism. Associated with the names Foucault, Lacan, Derrida, Lyotard, and de Man, postmodernism theorizes that the mind cannot grasp things in themselves but understands only concepts as expressed in cultural language. We cannot get beyond these forms, one of which is the social construct of gender. Objective truth is beyond us because we are trapped in a web of language, reflecting a plurality of perspectives that are uncertain, ambiguous, and unstable.

Ethics is a second area of concern, where a woman's perspective has been slighted. In most traditional approaches, the emphasis has been on rights, obligations, and autonomy. The ethical theories of Plato, Mill, and Kant in particular apply broad principles and reasoned responses to moral issues. Their schemes are constructed in terms of maxims and obligations, strict deductions that are almost mathematical. Objective judgments are made as to what is worthwhile and what is worthless, and these judgments are tested and defended with evidence and argument.

Feminists charge that this is a characteristically male approach, in which principles, duties, and moral laws are all-important. But women are more concerned with "virtue," especially the values of caring, nurture, relationships, cooperation, love, community, openness, and trust.

Feminist ethics is based on more subtle and empathetic modes of understanding, not on rational systems of thought. Feminist philosophers prefer a collaborative attitude, hoping to reach a compromise on ethical differences so that all factions can agree. They want to resolve conflict in ways that take every party's interests into account. Ethics, they maintain, is not a matter of finding the right answer but one that everyone can live with. We all have a right to representation, so questions of who is correct pale beside the need for cooperative strategies.

Carol Gilligan, a developmental psychologist, has been an influential figure in the feminist movement, and her book *In a Different Voice* describes a more female-centered morality that is founded on caring, attachment to others, and personal connectedness. She writes,

> This conception of morality as concerned with the activity of care centers moral development around the understanding of . . . relationships, just as the conception of morality as fairness ties moral development to the understanding of rights and rules.

The difference in mentality has been characterized as follows: Men function competitively; women cooperatively. Men use logical arguments; women prefer their inner feelings. Men operate in terms of general rules; women, according to their experience. Men talk about their obligations; women, specific situations. Men want action based on good reasons; women want understanding in accordance with their insights. Men refer to principles; women to humane values that emerge from personal interaction. Men value culture; women nature. Men trust their minds; women their bodies. Men are driven by principles; women respond to situations. Men prefer the mechanical; women the organic. Men function in terms of heavenly excellence; women, earthly satisfaction.

Most feminist writers agree, rejecting the detached, impartial, cerebral ethic in favor of a subjective, emotional, personal approach that allows the free play of moral sentiments in particular situations. One feminist rejects objective principles, such as truth telling and promise keeping in favor of a situation-based compassion; another stresses the importance of birthing, caretaking, and family relations; and still another emphasizes the virtues of sympathy and compromise as particularly female approaches.

Caring and nurture are preeminent virtues in the feminist lexicon, especially the care of children, the old, the sick, the disabled, and the needy. We should respond to people's pain, evincing a sympathetic understanding based on feeling, not people's moral rights. Relationships are also celebrated, especially love and friendship, which can be more fulfilling between women. Lesbians point out that we fall in love with people, not their sex. We should be mutually supportive and interdependent, not independent, because our very humanness depends upon social interaction.

In both friendship and love we share intimate parts of ourselves, trusting the other not to take advantage of our vulnerability. Within the safe haven of friendship, we can expose our dreams, weaknesses, and shameful secrets, and find validation of ourselves through relationships. Men are more protective and defensive with one another, while women are open, responsive, and supportive. To men the display of emotion is often felt as weakness, whereas for women tears and embraces are socially acceptable. Women bond more easily, whereas men can feel compromised by dependence, which can lead to isolation. To feminists it is time to recognize and reward female attitudes in place of a male, principle-centered ethic.

An Evaluation
In terms of knowledge being "situated," the main criticism is that this means feminism itself reflects only the female viewpoint and cannot be judged as

objectively true. It is only a function of the attitudes, assumptions, and interests of women, who see the world from a disadvantaged perspective. If all knowledge is biased, why prefer the feminist bias? Women's experience has no greater claim than men's as a reference point for life's meaning.

In a sense, feminists cut off the limb on which they sit by denying that any claims are actually true, because that must include feminist claims. There may not be absolute certainty, but we do get to the moon, after all; reality does seem accessible to some extent.

While people's ideas are inflected by their background, nevertheless that does not imply our beliefs are determined; ideas might be accepted on their merits. And the fact that men may have had something to gain by understanding the world in a particular way does not mean they understood the world this way in order to gain something. Some feminists who are pro-women are anti-men, but an affirmation here need not mean a negation there. Ethicists have also raised questions about the "privileging" of emotion and personal experience and the rejection of moral rules and principles as male bias.

Although ethical theories have tended to neglect context and feeling, that oversight does not justify rejecting moral standards altogether. No matter how hard we focus on particular circumstances, the similarities between situations allow them to be grouped under common principles. And even extreme feminists want equal pay for equal work, suffrage for all citizens, rules against sexual harassment, and so forth. Furthermore, feminists want impartiality in the law to prevent discrimination, and consistency so civil rights are guaranteed for all people. Such standards may not be generated by emotion but by rational thought. In fact, the emotions can lead to intolerance and injustice. In short, moral principles seem an indispensable part of any ethical system, protecting people from unfair treatment.

When push comes to shove, feminists themselves want transcultural norms that condemn such practices as clitoral circumcision, pride killings, compulsory child marriage, the immolation of widows on their husband's funeral pyre, and the general subordination of women. They might want to endorse the UN's Universal Declaration of Human Rights, which specifies minimal standards for all human beings on earth. It includes the rights to life, liberty, and security of person; to family and a political voice; to peaceful assembly and religious expression; to work and the ownership of property; and to privacy, health, and education. It even states

> the peoples of the United Nations reaffirm their faith in fundamental human rights, in the dignity and worth of human persons and in the equal rights of men and women. . . .

Finally, gender roles may be more affected by a person's sex than feminists suggest. Research into brain function and behavior patterns show a biological as well as a social foundation for gender differences.

Although men and women score about the same on intelligence tests, men have larger brains (and not just proportionally) with more white matter, while women, with smaller brains, have more gray matter. This becomes significant because white matter gives men an advantage in spatial reasoning and the ability to focus more narrowly on abstract problems; it enables men to concentrate on work without as much mental interference. Furthermore, this brain difference causes men to analyze the world in terms of the rules governing events, and to do so in a more detached way.

A woman's brain, with more gray matter, densely packed with neurons and dendrites, processes information equally well, but in terms of contexts. For example, in finding a destination, women remember landmarks, while men remember the map, the layout of the roads. Women seem to have greater awareness of cues and subtle messages, the ability to infer other people's thoughts and feelings, and to perceive facets of situations and offer creative solutions to problems. The language centers in the brain are also more highly developed in women, allowing greater verbal fluency and reading comprehension, as well as the assimilation of foreign languages. Women perceive the nuances and ambiguities of conversation, the complexities of relationships, and meanings much more successfully than men.

Women's perceptual skills, therefore, have been called "intuitive," as opposed to men's "conceptual" skills, which are usually classified as logically sequential. In the simplistic formula, women empathize and men systematize.

In addition to the differences of spatial cognition versus empathetic understanding, the male Y chromosome stimulates the brain to develop extra "dopamine" neurons, responsible for motivation and rewards. These induce adventure seeking and risk taking, as well as make drug addiction more pleasurable. Women, on the other hand, are prone to depression, and the stress hormones are more difficult to turn off. Of the millions across the world who suffer from depression, two out of three are women.

The biological differences are extensive and heavily questioned, but if these findings are accurate, then the *behavioral* differences between the sexes can be explained, not just in terms of social influences, but in terms of genetic inheritance as well. This is borne out by numerous behavioral studies that cut across cultures, historical periods, developmental stages, and even species, thereby controlling for the effects of socialization.

In cross-cultural studies of play patterns, boys prefer tools and problem solving, gravitating to blocks and toy cars, taking things apart and putting them together, banging and throwing objects. Male infants even show a preference for mechanical mobiles over human faces. Among all primates, including human beings, young males engage in rough-and-tumble play much more commonly, in vigorous mock fighting and physical action aimed at domination. Across the spectrum of primates, females play at parenting most frequently, and in humans, a girl's fantasy play has to do with relationships, while boys imagine action and power. Males are more physically active from the time of infancy, and this becomes more pronounced with maturity. Boys have greater running speed and throwing skills: they are able to hurl objects farther and faster from age two. This seems related to upper body strength and differences in skeletal structure, which encourage such behavior. Girls are oriented toward faces and voices, maintain more eye contact, and react with greater empathy to the distress of others. Women speak more words than men and interact with others more frequently. They will attend to objects and their properties mainly in terms of consequences, and female-female competition takes the form of shunning, gossiping, excluding. Women's bodies are more flexible and age better, with superior small-motor coordination.

All these gender differences are heavily modified by cultural forces and vary between societies, but the differential seems significant, and some biological basis is difficult to deny. As with many social issues, it isn't a matter of either/or. Gender seems a product of nature as well as nurture, heredity times environment, and the interesting question is how much weight to assign to each. The research and the argument are ongoing, contaminated by politics, and we have yet to arrive at a definitive answer.

Current Moral Issues: Abortion and Racism

Our exploration of philosophy would not be complete if we neglected contemporary ethical issues that are hotly debated today—issues such as contraception and abortion, racism (including affirmative action), environmental pollution, global warming, euthanasia, cloning, capital punishment, war and terrorism, health care, animal rights, homosexuality, business ethics, and so forth. Philosophers have taken up these issues in what is called "applied ethics" and have contributed their analyses. The first two issues, abortion and racism, can be taken as representative.

Abortion
The abortion issue begins with our vocabulary: when women have an abortion, do they abort an embryo or an unborn child, living tissue that will

become a human being or a person who has a right to life? Obviously, more than semantics is at stake, because the label reflects our attitude about the nature of that organism and, to some extent, our judgment about abortion itself. By and large those in favor of a woman's right to choose prefer the term "embryo," while antiabortionists refer to the "unborn child." Deciding on vocabulary does not settle the abortion issue, but it does inform it in subtle and significant ways.

Are frozen embryos (now in the hundreds of thousands) actually frozen people? Should a pregnant woman count as two in the U.S. census? Should we celebrate a baby's birthday at three months? Should there be funerals for miscarriages (about 35 percent of all pregnancies)? Should we conduct therapeutic research on embryonic stem cells, or are they human subjects?

The root issue is whether a person is present in the womb (uterus). "Human being" is more of a biological classification, whereas "person" is a metaphysical category, with moral rights and legal protection. The issue, then, is what constitutes a person, and when in the gestation process does personhood begin.

The conservative and Catholic answer is "at the moment of conception." Unlike other stages of pregnancy, which are part of a continuum, here sperm and egg join to start a new organism. And this organism will not become a bear or kangaroo, but a person; therefore we can say that personhood begins at conception.

However, some philosophers challenge this reading because it confuses potentiality and actuality. In other words, what something will be is not what it is already. As mentioned previously, an acorn is not an oak and an egg is not a chicken, even though they possess the potentiality to become these things. To claim that potentiality is actuality requires a specialized argument based on the Aristotelian notion of a final cause. If someone has construction materials and hires an architect for the purpose of building a house, we cannot say that it is already a house, and if a boy presents his girlfriend with a seed packet, he is not giving her flowers, even if the seeds have germinated.

Implantation, which occurs between one and four weeks, is an alternative to the theory of personhood—the time when the embryo attaches itself to the wall of the uterus. Then, it is argued, the embryo is well on its way to full development. But although the embryo has a better chance of becoming a person, that does not mean it is a person at that point. Besides, one half is the embryo proper; the remainder becomes placenta.

Between two and four months body parts develop—buds for legs, arms, hands, and feet—and the reflexes of swallowing, kicking, and thumb sucking. Spontaneous movements occur, sometimes called quickening, in which the fetus nods its head and balls its fingers into a fist. Above all, a heartbeat can be detected. All these features suggest that a person is present, not just a mass of cells. In addition, a separate heartbeat indicates the fetus is not a part of the woman's body, but only dependent on it, as a parasite feeds off its host.

However, none of these features are distinctively human, much less characteristics of a person. If we want to define a zebra, it isn't enough to say it is warm-blooded and four-footed. We have to specify the attributes unique to zebras, qualities that separate zebras from other animals; this is what Aristotle called the differentia in addition to the genus. And not only is the fetus not differentiated from other mammals at this stage, but it has gill depressions, webbed feet, and a tail, and it subsequently develops fine white hairs over its entire body, called lanugo. This suggests our kinship with lower organisms and the evolutionary development of the species.

Some philosophers have proposed that a functioning brain is central to persons, and brain development takes place between five and six months. Rapid growth does not occur until eight months, and even then the fetus does not solve mathematical equations. This suggestion is reinforced by the Harvard definition of death as a flat electroencephalograph, that is, the point at which brain waves cease. It also coincides with the *Roe v. Wade* decision of the Supreme Court. According to this landmark case, a woman is entitled to an abortion during the first six months of pregnancy, which could imply that after that period a genuine person is present.

However, that might be a bit rigid, even though the Greeks generally thought of rationality as the hallmark of human beings. After all, some people fall below the threshold of human brain functioning, such as the mentally retarded or patients in comas; nevertheless, we regard them as persons.

Still another proposal is viability—the capacity to live independently outside the womb. This normally occurs at eight and a half to nine months, but there are premature births, with babies supported by incubators. However, dependence on an incubator is not independence, and it would be odd if personhood was a function of technology, that is, the sophistication of our incubators. Now it is as early as five months, but in the future perhaps it will be three months, or the gestation process could take place outside the woman's body altogether, in an artificial uterus. What's more, some people are not self-sufficient at age forty but depend on parents or spouses to survive; nevertheless, they are considered persons.

Some philosophers have suggested that, rather than looking for a unique characteristic, we should use a "clusters" approach. We could say, for example, that a person possesses reason, consciousness, emotion, volition, language, and self-awareness. Perhaps three out of six features would be sufficient to call an organism a person. But the fetus has none of those traits, so we are back to square one.

Throughout history defining "man" has been an intellectual enterprise, and almost everyone has had a crack at it. We have been labeled the political animal (Aristotle), the tool-making animal (Samuel Johnson), the religious animal (Edmund Burke), the social animal (John Locke), the animal that destroys its own kind (Thomas Hobbes), and the creature that consumes without producing (George Orwell). We are the bored or playful animal; we want to know; we laugh at ourselves; learn from our mistakes; eat when we aren't hungry, drink when we are not thirsty, and make love all year round. We are apes or angels (Benjamin Disraeli), heaven's masterpiece (Francis Quarles), nature's sole mistake (W. S. Gilbert), the beast that makes progress (Robert Browning), a bundle of contradictions (C. C. Colton), or the only creature that is ashamed of itself—or needs to be (Mark Twain).

How are we different than (other) animals? Whales possess intelligence, chimpanzees use sign language, elephants paint pictures, rats can laugh, most young animals play, and many species live in social and political groups. Bees, lions, and birds keep track of numbers and do basic arithmetic, which is useful in looking after eggs. In what way are we "poised between heaven and earth"?

In the light of the welter of choices and the debate over human being and person, the status of the fetus is unclear—which does not mean it is merely a collection of cells and that abortion is always permissible. The fetus is at least a potential person, so an abortion should be performed only for good reasons. Equally, we should not assume the fetus is a person from the outset and that abortion is murder, for the fetus does not exhibit any of the characteristics associated with persons, at least until the third trimester.

Reliable statistics on abortions are difficult to obtain, partly because the issue is so politicized, but probably 43 percent of American women have had abortions, which represents a decline since the 1980s, and in the United States, which has 5 percent of the world's population, 3 percent of the world's abortions are performed. There are virtually no elective abortions in the third trimester (partial-birth abortions). Some 90 percent occur during the first trimester; since the pain sensors have not developed, the fetus does not suffer.

The "Pro-Life" Arguments

Those who are opposed to abortion are mainly concerned about protecting the life of human beings or persons. They argue that the fetus is a person from conception onward, and that "Thou shalt not kill" is a fundamental rule (even though the Bible is silent on abortion per se). Some extend the principle to potential human life, vegetarians extend it to animals, and some Eastern religions to insects. In any case, a basic principle of civilization is the preservation of life, which usually means human life.

Although we sometimes feel justified in killing people, we treat those deaths as a justified response to wrongdoing, not as murder. We say that those people deserve to die because they have committed some heinous offense. We execute murderers, kill in self-defense, and fight wars when we are threatened by other nations. However, the "unborn child" is completely innocent. It has not done anything that would merit the death penalty, and therefore its life should be protected. Otherwise, we establish a precedent of killing those who are not guilty, which is a long slippery slope.

Not only should we not kill the innocent, but we also have a special obligation to support the weak, the vulnerable, and the helpless. Rather than taking advantage of our power, we have a moral duty to help those who cannot help themselves. In the same way, the unborn child is wholly reliant on its mother for life, and it would be immoral for her to destroy that infant who is wholly dependent on her. As a mother, her primary responsibility is to protect and nourish her baby. Adults safeguard children because they are stronger and have that responsibility.

Other arguments are less persuasive: that abortion will leave women with lifelong guilt (but that does not seem borne out by the evidence), and that abortion will be used as birth control (which is uncommon). Another argument is that abortion will encourage sexual activity before marriage, but a prior case must be made that sex before marriage is immoral. It was formerly argued that premarital sex is wrong because it can produce unwanted children, whereas here it is argued that we should not abort unwanted children, because it will lead to premarital sex. That is circular reasoning.

The "Pro-Choice" Response

Those on the other side of the controversy do not say abortion is a good thing but stress a woman's right to choose. The dispute is bitter and divisive because two significant, opposing values are at stake, freedom and life, although those who are pro-choice generally treat that life as a fetus rather than a child.

Since it is an important matter, the pro-choice faction usually specifies the conditions under which abortion is permissible. At the top of the list is danger to the mother's life or health if the pregnancy were to continue. In such circumstances it seems unreasonable to ask a woman to sacrifice herself, to die so her baby can live. Some Catholics believe that if there is a choice, the baby should be given preference, because the mother has had her chance at life and the baby has not. The mother's death is a "foreseen but unwilled side effect" of saving the child. However, the mother may have other children dependent on her, and she may have relationships within the social community. Furthermore, the father might be involved in the decision, and he would almost certainly choose his mate over his offspring. Above all, the woman has a right to protect her life and well-being; it is a matter of self-defense.

Another circumstance that might allow abortion is rape and/or incest. Rape is not consensual sex, but an act of violence, and a woman who becomes pregnant as a result of rape should not have to bear a child conceived in that way. Although the new life is innocent and could not help the circumstances of its conception, the woman should not be obliged to carry that life to term, especially since it could resemble the rapist. That is asking too much. As for incest, it can be pedophilia, and children are not able to give consent. In any case, there is a general abhorrence and a high risk of genetic abnormalities.

In a well-known article the philosopher Judith Jarvis Thomson uses an analogy to address the issue of whether preserving innocent life takes precedence over individual freedom:

> Let me ask you to imagine this. You wake up in the morning and find yourself back to back in bed with an unconscious violinist. A famous unconscious violinist. He has been found to have a fatal kidney ailment, and the Society of Music Lovers has canvassed all the available medical records and found that you alone have the right blood type to help. They have therefore kidnapped you, and last night the violinist's circulatory system was plugged into yours, so that your kidneys can be used to extract poisons from his blood as well as your own. The director of the hospital now tells you, "Look, we're sorry the Society of Music Lovers did this to you—we would never have permitted it if we had known. But still, they did it, and the violinist now is plugged into you. To unplug you would be to kill him. But never mind: it's only for nine months. By then he will have recovered from his ailment, and can safely be unplugged from you." Is it morally incumbent on you to accede to this situation? No doubt it would be very nice of you if you did, a great kindness. But do you *have* to accede to it?

Obviously, this is a rhetorical question. Thomson is using an analogy to illustrate that freedom has a higher value than life, even the life of an innocent person, especially in situations where there is no initial choice.

A third circumstance justifying abortion is when the child is diagnosed as having severe mental or physical defects. Suppose that, through imaging technology or amniocentesis, the fetus is diagnosed with anencephaly, a condition in which only the brain stem is functioning and most of the skull is missing; or suppose trisomy is detected, a chromosome abnormality with severe mental retardation and birth defects; or Tay-Sachs disease, a progressive disorder of the nervous system that causes brain damage, blindness, deafness, and death in early childhood. These are often considered good reasons for abortion. Other abnormalities are borderline, such as dwarfism, mongolism, and cystic fibrosis, although the impact on the rest of the family should be considered. But in the most serious cases the choice seems clear-cut. Quality of life must be evaluated, as well as life itself, and if that quality is minimal, then it is argued that abortion should be allowed, perhaps morally required.

Various other circumstances are debatable, for example, if the family is struggling financially, and is without adequate food, shelter, money, or time for another child; if the household has a number of children already and the parents cannot handle any more psychologically; if the mother is handicapped, an alcoholic, or a drug addict; in cases of early teenage pregnancy where a child would be raising a child; or in cases of overpopulation, such as in China, which enacted a law allowing one child per family. The most liberal position, of course, is "abortion on demand," where a woman does not need to justify herself but claims abortion as a legal and moral entitlement.

Philosophers have not settled the issue, but they have added light instead of more heat, making useful distinctions, citing values, and improving the reasoning process. When reason goes against people, people go against reason, but life and death matters require our best thinking.

Racism
Americans often feel apologetic, even ashamed, about the country's history of racism, beginning with slavery and continuing with institutional and personal discrimination. As a legacy, blacks are three times more likely to be poor (one out of three blacks but one out of nine whites), black family income is 55 percent that of whites, the median wealth of white households is ten times that of blacks, and unemployment is generally twice as high among blacks (in the inner city, black unemployment exceeds 40 percent). What's more, blacks are clustered in low-paying, low-prestige, dead-end work, whereas whites dominate in more desirable occupations—management, the professions, and technical fields. Only 1.5 percent of lawyers are black, 2 percent of engineers, and 3 percent of scientists and executives, even though blacks constitute 12 percent of the population.

Some people argue that blacks have themselves to blame for their situation. The Civil War ended in 1865, and with Emancipation, blacks had the same freedom to succeed as other groups. The Italians, Jews, Irish, Greeks, and Poles, and more recently, Latinos and Asians, immigrated to the United States, integrated into the society, and achieved success. Blacks, by contrast, have remained in the underclass, which suggests lack of motivation and effort, crying victim instead of working to achieve the American dream.

Perhaps blacks are partly responsible for their condition, but the prejudice and discrimination endemic to our culture have not allowed blacks the same opportunity for achievement. Furthermore, no other group began as slaves with broken families, little education, and even less wealth. With Emancipation we eliminated slavery, but it is difficult to eliminate slaves. To build motivation, there must be support, and that has been sadly lacking. As Lyndon Johnson said, "You do not take a man who for years has been hobbled by chains, liberate him, bring him to the starting line of a race, saying, 'You are free to compete with all the others.'"

In short, we have been a racist country, meaning by "racism" both prejudice and discrimination. Prejudice means a derogatory attitude; discrimination, harmful action directed at a person based on their membership in a group regarded as inferior. The same distinctions apply to gender, sexual orientation, religion, ethnicity, handicap, and even to looks. This raises a philosophic question: is it legitimate to classify individuals at all, or is this stereotyping and profiling? We do identify and generalize about makes of cars (Hondas, Fords, Nissans), and trees (elms, birches, oaks); we say giraffes are tall, circles are round, diamonds are hard, and green plants form starch in the presence of light. In fact, unless we generalize, we never achieve knowledge at all. But should every human being be regarded as an individual and not categorized?

This is a delicate question. It seems common sense for a security guard at an airport to be more suspicious of a man from Saudi Arabia than an old lady from Iowa, for although not all Arabs are terrorists, almost all terrorists are Arabs. In the same way, a police officer might regard a black teenager as potentially more dangerous because he knows that young blacks are seven times more likely to commit crimes, that blacks are incarcerated at a rate eight times higher than whites, making up over half the prison population (of two and a half million), and that 45 percent of those on death row are black. Is it racism to generalize based on those statistics?

Car insurance companies give lower rates to women than men, to older drivers over younger ones, because those populations are involved in fewer accidents. Supported by facts, the judgments seem fair. Why not, then, have the police stop motorists more frequently for "driving while black"?

In the same way, we identify national types and say, "Americans are friendly," "The French have good taste," "The Chinese are industrious" (in terms of productivity), and "Italians like pasta" (based on per capita consumption). We mean to say that these characteristics hold true of the group as a whole, while not being true of each and every member. In 2010 the citizens of fourteen nations were identified for "enhanced screening" for originating from terrorist nations, which smacks of profiling. But the field of sociology is based on categorizing people as Democrats, left-handers, Presbyterians, senior citizens, and so forth, and on describing their behavior accordingly. Market researchers do the same. Is all this unfair?

Perhaps the answer is that, insofar as possible, we should treat people as individuals. We cannot help generalizing to some extent, but it should be minimized, and stereotyping should be avoided altogether, that is, having an oversimplified picture, reinforced through selective perception. All human beings share traits in common, but at the same time no person can be duplicated, and each individual's uniqueness should be recognized. We must make an effort not to prejudge, but to regard people in terms of their individual merits.

Bias in the criminal justice system accounts for some of these statistics, even allowing for a higher crime rate among blacks. For example, although 14 percent of drug users are black, 37 percent of those arrested for drug offenses are black.

Race is a questionable category in any case because, as anthropologists have pointed out, there are greater differences within races than between them. Nevertheless, race is taken into account when doctors decide on the most effective medical treatment for racial groups, and when pharmaceutical companies target medications for African Americans. For example, a heart-failure drug was recently approved by the FDA as effective for blacks. This implies that race has a genetic basis. Social scientists have been reluctant to deal with biological differences, treating the topic as forbidden knowledge, because it could lead to rating races in terms of innate abilities, say in athletics, mathematics, and the arts, and in terms of general intelligence. The picture is unclear, but we do know that when individuals are *perceived* as black, then prejudice and discrimination often follow.

In 1961 President John Kennedy initiated an affirmative action policy as a remedy for racism in America, stating that we must "take affirmative action" to ensure that hiring and employment practices are free of racial bias. This policy was extended in 1964 by President Lyndon Johnson in the Civil

Rights Act, which prohibited discrimination based on race, color, religion, or national origin. Businesses and educational institutions were required to set goals and timetables for increasing participation by blacks, to actively recruit minority candidates.

The Supreme Court further defined the law, especially in two cases involving universities: in 1978, *Regents of the University of California v. Bakke*, and in 2003, *Gratz v. Bollinger*, which involved the University of Michigan. Allan Bakke, a white applicant to the University of California, Davis, School of Medicine, claimed he was denied equal protection under the law because he had been rejected for admission while a less qualified black applicant had been accepted. The court found in his favor, ruling that quotas, percentages, and set-asides are unconstitutional. However, the justices also said that race "can be a legitimate factor" in the admissions process.

Further clarification was made in the *Gratz* case, which involved similar circumstances. Although the justices agreed with the plaintiff, they declared "race can be a plus factor in admission." Michigan had simply been too "mechanistic" in awarding twenty points to black candidates (of the one hundred points needed for admission), and by crafting its policy too narrowly, the university had violated the Fourteenth Amendment. Nevertheless, diversity remained an educational value. As one of the justices, Sandra Day O'Connor, wrote

> Student body diversity is a compelling state interest that can justify the use of race in university admissions. . . . [There are] many possible bases for diversity admissions but we have a special commitment to racial and ethnic diversity . . . groups which have been historically discriminated against. Race cannot be a decisive criterion for admission but it is a legitimate factor.

Nevertheless, several states, including California, Florida, and Washington, now refuse to consider race at all for entrance to universities or for positions in business. This is the attitude of many Americans, who maintain that merit alone should govern our decisions. Otherwise, we are judging people according to race, practicing reverse discrimination toward whites, and making color a prominent factor, instead of being color-blind. For those who have achieved success through hard work, it is unfair to be denied entry simply because they happen to be born white, and it is equally unjust for blacks to be given preference because of their inherited skin color. We do not solve economic problems through racial means. The white coal miner's son deserves the same chance as the black doctor's daughter.

Opponents of affirmative action also deny the concept of "collective guilt," arguing that an entire race cannot be held accountable for the actions of some members. Besides, whites of the present generation were not slave owners, in fact, they may be recent immigrants, and blacks of the current generation were not born slaves. By operating in terms of racial preferences, we are burdening those who are not responsible for slavery, and benefiting those who did not suffer under it.

Therefore, educational institutions and business organizations should choose the best qualified applicants, otherwise the system is unfair. Those who have earned a place, who are the most deserving, should be selected. When we need an operation, we want a highly skilled surgeon, not one who attended medical school under affirmative action, and we want to drive across bridges that were built by qualified engineers, not those admitted to engineering school because they were black.

But the supporters of affirmative action think differently. Blacks are not as qualified for admission because of past discrimination, just as whites are more qualified because of past privileges. To insist on merit is to maintain the status quo. Blacks must be given priority in order to raise the race as a whole, to provide role models that can inspire the young. We should therefore admit blacks who are less qualified, not unqualified, and provide support systems so they can catch up; we do not want to set people up for failure. And since blacks are entering management positions later, it is inherently discriminatory to apply the principle of "last hired, first fired."

The point is that blacks and whites are not starting even, so fairness dictates that whites be handicapped, just as we impose handicaps on superior competitors in golf, horse racing, or sailing in order to make the chances of success more equal. As for collective guilt, whites have enjoyed advantages in our society in the past, as they will in the future, and to give blacks an edge at this point seems reasonable. It is not so much compensation for historical injustices as an attempt to balance out the good and the harm that have accrued now.

Besides, we live in an increasingly multicultural society, so colleges should prepare students to interact with different peoples. Diversity enriches education itself through varied perspectives in the classroom, the world in miniature, and global awareness should be part of a college's mission. Businesses, too, might thrive with a diverse workforce that can relate to a customer base that is multicultural, so being a member of a minority group might be a qualification for employment. Rather than decreasing efficiency, diversity could enhance communication and profitability. A police force in a heavily black area might be more effective if several of the officers were black, especially in community policing.

In some ways, the debate comes down to individual rights versus the general good. People should get what they deserve, which implies they should be rewarded for their achievements; merit should operate in admission and employment. On the other hand, for the sake of social justice, people should be able to compete evenly, and that means giving blacks preference, compensating them for their disadvantages. In that way the cycle will be broken.

Again, philosophy does not settle the issue but illuminates it so that an informed and rational decision can be made.

Epilogue
As we have seen, philosophy offers a pageant of ideas, some profound, some bizarre, some arresting, but all demanding a decision. In many ways the journey through philosophy is delightful, filled with intriguing notions and elegant reasoning, but in the end we must evaluate the theories, not just grasp them—theories about what is real and how we can know, what is human nature and how we should live, and whether our existence has any meaning. We are asked to reflect on right and wrong, the ideal form of government, justice and injustice, and on the presence or absence of a divine being.

These are critical questions that each of us must answer for ourselves, using our clearest, subtlest, and most insightful analysis. Once we are aware of the options, that is, what the philosophers have to say, and can judge their claims according to canons of rationality, we are in a better position to reach sound conclusions.

Overall, a standard of *reasonableness* should govern our decisions. A theory that contradicts itself is less reliable than one that is consistent, and having a foundation in facts and a valid interpretation of experience are critically important.

We cannot be self-contradictory, claiming that something is and something isn't at the same time. We cannot, for example, talk about a square circle or the larger half; say that all generalizations are false, which is itself a generalization; or assert that there's an exception to every rule, which, of course, must have an exception. A self-contradiction makes no sense, while a consistent theory is at least plausible. In addition, the relevant facts must be considered, and to omit them is a defect. For example, there is no factual basis for claiming that fate or destiny rules our lives, even though it may reassure us when we are in danger. Similarly, if an uneducated slave boy can produce the Pythagorean theory, that should not be interpreted as proving innate knowledge, but only innate intelligence.

The conclusions we reach are a blend of the subjective and objective: what we can accept personally with good reasons for accepting it. On the one hand, we want to avoid wishful thinking, believing whatever is comforting, and on the other, feeling forced to admit what we cannot refute. Common sense should modify abstract thinking, while at the same time we should recognize that reality may not resemble our ordinary view of the world. Science certainly offers a very different picture of reality.

In short, we need to test our ideas in the light of reason, not accepting things at face value, and this is what the tortoise taught us. We must think carefully about questions that matter and not believe ideas simply because they are conventional. Our lives should be founded on truth, not illusion, and that means hard philosophic thinking.

Notes

Chapter 1
4. Herodotus, *The Histories*, trans. C.E. Godley (University of Oxford Press, 1998).
10. A. H. Coxon, *The Fragments of Parmenides*, trans. Rex Warner (Las Vegas: Parmenides Publishing, 2009).
14. Laertius Diogenes, *Lives of Eminent Philosophers*, trans. R. D. Hicks (Cambridge, MA: Harvard University Press, 1925).
14. Thucydides, *The Peloponnesian War*, trans. Martin Hammond (New York: Oxford University Press, 2009).
22. Plato, *The Apology*, trans. Benjamin Jowett (New York: Oxford University Press, 1891).

Chapter 2
35. Plato, *The Republic*, trans. Benjamin Jowett (New York: Oxford University Press, 1891).
38. Bertrand Russell, *A History of Western Philosophy* (New York: Simon and Schuster, 1945).
41. Aristotle, *Nicomachean Ethics*, trans. W. D. Ross (New York: Oxford University Press, 1925).
48. Epictetus, *The Handbook*, trans. Nicholas White (Indianapolis, IN: Hackett Publishing Co., 1983).
52. Boethius, *The Consolation of Philosophy*, trans. W.V. Cooper (London: J. M. Dent, 1902).

Chapter 3
61–62. Mary Clark, *An Aquinas Reader* (New York: Fordham University Press, 2000).
69–70. *King James Bible*, ed. Stephen Pinkett and Robert Carroll (New York: Oxford University Press, 1908).
79–80. Fedor Dostoevsky, *The Brothers Karamazov*, trans. Constance Garnett (New York: W. W. Norton, 1976).

Chapter 4
81. Bertrand Russell, *A History of Western Philosophy* (New York: Simon and Schuster, 1945).
86. René Descartes, *Meditations on First Philosophy*, trans. J. Cottingham (Cambridge: Cambridge University Press, 1996).
87. Descartes, *Meditations on First Philosophy*, trans. J. Cottingham.
92. Oscar Wilde, *The Picture of Dorian Gray* (New York: Oxford University Press, 2006).
93. John Donne, *Meditation XVII in The Major Works* (New York: Oxford University Press, 2000).
98. Thomas Hobbes, *Leviathan*, Project Gutenberg e-book, 2002.
102. Jean Jacques Rousseau, "The Confessions" in *The Collected Writings of Rousseau*, trans. Christopher Kelly (Hanover, NH: Dartmouth College Press, 1995).
102–103. *Writings and Speeches of Edmund Burke*, ed. P. Langford (Clarendon Press, 1981).

Chapter 5
119. Langford Reed, *The Complete Limerick Book* (New York: Putnam, 1924).
119. George Berkeley, *Principles of Human Knowledge* (Forgotten Books, 1957).
121. David Hume, *Essays, Moral, Political, Literary*, ed. Eugene Miller (Indianapolis, IN: Liberty Classics, 1985).
122. Hume, *Essays, Moral, Political, Literary*, ed. Eugene Miller.
125. Adam Smith, *The Correspondence of Adam Smith*. ed. E. C. Massner and Ian Simpson Ross (New York: Oxford University Press, 1976).
130. Hume, *Essays, Moral, Political, Literary*, ed. Eugene Miller.

Chapter 6
133. Manfred Kuehn, *Kant: A Biography* (Cambridge: Cambridge University Press, 2001).
140. I. Kant, *Lectures on Ethics*, trans. Louis Infield (Indianapolis, IN: Hackett, 1963).
144–145. J. S. Mill, "On Liberty" in *Collected Works of John Stuart Mill* (Toronto: Toronto University Press, 1963).
145. Patrick Devlin, *The Enforcement of Morals* (New York: Oxford University Press, 1965).

158–159. A. Camus, *The Myth of Sisyphus and Other Essays*, trans. Justin O'Brien (New York: Knopf, 1955).

Chapter 7

169. Aristotle, *The Politics* (New York: Oxford University Press, 1995–1999).

173. Carol Gilligan, *In a Different Voice* (Cambridge, MA: Harvard University Press, 1982).

185. R. Wasserstrom, ed., *Today's Moral Problems* (New York: Macmillan, 1975).

Selected Bibliography

Chapter 1
Barnes, Jonathan. *The Presocratic Philosophers*. London and New York: Routledge, Taylor and Francis, 1982.
Burnet, John. *Early Greek Philosophy*. New York: The Meridian Library, 1957.
Diogenes, Laertius. *Lives of Eminent Philosophers*. Translated by C. D. Yonge. Whitefish, MT: Kessinger Publishing, 2006.
Guthrie, W. K. C. *Socrates*. Cambridge: Cambridge University Press, 1972.
Herodotus. *Histories*. Translated by A. D. Godley. Cambridge, MA: Harvard University Press, 1920.
Kirk, G. S., and J. E. Raven. *The Presocratic Philosophers*. Cambridge: Cambridge University Press, 1957.
Luce, J. V. *An Introduction to Greek Philosophy*. London: Thames and Hudson, 1992.
Popper, Karl. *The World of Parmenides*. London and New York: Routledge, 1998.
Salmon, Wesley. *Zeno's Paradoxes*. Bloomington: Indiana University Press, 1970.
Taylor, A. E. *Socrates*. New York: Doubleday, 1953.
Taylor, C. C. W., R. M. Hare, and J. Barnes. *Greek Philosophers—Socrates, Plato, and Aristotle*. New York: Oxford University Press, 1998.
Vlastos, G., ed. *The Philosophy of Socrates*. Garden City, NY: Anchor Books, 1971.

Chapter 2
Bakalis, Nikolaos. *Handbook of Greek Philosophy*. Bloomington, IN: Trafford Publishing, 2005.
Barnes, Jonathan, ed. *The Complete Works of Aristotle*. Princeton, NJ: Princeton University Press, 1995.

Brennan, Tad. *The Stoic Life*. New York: Oxford University Press, 2006.
Field, G. C. *The Philosophy of Plato*. New York: Oxford University Press, 1969.
Foot, P. *Virtues and Vices*. Oxford: Blackwell, 1978.
Guthrie, W. K. C. *A History of Greek Philosophy*. Cambridge: Cambridge University Press, 1986.
Hamilton, E., and Huntington Cairns, eds. *The Collected Dialogues of Plato*. Princeton, NJ: Princeton University Press, 1961.
Hicks, Robert D. *Stoic and Epicurean*. New York: Russell and Russell, 1962.
Irwin, T. *Plato's Ethics*. New York: Oxford University Press, 1995.
Mason, Andrew, and Theodore Scaltsas, eds. *The Philosophy of Epictetus*. New York: Oxford University Press, 2007.
Ross, W. D. *Aristotle*. New York: Oxford University Press, 1955.
———. *Plato's Theory of Ideas*. Oxford: Clarendon Press, 1951.
Sellars, John. *Stoicism*. Chesham, UK, and Berkeley: University of California Press, 2006.
Shorey, P. *What Plato Said*. Chicago: University of Chicago Press, 1933.
Taylor, A. E. *Plato: The Man and His Work*. New York: Courier Dover Publications, 2001.
Veatch, Henry. *Aristotle: A Contemporary Appreciation*. Bloomington: Indiana University Press, 1974.
Vlastos, Gregory. *Plato's Universe*. Las Vegas: Parmenides Publishing, 2006.

Chapter 3

Adams, Marilyn M., and Robert M. Adams, eds. *The Problem of Evil*. New York: Oxford University Press, 1990.
Burill, D., ed. *The Cosmological Argument*. New York: Doubleday, 1967.
Copleston, Frederick. *Aquinas: An Introduction*. New York: Penguin Books, 1991.
Davies, Brian. *The Thought of Thomas Aquinas*. New York: Oxford University Press, 1993.
Helm, Paul. *John Calvin's Ideas*. New York: Oxford University Press, 2004.
Hick, John. *Evil and the God of Love*. New York: Harper and Row, 1966.
Larrimore, Mark, ed. *The Problem of Evil*. Oxford: Blackwell, 2001.
Lewis, C. S. *The Four Loves*. Fount, 2002.
Lull, Timothy, ed. *Martin Luther: Basic Theological Writings*. Minneapolis: Fortress, 1989.
McPherson, Thomas. *The Design Argument*. New York: Macmillan, 1972.
Oord, T. J. *The Altruism Reader*. West Conshohocken, PA: Templeton Foundation Press, 2008.
Oppy, Graham. *Ontological Arguments and Belief in God*. Cambridge: Cambridge University Press, 1995.
Stump, Eleanor. *Aquinas*. New York: Routledge, 2003.
Swinburne, Richard. *The Existence of God*. Oxford: Clarendon Press, 1991.

Chapter 4
Beck, L. J. *The Method of Descartes*. Oxford: Clarendon Press, 1952.
Chappell, Vere. *Descartes's Meditations*. Lanham, MD: Rowman and Littlefield, 1997.
Cottingham, J., ed. *The Cambridge Companion to Descartes*. Cambridge: Cambridge University Press, 1992.
Dent, Nicholas. *Rousseau*. New York: Routledge, 1992.
Gale, Richard M. *The Blackwell Guide to Metaphysics*. Oxford: Blackwell, 2002.
Gankroger, Stephen. *Descartes: An Intellectual Biography*. New York: Oxford University Press, 1995.
Garber, Dennis, and Michael Ayers. *The Cambridge History of Seventeenth Century Philosophy*. Cambridge: Cambridge University Press, 1998.
Gauthier, David. *Rousseau: The Sentiment of Existence*. Cambridge: Cambridge University Press, 2006.
Lowe, E. J. *A Survey of Metaphysics*. New York: Oxford University Press, 2002.
Malcolm, Noel. *Aspects of Hobbes*. New York: Oxford University Press, 2002.
Robinson, Dave, and Judy Groves. *Introducing Political Philosophy*. Cambridge: Icon Books, 2003.
Sorrell, Tom. *Descartes*. New York: Oxford University Press, 1987.
Strauss, Leo. *The Political Philosophy of Hobbes*. Oxford: Clarendon Press, 1936.
Wokler, Robert. *Rousseau*. New York: Oxford University Press, 1995.

Chapter 5
Atherton, Margaret, ed. *The Empiricists: Critical Essays on Locke, Berkeley, and Hume*. Lanham, MD: Rowman and Littlefield, 1999.
Bennett, J. *Locke, Berkeley, Hume: Central Themes*. Oxford: Clarendon Press, 1971.
Berkeley, George. *The Works of George Berkeley, Bishop of Cloyne*. Edited by A. A. Luce and T. E. Jessop. London: Thomas Nelson, 1948–1957.
Dancy, Jonathan. *Berkeley*. New York: Oxford University Press, 1987.
Flew, Anthony. *David Hume: Philosopher of Moral Science*. Oxford: Blackwell, 1986.
Hume, David. *An Enquiry Concerning Human Understanding*. Selby-Bigge, L. A., ed. New York: Oxford University Press, 1979.
Mossner, E. C. *The Life of David Hume*. New York: Oxford University Press, 2001.
Norton, David. *David Hume: Common Sense Moralist*. Princeton, NJ: Princeton University Press, 1985.
Pappas, G. S. *Berkeley's Thought*. Ithaca, NY: Cornell University Press, 2000.
Smith, Norman Kemp. *The Philosophy of David Hume*. New York: Macmillan, 1941.
Stroud, B. *Hume*. London: Routledge, 1977.
Winkler, K. P. *Berkeley: An Interpretation*. Oxford: Clarendon Press, 1989.

Chapter 6
Acton, Harry. *Kant's Moral Philosophy*. New York: Macmillan, 1970.
Barrett, William. *Irrational Man: A Study of Existential Philosophy*. New York: Doubleday, 1962.

Bree, Germaine. *Camus*. New Brunswick, NJ: Rutgers University Press, 1959.
Broad, C. D. *Kant: An Introduction*. Cambridge: Cambridge University Press, 1978.
Crisp, Roger. *Mill on Utilitarianism*. London and New York: Routledge, 1997.
Kaufmann, Walter. *Existentialism from Dostoevsky to Sartre*. New York: Meridian Books, 1968.
Kierner, George C. *Three Philosophical Moralists: Mill, Kant, and Sartre*. New York: Oxford University Press, 1990.
Lyons, D. *Forms and Limits of Utilitarianism*. Oxford: Clarendon Press, 1965.
Paton, H. J. *The Categorical Imperative*. Philadelphia: University of Pennsylvania Press, 1971.
Plamenatz, J. *The English Utilitarians*. New York: Oxford University Press, 1949.
Rosen, Frederick. *Classical Utilitarianism from Hume to Mill*. London and New York: Routledge, 2003.
Ross, W. D. *Kant's Ethical Theory*. Oxford: Clarendon Press, 1954.
Schilpp, Paul Arthur, ed. *The Philosophy of Jean-Paul Sartre*. La Salle, IL: Open Court, 1981.
Smart, J., and B. Williams. *Utilitarianism: For and Against*. Cambridge: Cambridge University Press, 2002.
Taylor, Charles. *The Ethics of Authenticity*. Cambridge, MA: Harvard University Press, 1991.
Warnock, M. *Existential Ethics*. New York: Macmillan, 1967.
Watson, John. *Hedonistic Theories from Aristippus to Spencer*. Glasgow: John Maclehose, 1896.
Wood, Allen. *Kant's Ethical Thought*. Cambridge: Cambridge University Press, 1999.

Chapter 7

Baird, Robert M., and Stuart E. Rosenbaum, eds. *The Ethics of Abortion: Pro-Life vs. Pro-Choice*. Buffalo, NY: Prometheus Press, 1989.
Beckwith, Francis J., and Todd E. Jones, eds. *Affirmative Action: Social Justice or Reverse Discrimination?* Amherst, NY: Prometheus Press, 1997.
Boonin, David. *A Defense of Abortion*. Cambridge: Cambridge University Press, 2003.
Cahn, Steven, ed. *The Affirmative Action Debate*. New York: Routledge, 2002.
Callahan, Daniel. *Abortion, Law, Choice, and Morality*. New York: Macmillan, 1970.
de Beauvoir, Simone. *The Second Sex*. New York: Vintage Books, 1973.
Feagin, Joe. *Systemic Racism*. New York: Routledge, 2006.
Feinberg, Joel, ed. *The Problem of Abortion*. Belmont, CA: Wadsworth, 1984.
Gatens, M. *Feminism and Philosophy*. Bloomington: Indiana University Press, 1990.
Greer, Germaine. *The Female Eunuch*. New York: HarperCollins, 1970.
Lewis, David Levering. *W.E.B. Du Bois: Biography of a Race*. New York: Owl Books, 1994.
Macdonald, D. L., and Kathleen Scherf, eds. *Mary Wollstonecraft: The Vindications: The Rights of Men and the Rights of Women*. Toronto: Broadview, 1997.
Memmi, Albert. *Racism*. Minneapolis: University of Minnesota Press, 1999.

Ryle, Gilbert. *The Concept of Mind*. Chicago: University of Chicago Press, 2000.
Singer, Peter. *Practical Ethics*. Cambridge: Cambridge University Press, 1998.
Soames, Scott. *Philosophical Analysis in the Twentieth Century*. Princeton, NJ: Princeton University Press, 2003.
Sommers, Christine H. *Right and Wrong*. San Diego: Harcourt Brace, 1986.
Sterba, James P. *Morality in Practice*. Belmont, CA: Wadsworth, 1988.
Strawson, P. F. *Individuals*. London: Methuen, 1959.
Stroll, Avrum. *Twentieth-Century Analytic Philosophy*. New York: Columbia University Press, 2000.

Index

abortion, 177–183; personhood of fetus, 177–180; pro-choice, 181–183; pro-life, 180–181
Academy, the, 27–29; curriculum, 29
air, earth, fire, and water, 4
Albertus Magnus, 60
Alcibiades, 14
Alexander the Great, 37–38, 47
Anaximander, 6
Anaximenes, 6
ancient philosophy, 1–10
apatheia, 51
Aquinas, St. Thomas, 40, 58–66, 84, 85, 140; five ways, 63–64; God, nature of, 61–62; *Summa Theologica*, 40, 63; theology, 61–62; works: *On Being and Essence, On the Principles of Nature, Summa Gentiles, Summa Theologica*, 62
argumentum ad absurdum, 19
Aristophanes
Aristotle, 3, 25, 37–45, 131, 169; and Plato, 37; art, 44–45; ethics, 40–41; eudaimonia, 41; function, 41, 42–43; golden mean, 41–42; Lyceum, the, 38; metaphysics, 39–40; politics, 44–45; teleologism, 39–40; works: *De Anima, Nicomachean Ethics, Poetics. Politics, Physics*, 39
Athens, 14–15, 23; nobility, 15; persecution, 18; slavery, 15; women, 15;
Aubrey, John, 97
Ayer, A. J., 163–164

Beethoven, Ludwig, 69
Bentham, Jeremy, 142, 146–147; hedonic calculus, 146–147
Berkeley, George, 113–120; philosophy, 115–120; Rhode Island, 115; subjective idealism, 116–119; works: *Alciphron, Essay Toward a New Theory of Vision, Siris, Three Dialogues Between Hylas and Philonous, A Treatise Concerning the Principles of Human Knowledge*, 114–115
Bible, 69–75
big bang, 66, 68
Burke, Edmund, 102–103
butterfly effect, 7

Camus, Albert, 152, 155, 158–159
Carlyle, Thomas, 148
change, 6–9
chaos theory, 7
Chesterton, G. K., 58, 61
Christianity, 44, 72–73; agape love (and eros), 73–75; divine justice, 75–76; ethics, 72–79; impracticality, 77; spirit and letter, 78
Christina, Queen of Sweden, 84
Cicero, 36
cosmological argument, 63–64
Cynics, the, 45–47; representatives: Antisthenes, Cratus, Diogenes, Hipparchia, Zeno of Citium, 46

Darwin, Charles, 66–67
de Beauvoir, Simone, 152
Debbs, Eugene, 93
Democritus, 3, 6
Descartes, René, 81–91, 111; Cartesian circle, 88–89; cogito, ergo sum, 85–87; God, existence of, 86–88; mind/body split, 89; works: *Discourse on Method, Meditations on First Philosophy, Philosophical Essays, The Passions, The World*, 84–85
de Warren, Louise, 101
Diderot, Denis, 101
Diogenes Laertius, 27
Dodgson, C. L. (Lewis Carroll), 163
Donne, John, 93
Dostoevsky, Fedor, 30–31, 79, 155
Dryden, John, 53

Elea (Eleatics), 9
Empedocles, 3, 6
empiricism, 109–111
Ephesus, 6, 7
Euclid, 27
existentialism, 153–159; anxiety (nothingness), 154; existence precedes essence, 155–156; free will, 155–157

fallacy of composition, 53
forbidden knowledge, 18
free will, 49–50

Genesis, 8, 18
Genet, Jean, 152
Gide, Andre, 152
Glaucon, 33
Gaugin, 44
Gibbon, Edward, 48
Gilligan, Carol, 173–174
God of the gaps, 67

Hawking, Stephen, 68
hedonistic paradox, 151
Hegel, G. W. F., 164
Heidegger, Martin, 152
Heraclitus, 6–9; change, 7–8; logos, 8; unity of opposites, 9
Hermias, 37
Herodotus, 2
Hippocratic oath, 140
Hobbes, Thomas, 96–101; political philosophy, 97–99; social contract, 98; state of nature, 98–100; works: *Human Nature, Leviathan, Objections, Of Liberty and Necessity, Short Tract on First Principles*, 97
Homer, 36
human nature, 95, 96–107
Hume, David, 103, 116, 120–130; causation, 126–127; matters of fact and relations of ideas, 126; miracles, 127–129; philosophy, 125–130; works: *Dialogues Concerning Natural Religion, Enquiry Concerning Human Understanding, Enquiry Concerning the Principles of Morals, History of England, My Own Life, The Natural*

History of Religion, Political Discourses, A Treatise of Human Nature, 122–123
Huxley, Thomas, 66

Iambichus, 3
Ignatius, St., 13
Indian philosophy, 52, 94, 112
intelligent design, 67
intuitionism, 112–113
Ionian, 3

James, William, 112
Jaspers, Karl, 152
Johnson, Samuel, 119
Judaism, 69–72; covenant relation, 70; the flood, 7; forbidden fruit, 70; prophetic tradition, 71; Ten Commandments, 71–72
Jung, C. G., 111

Kant, Immanuel, 130–142; categorical imperative, 138; epistemology, 135–136; ethics, 136–141; a good will, 137; practical imperative, 138–139; religion, 136; works: *Critique of Judgment, Critique of Practical Reason, Critique of Pure Reason, Groundwork of the Metaphysic of Morals*, 134
Kierkegaard, Soren, 252
King, Martin Luther, 93
Knox, Ronald, 119

Lewis, C. S., 165
linguistic philosophy, 162–168; linguistic analysis, 165–168; representatives: J. L. Austin, G. E. Moore, R. M. Hare, Peter Strawson, Ludwig Wittgenstein, 165
logical positivism, 163–165; representatives: Rudolf Carnap, Moritz Schlick, Otto Neurath, 163
Locke, John, 116

Marcel, Gabriel, 152
Meletus (Anytus and Lycon), 18–20
Miletus (Milesian), 3
Mill, John Stuart, 142–151, 162, 169; politics (liberty), 144–146; qualitative happiness, 147–149; utilitarianism, 146–150; works: *Autobiography, On Liberty, Principles of Political Economy, The Subjection of Women, A System of Logic, Utilitarianism*, 143–144
Monet, Claude, 69
Moore, G. E., 120

Niebuhr, Reinhold, 77
Nietzsche, Friedrich, 152

Occam's razor, 67
On Nature, 7
Orphic Brotherhood, 6–7

Paley, William, 63–65
Parmenides, 3, 9–11, 31; unchangingness, 10–11
Pascal, Blaise, 152
Peloponnesian War, 14, 17
Pericles, 15, 23
peripatetics, 38
Plato, 3, 13, 25–37, 131, 169; allegory of the cave, 32–34; dialogues: *Apology, Crito, Meno, Parmenides, Phaedo, Protagoras, Sophist, Symposium, Timaeus*, 17; *Euthyphro*, 17, 29–31; justice, 32–33; learning is recollection, 25–29; philosopher kings, 34–35; religion, 29–31; and Socrates, 25; state, ideal, 34–37; theory of forms, 31–34
Plutarch, 3, 37
Pope, Alexander, 114
pre-Socratics, 1–13
Pythagoras, 6, 27

racism, 183–188; affirmative action, 186–188; profiling, 184; wealth differential, 183–184
rationalism, 111–112
Rousseau, Jean-Jacques, 101–106, 123; cyborgs, 106–107; human nature, 104–105; music, 105; works: *Apology for my Life, Confessions, Discourse on Science and the Arts, Émile, Reveries of the Solitary Walker, The New Heloise, The Social Contract*, 102–103
Rudolf, St., 13
Russell, Bertrand, 13, 62, 81, 112, 164

Sagan, Carl, 68
Sartre, Jean-Paul, 152–157; works: *Being and Nothingness, Dirty Hands*, "Existentialism is a Humanism," *The Flies, Nausea, No Exit*, "The Wall," *The Words*, 153
Sebastian, St., 13
self, 90–94, 126, 129; space and time, 92–94
Seneca, 3
Shakespeare, William, 74, 109, 149
Socrates, 9–10, 13–23, 149; *Apology*, 18–22; daimon, 15; dialectic, 16; gadfly, 17; problem of Socrates, 17
Sophists, 14
standard of reasonableness, 188–189
Stoicism, 45–55; destiny (fate), 49–52; Epictetus, 47–48; lazy argument, the, 53–54; Marcus Aurelius, 48; *Meditations*, 48; representatives: Cleanthes, Chrysippus, Marcus Aurelius, Seneca, 47
Swift, Jonathan, 114

Taylor, Harriet, 143–144
teleological argument, 65–66
Thales, 1, 3–5; water, 4–5
Thomson, Judith Jarvis, 182
Tillich, Paul, 154

Vienna Circle, 163
virtue is knowledge, 28

Wessel, J. H., 150
Wilberforce, Samuel, 66
Wilde, Oscar, 92
Wollstonecraft, Mary, 169; works: *Thoughts on the Education of Daughters, A Vindication of the Rights of Women*, 170
women philosophers, 168–171; caring and nurture, 174; ethics, 173–174; feminist thought, 171–174; representatives: G. E. M. Anscombe, Susan B. Anthony, Aspatia, Mary Astell, Simone de Beauvoir, Germaine de Stael, Phillipa Foot, Hypatia of Alexandria, Susanne Langer, Rosa Luxemburg, Iris Murdoch, Martha Nussbaum, Simone Weil, Mary Wollstonecraft, 169; situated knowledge (gender), 171–172

Xanthippe, 15–16
Xenophon, 14

Zeno of Elea, 11–12, 31; Achilles and the tortoise, 12; dichotomy, the, 12; flying arrow paradox, 11–12

About the Author

Burton F. Porter is the author and/or editor of numerous books on philosophy, including *The Good Life, The Head and the Heart, Philosophy Through Film, The Voice of Reason, Personal Philosophy, Reasons for Living, Religion and Reason, Philosophy: A Literary and Conceptual Approach*, and *Deity and Morality*.

He holds a B.A. from the University of Maryland, and a Ph.D. from St. Andrews University, Scotland, with graduate study at Oxford University. Dr. Porter has taught at various institutions, including Russell Sage College and Drexel University, and he has served as department head and as dean of Arts and Sciences. At present, he is a faculty member at Western New England College in Springfield, Massachusetts, and a sometime visiting professor at Mount Holyoke College in South Hadley, Massachusetts.

Dr. Porter's area of concentration is ethical theory, contemporary moral problems, the philosophy of religion, and philosophy in fiction and film. He has published numerous articles and book reviews, and he received the award of Outstanding Educator of America. He lives in Amherst, Massachusetts, where he indulges his interest in literature, music, and philosophy.